THE
POLITE
REVOLU-
TION

THE POLITE REVOLU- TION

PERFECTING THE CANADIAN DREAM

JOHN IBBITSON

Library and Archives Canada Cataloguing in Publication

Ibbitson, John
    The polite revolution : perfecting the Canadian dream / John Ibbitson.

ISBN 0-7710-4351-1

    1. Canada – Politics and government – 1993-.   2. Canada – Economic policy – 1991-.   3. Canada – Social policy.   I. Title.

FC635.I23 2005   971.07   C2005-903694-X

We acknowledge the financial support of the Government of Canada through the Book Publishing Industry Development Program and that of the Government of Ontario through the Ontario Media Development Corporation's Ontario Book Initiative. We further acknowledge the support of the Canada Council for the Arts and the Ontario Arts Council for our publishing program.

Typeset in Bembo by M&S, Toronto
Printed and bound in Canada

This book is printed on acid-free paper that is 100% recycled, ancient-forest friendly (100% post-consumer recycled).

McClelland & Stewart Ltd.
The Canadian Publishers
75 Sherbourne Street
Toronto, Ontario
M5A 2P9
www.mcclelland.com

1 2 3 4 5   09 08 07 06 05

For my mother and father.

CONTENTS

PREFACE AND ACKNOWLEDGEMENTS

Darrell Bricker is to blame for this book. The president of Ipsos-Reid Public Affairs and I met for lunch in April 2004, on the cusp of a federal election whose outcome no one could predict. Canadian politics, we agreed, had reached Shakespearean levels of drama and intrigue: Paul Martin and Jean Chrétien were tearing the Liberal Party apart in a contest seemingly without quarter, even as the fragmented conservative parties attempted to coalesce. The federal sponsorship program in Quebec had turned into a cesspool of fraud and kickbacks, with the subsequent scandal reviving the fortunes of the Bloc Québécois, while the New Democrats were seeking new relevance under their new leader, Jack Layton. These political tempests raged over a national landscape of provincial discontents, alienated regions, and disaffected voters. "Someone needs to write a book about all this," Bricker declared, "and it might as well be you." One thing led to another.

As the idea of this book evolved over the following weeks, ultimately encompassing the June federal election, it seemed clear that a simple political narrative was not sufficient. Politics matters because it reflects the strengths and divisions of the society politicians are meant to serve. Political conflicts mirror our own personal conflicts – with each other and within ourselves. Canada is at an apex of growth and change; the tumult in our legislatures reflects nothing less than our own strivings and internal contradictions. As we talked about and tussled over the themes the book should explore, John Pearce became, not only my agent, but my confidant, counsellor, and friend. When Doug Pepper, newly installed as president and publisher of McClelland & Stewart, heard of what we had in mind, he decided this book would be his first acquisition, and that he would edit it himself.

If these three were responsible for this work's genesis, many others helped bring it to fruition. Edward Greenspon and Patrick Martin, respectively the *Globe and Mail*'s editor-in-chief and Comment editor, gave the book their full support. *The Polite Revolution* is by no means a mere repetition of ideas contained within the political-affairs column I write for the *Globe*, but without the column, there would have been no book. And thanks to them, I have the best job in Canadian journalism.

Both column and book are also in debt to my friends and colleagues in the *Globe*'s Parliamentary bureau. This page affords an opportunity to thank all of them publicly for the help, advice, and good sense they provide every day, and for never seeming to mind when I steal their ideas and exploit their insights. I owe two special debts: to Jeffrey Simpson, the *Globe*'s national affairs columnist, who over the past three years has been an invaluable and generous guide to the intricacies of federal politics, and to Brian Laghi, our bureau chief. The secret to staying on top of the Ottawa game is simply to drop into Brian's office first thing every morning and ask: "So, what's going on?"

Many others provided comments and criticisms as the chapters evolved. Most would rather not be cited, but I hope David Naylor, the former Dean of Medicine at the University of Toronto, and now its president, won't mind public thanks for the advice he offered on the section devoted to social policy. Robin Wortman, a passionate advocate for native rights, debated via many an e-mail over that issue. Paul Cappon, president of the Canadian Council on Learning, offered wise insights on education as a national priority. None of them agree with all (or perhaps any) of the arguments and suggestions put forward in this book, which makes their assistance all the more generous.

Bryan Mullan — a producer at TVOntario's *Studio 2*, a good friend but an indifferent squash player — stepped in at a critical juncture to chase down statistics, citations, and sources. Without him the book would never have been completed on time. Jenny Bradshaw, at McClelland & Stewart, provided a meticulous and clear-eyed copy edit. Finally, I owe a special debt to Grant Burke, for his unique and invaluable contribution.

To all of the above, many thanks. For any errors or outrages that might nonetheless have made their way into the text, the author ruefully claims sole responsibility.

Ottawa
July 2005

THE
POLITE
REVOLU-
TION

AND
HERE
WE
ARE

Sometime, not too long ago, while no one was watching, Canada became the world's most successful country.

It might have happened in the late 1990s, when this nation perfected the unique and virtuous circle of low interest rates, low inflation, balanced budgets, and paid-up pension funds. Or perhaps it emerged in 2001, when the latest census revealed we had become possibly the world's most urban country (80 per cent of us live in cities);[1] that nearly one Canadian in five arrived here from somewhere else; that Toronto, with 44 per cent of its population foreign-born, was more diverse than Miami, Los Angeles, or Sydney;[2] and that by 2017, when Canada celebrates its 150th birthday, one Canadian in five will be a member of a visible minority.[3]

It might have been celebrated in any of those years over the past decade when the United Nations Human Development Index ranked Canada as one of the world's most desirable countries in which to live.[4] For the culturati, 2002 was a particularly good year: three of six finalists for the Booker Prize for best new novel were Canadian – our Yann Martel won for *Life of Pi* – and Margaret Macmillan's *Paris 1919* was praised on both sides of the Atlantic as the best non-fiction book in years, while jocks rejoiced over Canada's gold medal in hockey at the Winter Olympics. Pop-music buffs may insist Canada reached its zenith in 2005, when *Spin* magazine, the *New York Times*, and *TIME* Canada all declared that Montreal offered the most influential independent music scene in North America.[5]

Canadians fret about the country: about its regional and linguistic divisions; about a lack of identity, whatever that may mean; about being perpetually overshadowed by the United States; and, of course, about the weather. But while there's not much we can do about the weather, the progress of the nation in the past generation has been simply astonishing. This country works better than it has ever worked before. Choose an area of endeavour: business success, standard of living, culture, scientific discovery, and you'll find that Canada is almost invariably performing at a level equal to or surpassing that of most other developed countries.

In 1904, Sir Wilfrid Laurier proclaimed that, while the nineteenth century belonged to the United States, the twentieth century would belong to Canada.[6] He was a tad off the mark. It is obvious that this country will never boast a population and economy sufficient to warrant Great Power, let alone superpower, status. But greatness can be more than strength of arms or size of GDP. Canada's greatness, which we are only now beginning to fully realize, lies elsewhere.

Here is a prediction: A century from now, historians and anthropologists will cite Canada as the harbinger of a new age. This new age will be marked by a steep reduction in intolerances so deeply ingrained in human culture that for millennia we have shaped our caste systems and fought our wars based on them, to the point in the last century where we came close to destroying ourselves. It is the intolerance of the clan, which stipulates that the further a person is removed from your own family, tribe, village, the likelier that person is to be alien and threatening. It is intolerance toward the other, whose God is not yours, whose economic system is not yours, whose sexuality is not yours, whose language is not yours. September 11, 2001, demonstrated once again the horrors of which modern technology married to barbarous hatred are capable.

Canada, more successfully than any other country in the world, is finally defeating that intolerance. We are a nation of strangers, bringing in more strangers by the hundreds of thousands each year, from every region of the globe, who then learn to live together as friends. Already 70 per cent of our labour-force growth is attributable to new immigrants. It is estimated that by 2011 that will rise to 100 per cent, and by 2026, immigrants will account for all net population growth in this country.[7]

Canada is the world's most successful country because it is profiting from the explosive creative forces that are unleashed when people of different races, cultures, and lifestyles live together and bond. Just as English has emerged as the world's most robust language by virtue of its being a mongrel tongue,[8] so too are

Canadians a mongrel people, a mélange. And while once such intermixing of bloodlines was abhorred, even outlawed, today most Canadians don't even know the meaning of the word *miscegenation*. We have discovered the golden secret of the third millennia: They who don't simply tolerate diversity, but embrace it, thrive.

Those who consider this a slender accomplishment need turn only to other liberal societies to witness their agonizing struggles. Racial tensions are tearing at the social fabric of the Netherlands, where mosques are being pushed to conduct their services in Dutch[9]. Secular extremism in France forces Muslim girls to doff their hijab on school property. But where are the Canadian headlines? Even the most militant Quebec separatists have never advocated forcing churches and mosques to conduct their activities only in French, while the controversy in 1990 over whether Sikh RCMP officers should be allowed to wear turbans now seems positively quaint.

Because of this, because of our embrace of diversity and our triumph over intolerance; because we successfully evolved from a rural, resource-based scattering of peoples into a cosmopolitan, urban polyglot; because that transformation itself served as a catalyst for a cultural explosion made manifest in the arts and on the street; because Canada and Canadians have largely mastered the art of getting along, the twenty-first century will be Canada's century. We shall be an example, a template, a lesson. Canada should, and hopefully will, be known throughout the world as the exemplar of what can be achieved when chauvinism gives way to accommodation, when the obsessions with shared race, shared blood, shared history are transcended by an infinity of permutations.

Mostly it was luck, especially in our historical origins. While the English and the Spanish competed for control of the southern half of our continent throughout the eighteenth and nineteenth centuries, the English and the French had the matter resolved in the northern half by 1763. The result in the South, at least for the Spanish, was dismal. The English and their American successors lucked into or expropriated everything worth having, relegating the Spanish and their Latin American successor states to the poorest, hottest, most disease-infested regions. Between its geography and the bad luck of having Spain and Portugal as the metropolitan powers – themselves backward and rapacious at the time – Latin America was doomed to poverty and stagnation, from which that region is only slowly and uncertainly beginning to emerge. For their part, the American conquerors – embracing their English heritage, settler culture, and manifest destiny – went from strength to strength, imposing a uniform myth of Americanness on all who entered, while trying to ignore the scourge of slavery and its legacy, which made a mockery of everything America was supposed to stand for.

Up North, however, the story was different. France was never the best of colonial powers, often neglecting or actively impeding the interests of the sparse settlements in New France, but Paris was far more beneficent than Madrid or Lisbon.

And the English, who competed with and ultimately defeated France in North America, were the most successful colonizers in history. The nations forged by British settlers – the United States of America, Canada, Australia, and New Zealand – are virtually the only former colonies to equal the economic and social success of Western Europe.[10] And again, by accident as much as design, it was the English who came up with a solution to the problems

5

of integrating a mature French colony with an emerging English one – a solution that, three hundred years later, would produce spectacular dividends.

It's not as though they had much choice. When Great Britain assumed responsibility for British North America following the Treaty of Paris that ended the Seven Years War, it faced a distinctly uncomfortable situation. In the lands north of their already restive American colonies, the British inherited a territory consisting of seventy thousand French-speakers and three thousand English-speakers, with most of the latter clustered in Halifax. Apart from fur traders, there was little European penetration of the lands west of the Ottawa River. However, Lower Canada, as it would soon be called, was a stable, reasonably prosperous, and mature colony, already more than a century old. Very quickly, the English decided that the best solution was to leave well enough alone.[11] The French language, French legal code, and French customs would remain intact in Quebec; elsewhere, English language and customs would be the order of the day. This sensible compromise – remember that in human affairs, sensible compromises are rarely arrived at without the preliminary of several decades of war – became strained after the thirteen American colonies fought for and achieved independence. Following the British defeat, thousands of Americans loyal to the Crown, and many more thousands of retiring British soldiers, occupied the Maritime colonies and the emerging lands west of Quebec. In turn, further waves of discharged soldiers and fortune seekers emigrated from Great Britain in the wake of the Napoleonic wars. By the middle decades of the nineteenth century, the new Upper Canada was more populous and prosperous than either the old Lower Canada or the Maritime colonies.

After several failed experiments at joint government, the local leadership decided that the two great colonies of Canada East and Canada West (as they were known at the time) needed to dissolve the temporary union that had been forced on them by their colonial masters, and instead confederate into a Dominion that would leave each free and autonomous, with the general government looking after matters of joint interest. The idea was sufficiently appealing to convince, first the Maritime colonies, then the emerging Western territories, and finally Newfoundland and Labrador to sign on. And here we are.

The point of this potted history is to remind the reader that Canada, unlike the United States, was forged not in revolution, but in compromise, between two national groupings, the French and the English, who back in Europe had been at each other's throats, on and off, for several hundred years. The American Declaration of Independence established, for that great nation, a founding mythology of inalienable rights. The British North America Act provided Canada with the more elusive mythology of getting along.

Because Canadians chose accommodation over contest, our history is rather dull. But when it comes to history, dull is a blessing. The Americans slaughtered six hundred thousand of their own people in a civil war over slavery and the rights of states. The Northwest Rebellion of 1884 lasted two months and cost 150 lives, including that of its leader, Louis Riel. In any other nation, the incident would have been a footnote. Central and Eastern European governments in the twentieth century showed us the horrors of which people are capable when cultural intolerance and political immaturity are exacerbated by industrialization. Canada's dealings with its aboriginal peoples are not a matter for pride,

7

but our country has never been riven by hatred, the majority has never sought to eradicate the minority, and (since 1814) we have never experienced the worst of all horrors: war on our own soil.

A society founded on principles of accommodation, and free of external or internal trauma, is capable of great things. And Canada has repeatedly achieved greatness. We helped defend the values of liberal democracy against its many twentieth-century challengers, in both world wars and the Cold War. We built, or helped build, such engineering marvels as the Canadian Pacific Railway, the St. Lawrence Seaway, and the TransCanada Pipeline. We gave the world insulin, new treatments in radiation and chemotherapy, and the first coronary care units. We were the first country to employ space satellites for the purpose of domestic communication. Though we are relatively few in number, and though the land is harsh, our achievements surpass the sum of us.

The greatest Canadian achievement of all is the world's most enlightened immigration policy. Canada has generally been more welcoming of immigrants than the other great settler culture to our south – taking in, per cápita, more people per year, and from a wider ethnic pool. (In the 1950s, for example, the Americans took in 2.5 million immigrants, while Canada, with about a tenth of the population, took in 1.5 million.[12]) In part, we were compelled to. Canada has historically been a second choice for immigrants, many of whom would have preferred, but couldn't get into, the United States. (During parts of this country's history, emigration from Canada to the United States rivalled or even exceeded emigration from other countries to Canada.) That, coupled with periodic labour shortages – of everything from farmers for prairie lands to construction hands for subway and sewer systems – forced federal and provincial officials to accept immigrants that the ruling British Protestant hierarchy would, frankly, rather have kept out.

But they could not be kept out, and wave after wave of them came to push back the frontier and fill the cities. First the Irish, then the Germans and the Poles; then a great agglomeration of Jews, Ukrainians, Italians, Portuguese, Spanish, Hungarians, Czechs, Greeks, and on and on. The flood was so great that, today, Toronto's Italian population is greater than Bologna's, the seventh-largest city in Italy.[13]

Finally, in the 1960s, an enlightened federal government (enlightened perhaps by the fact that the pool of available immigrants from European territories was dwindling) lifted the restrictions on immigration from Asian and other Third World lands. In the 1970s, for the first time, non-European immigrants surpassed European immigrants in number, a trend that continued and accelerated over the succeeding decades.

There were tensions. In English Canada, WASPs who had grown up in towns dominated by the Orange Lodge chafed at the weakening of the Imperial ties, as the Union Jack gave way to the Maple Leaf, and the Queen found it harder and harder to get her face on a stamp or a banknote. The young who waged a Quiet Revolution to modernize Quebec society did not always welcome new arrivals, who lacked their exquisitely honed resentment of *les maudits Anglais*. Those redder of neck resented multiculturalism as much as they abhorred bilingualism, the two great exercises in toleration launched by Pierre Trudeau. It was bad enough that there was French on one side of the cereal box, but even worse that the guy on the box was Chinese.

Still, all things considered, the country got through the traumas of universal immigration relatively unscathed. As well, twice we have faced – and met – the ultimate challenge of debating the dissolution of the country itself, through the Quebec referenda of 1980 and 1995. To their enormous credit, the Czechs and the Slovaks went through the same process – which ended in the separation of Czechoslovakia into the Czech Republic and Slovakia – in the early 1990s. But the handful of nations who can debate dissolution without reaching for the cudgels is minuscule.

The benefits of our bicultural heritage and multicultural present are enormous, though in part intangible. Today, new arrivals tend to be between the ages of thirty and fifty, their peak working years. Their education levels are generally higher than those of native-born Canadians. Although they often have to start at the bottom and work their way up, their energy and enthusiasm for their new homeland infuse society. As the cultural isolation that generally attends the first generation of any immigrant group breaks down, the second and third generation blend seamlessly with more established populations, leading to an increase in intercultural and interracial mingling – not least through marriage – that creates unique perspectives and a unique open-mindedness. According to Statistics Canada, the number of interracial couples in Canada increased by 35 per cent in the 1990s, reaching 3 per cent of all couples.

This open-mindedness, now entrenched in an ethos of diversity, eventually pushed Canada toward, not simply putting up with, but embracing, the contribution of gays and lesbians. In July 2005, Canada became the fourth country in the world – after Belgium, Holland, and Spain – to legalize same-sex marriages nationwide. For the first time in human history, it can be comfortable to be homosexual, and nowhere on earth is it more comfortable than in Canada.

Through all these transformations, Canada continued the most important transformation of all, expanding from a rural, resource-based economy to one based on cities and knowledge. (By 2020, 90 per cent of Canadians will live in cities.[14]) Again, apart from the economic benefits that accrue from changing from drawers of water to drawers of animated film, the urbanization of Canadian culture has promoted, not the ghettoization and urban anomie that so many feared, but greater social integration. Today, the urban agglomerations centred on Toronto, Montreal, Vancouver, Ottawa-Gatineau, Calgary, and Edmonton account for almost half of the Canadian population. And these sprawly cities are marvellous. Fusion restaurants abound, men with pierced eyebrows wait in line for the bus behind women in burkas, enormous new Orthodox and Hindu temples supplant the crosses that once dominated the landscape.

In a rare example of the law of unintended consequences producing a benefit (that law usually begets gremlins), immigration and urbanization have also laid to rest that agonizing debate about what was wrong with Canadian culture. The answer, it turns out, is that it was just too white and uptight. Remember those dreary Canadian novels they made us read in school? Today, we publish a cosmopolitan literature dominated by authors with such exotic names as Michael Ondaatje and Rohinton Mistry – books that are read and admired around the world. Remember those execrable, incestuous documentaries that the National Film Board inflicted on prisoners and students? Or the endless stream of plays about Newfoundland boys angry at their fathers? Or those agonizing new compositions they always played first at symphony concerts, so you wouldn't feel you'd missed anything if you had trouble parking your car? Think Le Cirque du Soleil,

The Drawer Boy, John Estacio. Remember when state censors snipped the naughty bits out of the movies, the Sabbath was kept holy (whether you were or not), and you had to write down your choice of bad wine on little slips of paper at the liquor store? Now it's no crime to smoke pot after renting an unrated movie during your same-sex honeymoon. Canada has loosened up.

We have one additional, crucial advantage over most developed nations, one that will become more apparent with each passing decade. Almost all developed countries have reached, or will soon reach, the point where they are no longer able to maintain current population levels. With the exception of the United States,[15] all developed countries will experience sharp population declines over the coming decades. Because of an extremely low birth rate, coupled with a xenophobic reluctance to admit newcomers, Japan's population will decline by 20 per cent between now and 2050. Europe will lose 100 million people.[16] There will ever-fewer young workers to finance pension plans, and to purchase the houses and appliances that drive a domestic economy. In the first nine months of 2004, Russia lost half a million people.[17]

These countries, with their racially and culturally fixed identities, have great trouble assimilating new arrivals. At a visceral level, many Danes simply don't believe Philippine immigrants, for example, could ever become truly Dane. In coming years, such nations will struggle to reconcile economic imperatives with cultural prejudices, with the attendant and inevitable social strain.

But our high immigration rate, our culture of integration, and perhaps even our loosey-goosey sense of national identity – after all, it's so *easy* to be Canadian; just obey the laws and learn most of the words to the national anthem – have provided Canada with a distinct competitive edge, which will become more apparent with each passing decade. As Europe, Japan, and Russia hollow out, our population will remain stable, the average age will remain younger, and social tensions will remain peripheral, giving us both a competitive and a cultural advantage. It's a joke and a stereotype that Canadians are polite. But politeness is not some accidental quality of being Canadian. It is at the core of what we are. It is the means by which we accommodate each other. It is the secret recipe for a nation of different cultures, languages, and customs, whose citizens all get along. Canadians have used politeness to foment a social revolution. And from that revolution, our Canada has emerged – young, creative, polyglot, open-minded, forward-looking, fabulous.

And yet this book is also about what's wrong.

For we are not without flaws. Some of these flaws are the regrettable but necessary by-product of the choices we have made. Canada is, for example, increasingly ahistorical. Haitian arrivals in Montreal know nothing and care less about the Papineau rebellion. The Hong Kong community in Vancouver is decidedly uninterested in the tumult that led to the creation of the Charter of Rights and Freedoms. Few are the Guatemalans in Toronto who could describe the Family Compact.

The price of a truly cosmopolitan society is ahistoricism – an absence of collective cultural memory. That's not so bad, since much of history is misery, and the lessons learned are often swamped by the resentments rekindled. Yet those of us who have devoted our lives to chronicling this country's past, both recent and distant, cannot help but stifle a regretful sigh.

Other problems, however, are more intractable, and some of them threaten to compromise, or even undermine, our past and recent achievements. Our weak federal structure, abetted by shameful political evasion, has robbed our major cities of needed tax revenues. As a result, even as these cities take in fresh millions with each passing decade, there are fewer dollars to preserve existing infrastructure, let alone expand it to meet growing demand. Our once-pristine streets are increasingly filthy; our once-cohesive social contract has deteriorated to the point where the homeless litter the sidewalks; Southern Ontario is at risk of chronic brownouts and blackouts; it can take more than an hour to get to work.

We are a trading nation, yet we have lost interest in finding new markets for our goods. While the United States has signed more than a dozen free-trade agreements since 1993, the year of NAFTA, Canada has signed only three.[18] As a result, our continued prosperity is precariously dependent on trade with an American economy that, thanks to a multitude of deficits, could be headed in the coming decades into a prolonged decline. Even those who promote a closer integration with the United States worry about the federal government's lack of boldness in pursuing new and emerging markets. Within our own country, barriers to internal trade weaken the federation, making us all poorer.

Prosperity within Canada is not equally distributed. That is inevitable, for even were society to perfectly achieve that elusive goal of total equality of opportunity, results would vary according to circumstances. But within Canada, entire regions are falling farther and farther behind the leading edge. More significant still, the various regions of Canada are drawing apart from each other. The West, the English Centre, the French Centre, the East, are evolving into four separate solitudes. Not only is the federal government unable to reverse this estrangement, it contributes to the estrangement by its own policies.

And within those solitudes, the people of Quebec continue to struggle with the rest of the country for mutual recognition of the truth that Quebec is a nation within a nation. The inability and unwillingness of English Canada to accept that truth places the country at risk of another referendum on separation within a very few years, one that the separatist forces would be poised to win.

Finally, and worst of all, the entrenched and protracted refusal of federal, provincial, and native leadership to address the problem of poverty on and off reserve has led to an emerging aboriginal underclass: uneducated, unemployed, and angry. This tide can still be reversed, and it must be, for it threatens to make a mockery of everything this country professes to believe in and that it has achieved.

These strains are the result of old thinking, of applying shopworn solutions to fresh problems. The ties that once bound us – a protected economy, subsidized communications (be it via railroads or radio waves), a coddled and protected cultural sector – fray further with each passing day. And a federal government that believes it has a monopoly on the national dream cannot comprehend that there are fewer and fewer left to dream it.

We need a new dream. We need to refashion Canada's political superstructure to reflect evolving realities. Much of this will entail loosening the ties that artificially bind. Yet new bonds can be forged, ones that leave the federation stronger politically and the people of Canada even more united in common cause. And we need to chart a new role for the federal government, one that allows it to focus on its core responsibilities of defence and foreign policy, while minimizing its intrusions into matters best left to provincial governments.

As we embark on this debate, let us set two rules. First, let us exclude from the conversation all of the whiners. Let us bar the door to those who claim victimhood, who profess to be alienated, abused, and misunderstood. You have problems? We all have problems. But we're here in search of solutions, not to wallow in a stew of complaints.

Second, let us never forget that we are not trying to fix a country and a culture that are broken. Because Canada is not broken. We're one of the least broken countries on earth. And we have demonstrated in recent years an astonishing capacity to solve the seemingly insoluble. Twenty years ago, Canada appeared to be locked in a vicious economic cycle of deficit and debt. But in the 1990s, tough-minded federal and provincial governments restored fiscal balance, while preserving the most important features of universal public health care, comprehensive public education, and aid to those most in need. At the same time, the federal and provincial governments took steps to correct the emerging insolvency of the Canada Pension Plan. Today, while American and European unfunded pension deficits threaten the very economic future of those countries, Canada is one of a small handful of developed nations[19] not facing the so-called generational imbalance.

One other example: this exemplar of trading nations – trade accounts for 65 per cent of the Canadian GDP[20] – clung for too many years to the tariffs that protected a weak Canadian manufacturing sector from American competition. But the Free Trade Agreement of 1988 and the North American Free Trade Agreement of 1993, which created the world's largest trading bloc, opened the Canadian economy to free and fair trade. Despite glitches (mostly occasioned by latent American protectionism), free trade and globalization have been a boon to the Canadian economy, doubling trade over the course of the decade,[21] gen-erating the longest sustained period of economic growth since the 1950s, and reducing unemployment from 9.5 per cent in the 1980s to a current level of around 7 per cent.

The point here is not to rehash old arguments, but to demon-strate that our country possesses a robust capacity to identify, con-front, and resolve apparently intractable problems. Even with a few cylinders misfiring, we have raced to the front of the pack. Most of this book focuses on the challenges facing the Canadian future. But we only damage our prospects by exploring the flaws of the federation, unmindful of its many successes. This country could work better, but this country works.

Bearing that in mind, let's begin.

CHAPTER ONE

THE POLITICS OF DYSFUNCTION

The atmosphere in the House of Commons was stifling, thick with tension and the heat from television lights and the hundreds of bodies that packed the Chamber and filled the surrounding galleries. The press gallery, normally empty but for the smattering of scribes who sat vigil during the theatrics of Question Period, was standing-room only, each reporter craning to make out the body language, gestures, or any other possible telegraphing signals of Chuck Cadman, the Independent MP on whom the fate of the thirty-eighth Parliament of Canada rested. But Mr. Cadman, with his long white hair, full beard, and kind, lined face, sat motionless, head bowed, hands folded, chewing gum.

Even people who normally ignored politics had been gripped

by the crisis of April and May 2005: the astonishing allegations from the Gomery inquiry of kickbacks and payoffs between the Liberal Party and the advertising industry in Quebec; the determination of Conservative leader Stephen Harper and Bloc Québécois leader Gilles Duceppe to bring down the Paul Martin government; the prime minister's desperate televised plea for more time; the promise of support from NDP leader Jack Layton, in exchange for massive new spending promises in the 2005 budget; the parliamentary manoeuvring – MPs crossing or threatening to cross the floor; House leaders jockeying to force or prevent a vote of confidence; allegations of attempted vote-buying; and the shocking, thrilling defection of billionaire Conservative MP Belinda Stronach, straight into the arms of the Liberal cabinet.

Stronach's switch had saved the government, *unless*: unless Cadman, a former Conservative MP who had run and won in 2004 as an Independent after the nomination in his suburban Vancouver riding was snatched out from under him, voted with his former party. He was ill, receiving chemotherapy, and undecided, claiming he would vote as his constituents wished. What did they wish?

The motion on the budget would decide everything. Liberal and NDP MPs rose, one after the other, as the Opposition watched in silence. Carolyn Parrish, a former Liberal who had been kicked out of caucus for her anti-American diatribes, cast her vote in support of her former colleagues, and then looked straight across the House, where Cadman sat. A pause. An infinity. And then he rose.

The Liberals leapt to their feat, exultant, cheering, hugging, throwing papers in the air. They had survived. Stephen Harper watched, impassive, hiding his disappointment. Behind him, some of his Conservative colleagues sighed with relief.

For many Conservatives were far from certain that forcing an election was a good idea. The polls were yo-yoing all over the place, with Liberal support spiking and plummeting with each day's headlines. Yet Conservative support remained stubbornly fixed at around 30 per cent, and most polls showed the Liberals well ahead in Ontario, which the hacks of the press were incapable of describing as anything other than "vote-rich." Quebec, for the Tories, remained a wasteland. An election victory was no sure thing, MPs and strategists confided to each other; some of them even shared their concerns with journalists, after a few strategically purchased drinks.

How could this be? How could the Liberal Party of Canada – in power for twelve years, led by a prime minister who had failed to meet the high expectations he had himself encouraged, mired in scandal, and underperforming in Parliament – remain competitive with a united Conservative Party captained by an intelligent, skilful leader who had moderated many of his party's most socially contentious policies?

With another hung Parliament – led by an unstable minority government of whatever hue – the likely outcome of the next vote, whenever it might be, close observers of Canadian politics were asking themselves another, even more troubling, question.

Why had federal politics become so dysfunctional?

Political parties are coalitions. They unify groups with differing but compatible agendas in common cause. To the extent that the largest and most important groups within a society find common cause in one political party or another, the sum of the parties can be said to broadly represent the interests of a society.[1] Labour and Conservatives in Great Britain. Conservatives (of one kind or another) and Socialists in France. Democrats and Republicans in the United States. Christian Democrats and Social Democrats in Germany. These great parties contest for power, supported by large portions of the voting public, with specialized interests represented by smaller, boutique parties that, in some instances, hold the balance of power.

Canada is different. Canada is Sweden. Canada is Japan.[2]

That is to say, Canada historically has only been able to generate one political party, the Liberal Party of Canada, that represents a coalition sufficiently large and sufficiently geographically dispersed to lay claim to the title of national political party. The alternative governing party, currently named the Conservative Party of Canada, is an unstable, mercurial creation, constantly dissolving in faction and then regrouping, only to dissolve again. For it to gain power, two circumstances must conjoin: voter disgust at the Liberal hegemony must approach critical mass, and – perhaps sensing the opportunity – the conservative factions must unite under a single, strong leader.

Such a combination is almost impossible to achieve: since the First World War it has occurred only thrice. The first was during the Great Depression, when economic malaise and a decade of Liberal rule brought about the election of R.B. Bennett; the second came in the late 1950s, when Canadians reached their limit after more than twenty years of Liberal government and elected John Diefenbaker; the third arrived in 1984, after a decade and a half of economic decline and political turmoil, with the election of Brian Mulroney.[3] All three prime ministers were political failures, all three left their parties weakened by factional infighting, guaranteeing another long, Liberal reign.

In June of 2004, Canadians almost gave the Conservatives a fourth chance. Then they drew back, ensuring that the Liberal hegemony, even if weakened, would continue to dominate Canadian politics in the opening years of the twenty-first century.

Why? The answer lies in the composition of the political parties themselves, and in the social and political forces that determine their failure and success. Those forces were powerfully at work in June 2004, and the tumultuous year that followed.

Darrell Bricker stared at the numbers in amazement. It was Monday, June 28, the day of a federal election certain to produce a minority government. Only three days before, Bricker's polling firm Ipsos-Reid had put the Liberals and the Conservatives in a dead heat. Other pollsters were reporting similar results. Ipsos-Reid's seat projections had the Conservatives taking 117 seats to the Liberals' 101. Prime Minister Paul Martin, in power only six months, seemed headed for a humiliating defeat that could end his political career.

But Ipsos-Reid had continued polling over the weekend, and the latest results were difficult to fathom. Each day the Liberals had gained strength, particularly in Ontario. On Sunday, the spike was so sharp that it resembled an earthquake on a seismograph. After averaging the Friday, Saturday, and Sunday returns, Bricker issued a private poll Monday morning for his clients the *Globe and Mail* and CTV. Bricker still predicted a reduced Conservative minority. What he didn't realize was that a stampede was underway, with the Liberals gaining ground by the hour.

Other pollsters registered the same shift. Conrad Winn's polling firm Compas concluded that one voter in four made up their mind in the last twenty-four hours of the campaign, with most settling on the Liberals. The election-day outcome: 37 per cent of the popular vote for the Liberal Party, a good four percentage points higher than the last published polls had predicted; 30 per cent for the Conservatives, about 2 per cent below expectations; a respectable but disappointing 16 per cent for the NDP, who were shut out of their traditional base in Saskatchewan; a solid 12 per cent for the Bloc Québécois (49 per cent of the popular vote in Quebec), who captured 54 of Quebec's 75 seats; and a surprising 4 per cent for the Green Party.

The pollsters were embarrassed. No one had expected the Liberals to enjoy such a comfortable cushion of 135 seats to the Conservatives' 99. Frank Graves, of Ekos Research Associates, offered an intriguing post-election analysis: voters, he believed, were sloshing back and forth among the various parties, like water in a pail, but doing so in equal numbers, which hid the level of volatility. Come the weekend before the vote, a final slosh of undecided voters moved Liberal, producing the election-day result.[4] In the end, two percentage points of NDP voters shifted Liberal, thanks to left-leaning voters who feared a Conservative government, and another two percentage points of Conservative voters also went Liberal, having had second (or tenth) thoughts about the Conservatives themselves.

A year later, the situation hadn't changed a whit. Voters were even more disenchanted with the Liberals than they had been in the 2004 election. Paul Martin's approval rating had sunk, and most Canadians appeared to believe he either knew, or should have known, about the shenanigans of the Liberal Party in Quebec.

Yet they seemed no more willing to support the Tories than they had been in the last election. Fears of a federal government that would abandon medicare, or that would ignore and alienate Quebec, or that had some mysterious hidden social agenda were every bit as real in 2005 as they were in 2004. What was it about the Conservatives that people found so scary?

The Conservative Party of Canada that fought in the 2004 campaign was a jury-rigged affair, cobbled together in the six months leading up to the election call, a reunion of at least the English-speaking part of the schism that destroyed the Progressive Conservative Party in 1993. Although the PC's last leader, Peter MacKay, had fought hard to preserve his party's Red Tory fundamentals when negotiating the reunion with Harper's Canadian Alliance, it was the Alliance wing that would ultimately dominate.

The erupting sponsorship scandal gave the Conservatives ammunition for the election that quickly followed, but it was going to take more than voter disgust at Liberal arrogance and corruption to bring the latest version of the Conservative coalition to power. The Conservatives were still recovering from the union and the leadership convention. They hadn't had a chance to hold a policy conference, which meant the party leadership crafted policy on the fly during the campaign. The party was hampered by foolish remarks on bilingualism, abortion, and the role of the courts from loose-lipped MPs. Alberta premier Ralph Klein waded in, warning his province might abandon the Canada Health Act, which the Liberals exploited by painting Harper as Klein's secret ally. And there was the unpleasantness over child pornography, with the Conservative leader refusing to withdraw insinuations that Paul Martin was soft on perverts. The amazing thing, perhaps, is not that the Conservatives lost the election, but that they came so close.

But if the 2004 election was disappointing, the months that passed were frustrating in the extreme. The Conservatives had ample time to unite and discipline their caucus; a March 2005 policy convention further moderated the party's image by explicitly promising a Conservative government would not introduce abortion legislation. Meanwhile, the Liberal brand grew more and more tarnished. And yet Ontario would not be moved.

The reasons were twofold. The Conservative Party contained within itself an internal contradiction that alienated it from mainstream central Canadian voters. And that conflict was embodied in the leadership of the party's creator and leader.

In his memoirs, former American president Bill Clinton argues that 1968 marked "the year that conservative populism replaced progressive populism as the dominant political force in our nation."[5] In Canada, both movements had existed side by side for decades. Their roots lay in Prairie farms, small Ontario towns, and the hinterlands of both British Columbia and Quebec. Prairie populism, married to labour solidarity, spawned the uniquely Canadian brand of democratic socialism that was ultimately embodied in the New Democratic Party. Prairie populism married to religious conservatism spawned the Social Credit Party, the extreme right of the Progressive Conservative Party, and ultimately the Reform and Alliance parties. Because the Alliance dominated the merger, that same populism lay at the core of the new Conservative Party of Canada. The irony is, Stephen Harper is not himself a populist.

Harper was born and raised in Leaside, a comfortable enclave of old, WASP Toronto. As a youth, he was troubled by asthma, leaving him surprisingly introverted for someone with political ambitions. After an unsatisfying academic start at the University of Toronto, he moved to Alberta, eventually enrolling in economics at the University of Calgary, where he came under the spell, and contributed to the magic of, what has been dubbed the Calgary Mafia.

Tom Flanagan, Ted Morton, Barry Cooper, Rainer Knopff, David Bercuson, Roger Gibbins, and Robert Mansell are political scientists, historians, economists. Some are close friends and collaborators of Harper's, others mere acquaintances. Only Mansell actually taught Stephen Harper, but all of them knew him as a student, counselled him during his successful run for Parliament in 1993, supported him when he left Parliament – disgusted with leader Preston Manning's personal control and populist platitudes – and encouraged him when he ran for the leadership of the Alliance, and subsequently the Conservative, parties. By the time of the 2004 election campaign, Flanagan was the party's campaign manager, and Ken Boessenkool, another U of C alumnus, was policy director. The other members of the Calgary School – the mafia's more academically respectable name – enthusiastically supported their protegé, just as they had helped shape his thinking and his career.

Stephen Harper is an intellectual. Not only does he hold an M.A. in economics, he is steeped in the economic and political philosophy of Lévi-Strauss, Friedrich Hayek, Milton Friedman, and Allan Bloom. Not all of the red-meat intellectuals of the Calgary School – they hunt and fish, as well as teach and prose-lytize – adhere to the same economically neo-liberal and socially neo-conservative dogmas, but in general the Calgary School is the intellectual anchor for a collection of conservative principles now enshrined in the beliefs of Harper and his party. They include protecting and promoting the Canadian family as a stable heterosexual union dedicated to raising and nurturing children; rebuilding the Canadian military as a credible defensive and deterrent force; experimenting with, at the least, increased competition and private-sector delivery within the public health-care system; limiting federal involvement in areas of provincial jurisdiction, especially social policy; reforming or abolishing the Senate and curtailing the powers of the Supreme Court; lowering taxes; limiting transfers of wealth from richer to poorer regions of the country.

These policies can be sold at a populist level to disenfranchised voters angry at the elite accommodation that dominates the Canadian political process. Preston Manning, a preacher's son, was moderately successful at representing the package as a grass-roots rebellion by the common folk. But these ideas also have a home in the academy, and it was at the academy that Harper studied and embraced them. There is nothing new about this; the NDP has traditionally been dominated by a vanguard of the proletariat operating out of faculty clubs. In its way, Harper and the Calgary School are a vanguard of their own.

Partly to broaden his party's appeal, partly to placate moderate Tories, Harper has attempted to moderate or downplay many of the old Reform/Alliance nostrums. Yet economic and social conservatism is at the root of his being. He enumerated their values during what is now known as the Civitas Speech, delivered in the spring of 2003. In that speech, Harper argued that the economic tenets of neo-liberalism – low taxes, a balanced budget, a minimum of interference in the market – have been broadly adopted by the Liberal centre-left. The next fight, he maintained, will be a fight to instill the values of social conservatism in Canadian society, a conservatism that embraces "banning child pornography, raising the age of sexual consent, providing choice in education and strengthening the institution of marriage. All of these items are key to a conservative agenda."[6]

He added, however, that "rebalancing the conservative agenda will require careful political judgment.... We must realize that real gains are inevitably incremental.... Conservatives should be satisfied if the agenda is moving in the right direction, even if slowly."

And while the speech clearly outlines a faith-based conservative agenda, nowhere does it advocate repealing abortion laws, reintroducing capital punishment, or limiting the rights of homosexuals, although it would circumscribe their right to marry.

Nonetheless, the imprint is there, an imprint that has deepened with the success of activist Christian candidates who secured riding nominations from Vancouver to Halifax in 2005. Although the religious right has a long way to go before it can hope to dominate the Conservative Party, the party has a long way to go before it can hope to shed its image of backward-looking social intolerance. And that's a shame.

For whether you are by nature a conservative or a liberal in your own mind, you should probably hope for a Conservative victory in the next federal election. First and foremost, a healthy democracy rests upon the regular rotation of parties in power, which tempers the tendency for bureaucracies to favour one political party over another, and which bring fresh thinking to the policy conundrums of the day.

Besides, much of what the Conservatives are currently thinking is probably worth a try. The Conservatives are more willing than the Liberals to give the separate regions of Canada room to develop in their own, unique ways, unhindered by a controlling and paternalistic central government. They recognize the need to improve Canadian competitiveness by limiting the constraints on business and by further lowering taxes. They are less frightened at the thought of encouraging competition from the private sector in health care. They understand the terrible price Canada has paid in national pride and national will by allowing the military to deteriorate while Ottawa pursues Pollyannaish foreign policies. They comprehend the importance of strengthening both trade and defence ties with the United States. Canada could use a good strong dose of all of these policies, and the Conservatives are far more likely than the Liberals to provide them.

And yet, while the Conservatives may win the next election, or the election after that, their long-term prospects for political prosperity are bleak. For the Conservatives' social conservatism makes the party its own worst enemy. It means that the party will never win in the cities.

It is a mistake to analyze the 2004 results – or, for that matter, the results of 2000, 1997, or 1993 – in exclusively, or even primarily, regional terms. Yes, the West tends to support parties of the right – though it also elects Liberals and New Democrats. And yes, the Liberals are more popular in Ontario and in Quebec, although the Bloc continues to dominate that province. But a far more profound schism underlies the conflicting power base of each party. The Conservatives dominate the rural, small-town parts of

English Canada, while the Liberals dominate the urban centres. The two parties fight for control of what could be called "transition ridings" – those ridings on the outer perimeter of cities with one border approaching the city centre and another the countryside – where elections are won or lost.

Consider British Columbia. The Conservatives dominated the province in 2004, with twenty-two of thirty-six seats. (The Liberals managed to take eight, and the NDP five, with Cadman the Independent.) They took the Okanagan Valley, Kelowna, Prince George, much of Vancouver Island, and most of the interior. The Liberals were confined to two bastions: Vancouver and Victoria. But there, they ruled. Liberals were elected in Victoria, Vancouver Centre, Vancouver Quadra, Vancouver Kingsway, Vancouver South, and North Vancouver.

The toughest fights were in the sprawling suburban ridings surrounding Vancouver. Communities such as Surrey, Richmond, and Burnaby have a high percentage of recent immigrants, especially from South and East Asia. Since their home societies were socially more conservative than the liberal Canadian norm, they should be attracted to the Conservative Party. But they also feel a debt to the open-door immigration policies of the Liberals. Non-immigrants in these ridings were pulled between the low-tax, Western-protest attraction of the Conservatives, and the Liberal commitment to invest in cities and to protect social programs, especially health care.

The splits were reflected in the results. In South Surrey– White Rock–Cloverdale, Conservative Russ Hiebert managed to take about three thousand more votes than Liberal Judy Higginbotham, while in Richmond, Raymond Chan took the riding for the Liberals over Conservative competitor Alice Wong.

Meanwhile the NDP held on to the Burnaby–Douglas, which had been vacated by disgraced incumbent Svend Robinson.[7]

The scene was repeated, magnified, in Ontario. The rural ridings of Eastern Ontario went Conservative, and Southwestern Ontario handed the party twelve seats, for a respectable provincial total of 24 of Ontario's 106 seats. But the Tories were shut out of the cities. Twenty-one of twenty-two Toronto ridings went Liberal; the exception went NDP. London elected three out of four Liberals; Ottawa elected five Liberals, two Conservatives, and one NDP (former party leader Ed Broadbent). And the immigrant community came through for the Liberals in the "905 belt," with its government-defining twenty-three seats, which sent eighteen Liberals, four Conservatives, and one NDP to the House. In the eighteen seats that went Liberal, immigrants and ethnic minorities made up at least 31 per cent of the riding. In the four ridings that went Conservative, they were less than 5 per cent.[8]

Only in Atlantic Canada did the Liberals manage to pick up hinterland seats, though they dominated the cities as well, taking twenty-two of the region's thirty-two ridings, compared to seven for the Conservatives and three for the NDP.

The message for the Tories should be clear: The party needs to stop asking itself why it cannot elect MPs in sufficient numbers east of Manitoba. The merged party managed to snag a decent catch of seats in Ontario and retained most of the former Progressive Conservative base in Atlantic Canada (although it dropped 11 per cent in the popular vote there). The real problem is that urban voters don't like the Conservatives. They don't like them in Vancouver. They don't like them in Toronto or Ottawa. They don't like them in Halifax. And let's not mention Montreal. The Liberals even managed to pick up two seats in Winnipeg, one in Regina, and two in Edmonton. Calgary is the only city in Canada that votes solidly Conservative, but then Calgary is a fascinating exception to most rules.

If the country were truly elected by representation through population, Conservatives would fare even more poorly. Fortunately for them, historical residue and contemporary guilt combine to tilt the House of Commons in favour of rural seats. The B.C. riding of Vancouver–Sunshine Coast, the most populous riding in the country, has a population of 124,572. The largest riding in Ontario (Mississauga–Cooksville) has 122,192. But the riding of Churchill River, in Saskatchewan, has a population of 64,416. The smallest riding in the country (Labrador) has a population of 27,864.

Political circumstances could easily conspire to deliver a Conservative minority government in the near future. But it will be, in a larger sense, an aberration. With Canada becoming evermore urban, with immigrants settling almost exclusively in a few major centres, and populations steadily flowing from the hinterlands to the cities, the odds against the Conservatives taking power will steadily increase.

Why don't urban voters like the Tories? Because the Tories don't like them.

The dominance of the hinterlands within the Conservative caucus and among its membership has a disproportionate influence on the party's counsels. Canada's cities are everything that many of these rural Conservatives hate. They resent the end of European-based immigration. They abhor the embrace of homosexuals as fully equal members of society. They lament the dilution of Protestant Christianity as the moral bedrock on which laws and customs are based. They detest the elimination of the death penalty, the easy access to abortion, the campaign to limit the rights of gun-owners. They are rural anachronisms trapped within an urban present. Some of them, especially those located in Alberta, think that the divide is not cities versus country but the West versus the rest. (They try not to think of how Liberal Vancouver actually is.) But they are wrong. Politically, the Conservatives control one city: Calgary. Even if the West were to separate from Canada – even if it were to exempt British Columbia from that separation – Prairie Canada would still be a region growing steadily more urban, with rural and small-town life disappearing, and with most urban centres growing more Liberal with each passing year. There is no escape from this inevitability.

There are leaders within the party who well understand this dilemma. And they see a way out. For them, the solution lies in turning the very immigrants who are currently bedrock supporters of the Liberal Party in suburban ridings. In essence, they seek to revive the suburban-rural coalition that propelled Mike Harris to power in Ontario in 1995, on a tax-cutting and crime-fighting agenda. That coalition, they believe, can be recreated, with the socially conservative new arrivals, especially from Asia, yoked in alliance with the European settler culture of the hinterlands. While city centres may remain a wasteland for conservatism, Richmond can be won; Mississauga can be won; Nepean can be won.

These strategists forget three things. The first is that such unions are unstable, as Ontario proved with the election of Dalton McGuinty's Liberals in 2003. Suburban ridings can quickly and easily revert to alliance with city centres, suggesting that a suburban-hinterland coalition is ephemeral. The second thing ambitious Conservatives forget is that social conservatism lasts but a generation. The children of Chinese or Indian parents imbibe a secular public education, they hang out in malls, they listen to hip-hop. Precious few eighteen-year-old daughters of Lebanese parents support the death penalty, want to limit abortion rights, or oppose same-sex marriage. Hands up everyone out there who has a child more socially conservative than they are. Conservatives who hope to appeal to the social conservatism of new arrivals in suburban ridings must accept that their base of votes will always be older, less affluent, and prone to generational seepage.

The third obstacle to Conservative recruitment of immigrants itself reflects the urban-rural cleavages of the country. Simply put, the Canada that exists outside the big cities is predominantly white, and happy to keep it that way.

Walk the streets of Quebec City in November, when few tourists are around. The provincial capital demographically resembles Toronto half a century ago. Asian faces are rare; African and Caribbean ones almost non-existent. The racial homogeneity becomes even more pronounced as you head north, into the Saguenay–Lac-Saint-Jean regions. That same mix – or lack of it – is visible in Fredericton, in the small towns of Ontario's cottage country, in rural Saskatchewan, in British Columbia's interior.

Immigrants shun these communities, because there are so few of their own kind there, and because there are so few economic opportunities. Those communities, in turn, display little zeal to attract immigrants, revelling instead in their so-called cultural heritage, which is really a desiccated remnant of Canada's colonial past. Because of the mutual lack of attraction, these regions are deprived of the entrepreneurial skill, the energy and the vitality that immigrants bring with them. Because they have no immigrants, these communities become even poorer and their populations continue to decline, as the young move out in search of the same opportunities that immigrants are in search of, and the remaining families have too few children to sustain their numbers. The population of Newfoundland declined by 10 per cent in the 1990s; the population of Saskatchewan is in decline; Quebec's population is expected to go into decline in the coming decade.

Not everyone within these homogeneous, declining populations is prepared to acquiesce in their fate. The Nova Scotia government and the Regional Municipality of Halifax, for example, are attempting to develop policies to encourage immigrants to settle in that city and province. Other strategies, however, actively deter immigration. Devoting resources to preserving schools and other facilities in small communities, rather than encouraging migration to larger centres, does more than simply waste money; it preserves a rural, European culture that, by its very nature, holds neither promise nor opportunity for new arrivals. An obsessive devotion to Nova Scotia's Celtic roots implicitly discourages cultural diversity. It would be the equivalent of Toronto officially celebrating the Glorious Twelfth.

In truth, there are two Canadas: the old, white one, clinging to the rock and soil of the Shield and Prairies, to Maritime moose pasture and the habitable patches of B.C.'s interior, a Canada that is insular and resentful and getting poorer; and the new Canada, polyglot, expansionist, affluent (or seeking to be), and in love with Montreal, Ottawa-Gatineau, Toronto, Calgary, Edmonton, Vancouver.

The Old Canada is the Canada of the Conservative Party.

The parallel is by no means absolute. Atlantic Canada is actually even more attracted to the Liberal Party, which devotes much of its existence to transferring wealth from other parts of Canada into that region. And there are Conservatives in cities: economic ones, who warm to Conservative policies of low taxation and deregulation; and social ones, who fear Canada is racing down a road to perdition. But the broad comparison holds. The Conservative Party does not thrive in cities, because the party's social conservative agenda does not resonate with urban voters, even immigrant ones. Conservatives might win an election here and an election there, as they did in the last century when the population lost its patience with the Liberals. But the long-term prospects hold little promise.

Consider one critical issue in the Conservative platform: opposition to the gun registry. Everyone agrees that it represents a dismal example of Liberal incompetence and mismanagement.[9] But for some Canadians, the resentments run deeper. For farmers, hunters, and even many rural residents who don't own weapons the gun registry represents an assault on their culture. For them, it is a draconian imposition of state regulation on what should be a fundamental freedom: the right to bear arms. It is, as well, a repudiation of the very settler culture of which they are the last remnants, an attack on nothing less than the country's own heritage.

Their anger is understandable. But it is an anachronistic argument that can have no resonance with a Sri Lankan arriving on our shores, having fled a country with far too many guns. How is the Conservative Party to appeal to that Sri Lankan, when so much of the party's psychic energy is taken up by such an issue? What is the gun registry to him?

One mystery that Conservatives cannot fathom is why rural Canada, evangelical Christian Canada, and urban neo-conservative Canada have failed to unite in a single party that mirrors the appeal of the Republican Party in the United States. One answer might lie in the relative emptiness of the Canadian midlands and the Far North, compared with the American midlands and the South. If America consisted of the big liberal cities of the Northeast along with Los Angeles in the West, with not much of anything to be found between the Appalachians and the Rockies except for lone, resentful Dallas, then American politics would look a lot more like Canadian politics. Another answer might lie – although this is a personal observation more than a researched phenomenon – in the preference of Canadian urban neo-conservatives to hang with, and vote with, urban liberals rather than with rural conservatives. Better to be taxed than to bring back the death penalty. Or, to put it another way, on Toronto's College Street West on a Saturday night, some may be of the left, and some may be of the right, but all are metrosexuals.

All of this, and we haven't even mentioned Quebec.

There are three schools of thought within the Conservative Party on Quebec. One, centred in Alberta, contends that it is possible to win power while ignoring the province. As long as the Bloc can split Quebec with the Liberals, goes the reasoning, and the West stays predominantly Conservative, a minority or even a majority government is possible, by swinging Ontario away from the Liberals. This argument is so flawed that it is hard to credit that so many of the party's right-wing ideologues hold to it. First off, it would be extremely dangerous for the country. The Liberals at least have a presence in Western Canada, with representation in all four provinces. To attempt to govern without any support from Quebec, however, would stoke the fires of separatism – which in a good year may be banked, but are never extinguished – into a full conflagration. It would mean an English-speaking government attempting to speak to a French-speaking nation. The nightmare scenario for this country – and it is an absolute bone-chiller – would be Stephen Harper leading a minority Conservative government, with the Bloc Québécois holding sixty or more seats in Quebec, and the Parti Québécois defeating Jean Charest's Liberals in the next provincial election. Who would speak for federalism in the 2008 referendum on separation? How much greater would be the chances, finally, of a Yes?

Besides being extremely dangerous, a Conservative victory without at least some support in Quebec might be impossible. Ontario voters are leery of Tories as it is. A conscious abandonment of Quebec by that party would keep many of them away from the Conservatives, no matter how upset they were with the Liberal hegemony. Joe Clark came close to winning a majority government in 1979, despite having almost no representation in Quebec, but the operative word in that clause is *close*, which in politics is no cigar. Ignoring Quebec is, for the Conservatives, a non-starter.

A second school of thought argues that, even without Quebec representation, the Conservatives could govern with the co-operation of the Bloc. After all, the Bloc is itself an offshoot of the Conservative Party, formed when Lucien Bouchard bolted the Mulroney coalition due to the failure of Meech Lake. The Conservative commitment to provincial rights, with its dis-avowal of federal intrusion in areas of provincial jurisdiction, would appeal to the Bloc. It might even convince the Bloc – or at least some of its members – to enter into a coalition with the Conservatives, in exchange for seats in cabinet.

The problem with this scenario is ideological. The great majority of the Bloc's members, as well as the party's platform, are to the left of the Liberals, never mind the Conservatives. Brian Mulroney's coalition held together as long as it did because the Progressive Conservative prime minister retained the status quo, as it then was, of the Canadian welfare state, and because nationalist Quebeckers were prepared to put aside their social agenda in exchange for a realignment of the powers within Confederation. It is unlikely that today's Bloc would make such a sacrifice again, especially because its soft-sovereigntist position has lost its adjective. Further, the Conservatives would risk alienating their Western base if they were seen to make too many concessions to Quebec nationalism, recreating the very schism that destroyed the last incarnation of a national conservative party. Yes, it's damned if they do and damned if they don't.

The third scenario is the one that is necessary (though not sufficient) to bring the Conservatives to power. The party must make a breakthrough in Quebec. It must win votes from Quebec federalists disgusted with the cronyism and corruption of the Liberal Party in that province, from nationalists who are ready to vote for a party that will respect the autonomy of all provinces, and from economic conservatives who want to curtail the power of the state, federal as well as provincial. One way to accelerate the process might be to convince the Action Démocratique du Québec (ADQ), led by Mario Dumont, to support the federal Conservatives. Failing that, the party must organize on the ground, establishing a network of riding associations, volunteers, and activists who will run for, and campaign for, the party in the next federal election.

And that's the problem. The ADQ has evinced no great interest in consorting with the Conservatives federally, nor displayed any evidence of being able to deliver seats if it did. Creating a viable political machine in a province with a language and culture foreign to much of the existing Conservative Party is a potentially insurmountable challenge. It could take several elections, if ever, before the Tories are once again a credible presence in Quebec federal politics. And the more energy the party apparatus and its leader spend on cultivating that presence, the more it will annoy Westerners who think the province isn't worth the effort.

Nonetheless, the third way is the only way, and Stephen Harper knows it. The Conservative leader has been taking extraordinary measures since June 2004 to build the party in Quebec. He appointed Quebec party strategists Josée Verner, Jean Fortier, and Nancy Pierre to the leader's office, charging them with the mandate of establishing a Québécois party apparatus. (The Conservative leader's office is more francophone than the Prime Minister's Office.[10]) Harper has also spent substantial time working the province: making contact with potential riding organizers, recruiting candidates. At its inaugural policy convention in March 2005, the party endorsed official bilingualism, to the delight of its surprisingly substantial Quebec contingent. In the 2004 election, senior officials in the Bloc were impressed with the quality of the Conservative campaign in certain ridings, such as Louis St. Laurent in Quebec City. A few even predicted that the Conservatives could take a few seats in the next election. Harper has dedicated much of the post-election period to the realization of that possibility. Harper's closest advisers, when asked about Quebec, put forward their two-election strategy: Win a minority government, with little or no Quebec support, govern well, and in the subsequent election win the federalist Quebec vote away from the Liberals. Harper's efforts at establishing an infrastructure in Quebec are clearly aimed at laying the foundations for that two-election breakthrough.

The Conservative leader has not confined himself to Quebec, however. Both during and after the election, Harper sought to moderate his party's image, making it more palatable for centrist voters, especially in Ontario, while trying not to dull the edge of its Western-based economic and social conservatism. Harper knows that a Conservative Party crafted in his own ideological image would never come to power. It would drive those Red Tories who remained with the party into the arms of the Liberals. It would extinguish the party in Atlantic Canada, and condemn it to a perpetual rural rump in Ontario.

This reasoning lay behind the tone of resolute moderation that permeated the March 2005 policy convention. In particular, Harper explicitly promised that a Conservative government would not introduce legislation limiting the right to an abortion, thus robbing the Liberals of one of their most potent Tories-are-scary weapons.

Perversely, Harper undermined all this good work with his categorical opposition to Bill C-38, the Liberal legislation legalizing same-sex marriage. Harper tried his best to present a reasoned alternative, proposing civil unions while keeping marriage itself a heterosexual estate. But the constitutional impossibility of his position,[11] coupled with the fervent support of evangelical Christians for his cause, only further entrenched the image of the Conservative Party as the handmaiden of the moral far-from-majority, while once again alienating Quebeckers, among whom support for same-sex marriage is strong. (The Quiet Revolution turned Quebec from the most socially conservative to the most socially liberal Canadian community in less than a generation.) The Tories' efforts to court immigrants from socially conservative countries through advertisements in the ethnic press only reinforced the opportunism of their campaign. In the long run, the Tory campaign against same-sex marriage probably did the party far more harm than good.

With these policies, this leader, and all this baggage the Conservatives will contest the next election. It is an open question whether the New Conservatives will win favour with enough voters to bring the party to power. Harper is a formidable organizer whose political skills have been consistently underrated by his opponents. But he has failed to form that ineffable, emotive bond with voters that marks a truly successful politician. He remains aloof and inscrutable – and that inscrutability leads voters to beware of him. Can we *really* trust the Conservative social agenda? How closely tied is the party to the radical ideologues in Alberta? What will happen to health care under a Conservative watch? Will Canada sell its sovereignty to the United States – or perhaps even just give it away? Will we go through the same-sex marriage debate again?

So daunting are the obstacles facing the Conservative Party, so fragile is its coalition, and so limited its prospects, that it is tempting to believe that it has no hope of ever forming a stable minority government, let alone forging a majority.

But the Conservatives do have one crucial weapon in their arsenal. They are fighting the Liberals. And rarely in its history has the Liberal Party of Canada been more vulnerable.

When we look at the Liberal Party, we see ourselves.

If Canada is a bilingual country, welcoming its French and English heritage, it is because Liberal governments from the days of Wilfrid Laurier on, fought to preserve and protect the French fact.

If Canada is a multicultural nation, embracing immigrants from every nook and cranny of the globe, it is because Liberal governments identified immigration as the first, best hope of filling this land's vast empty spaces.

If Canada is a welfare state unique in the world, with public health and education systems, a national program to even out economic disparities among regions, and a national commitment to welfare, old-age assistance, and subsidized housing for low-income families, it is because Liberal governments entrenched these policies.

If Canada has a cultural identity defined by paternalist compassion, a mythic (and largely imaginary) bond with the wilderness, and a sense of moral superiority toward the United States, it is because cultural institutions forged and subsidized by Liberal governments inculcated that culture.

If the fishing industry is on the ropes, it is because Liberal governments managed the fishery.

If Canadian productivity lags behind that of the United States, it is because Liberal governments chose high taxes and income redistribution over entrepreneurship and personal responsibility.

If Canada is respected around the world as a nation of peacekeepers, it is because a Liberal invented the concept and the word.

If Canada is derided as a nation militarily enfeebled and devoid of a coherent foreign policy, it is because Liberal governments gutted the army, navy, and air force, while attempting to be all things to all interest groups.

The Liberal Party *is* Canada, just like the Canadian cartoon strip: For Better or For Worse.

Long before Confederation, Liberals fought for responsible, autonomous, democratic government. John A. Macdonald's Conservatives were actually in a minority in Upper Canada, largely confined to the Tory bastions of Toronto, and propped up by the conservative *Bleus* of Lower Canada. But George Brown's Reform Party, an amalgam of moderate and radical reformers, dominated Canada West, and were increasingly impatient with the condescending coalition that they felt stifled real progress. Grit agitation finally forced a reluctant Macdonald to enter into a Grand Coalition that ultimately negotiated the terms of Confederation. And although the wily Father of Confederation was able to govern through most of the rest of his life, the latent power of the emerging Liberal Party predestined its ultimate dominance. Simply put, the Liberals understood Canada and the Conservatives did not.

First, capitalizing on Québécois outrage over the execution of Louis Riel, the Liberals made themselves the natural governing party of Quebec, severing the Tory/Bleu alliance. If Wilfrid Laurier taught his party nothing else, he taught it the essential truth that, without Quebec, no federal government could govern long or well. While the Conservatives have failed to choose a single francophone Quebecker as leader from the first day of Confederation until now, the Liberals have made it a practice to alternate between French and English chiefs. More important, the party contorted itself to ensure that Quebec interests were being accommodated by the federal government, that French minority rights would be respected in other provinces, that Quebec

would be able to protect its language and control its cultural institutions. Often that meant turning a blind eye to corrupt and
oppressive regimes in Quebec City, but it was the price of ensuring that Quebeckers were masters in their own homes, long
before they came to believe they weren't.

Protecting Quebec meant being comfortable with Catholicism,
which made Liberals both more religiously tolerant and more
attractive to immigrants, a great many of whom in the early years
of this country came from Ireland and Eastern or Southern
Europe, areas that were predominantly Catholic. The ongoing
alliance with the small farmers and business interests of Southern
Ontario – Toronto's Bay Street was free to support the Tories,
although the Liberals always kept the lines of communication (and
fundraising) open – ensured a continuing strong presence in
Ontario. The coalition of Ontario and Quebec interests guaranteed Liberal dominance in the House of Commons, although it
was also bound to make it more difficult to forge alliances in the
pioneer lands to the west, whose settlers resented what they saw
as oppression by the financial oligarchies in Montreal and Toronto.

The Liberals' third inspiration was to recognize the importance of industrialization. Mackenzie King, who took over the
leadership of the party in 1919 and finally surrendered it in 1948,
was a thoroughly modern man, a labour lawyer who consorted
with the Rockefellers and who recognized the importance of
urbanization, industrialization, and an enlightened social policy.
The Liberals had always supported free trade – in contrast to the
Tories' mercantilist fondness for high tariffs – and if King could
never break down the barriers entirely, he could at least promote
a modern, outward-looking Canada that would, under his prime
ministership, lay the foundations for the welfare state and take its

place on the world stage as an important and respected member of the Western alliance. Canada emerged as a great trading nation that sold its wheat and its wares to the world, backed up by a state-of-the-art infrastructure that expanded from roads and railroads to the St. Lawrence Seaway, the TransCanada Pipeline, and a national network of airports.

While the poor, bedraggled Conservatives fought to preserve the Union Jack and the Maple Leaf Forever, the Liberals under Lester Pearson and Pierre Trudeau capitalized on the social revolution already underway in the 1960s, expanding immigration to include new arrivals from all parts of the Third World, liberalizing the abortion laws while proscribing capital punishment, getting the government out of your bedroom while introducing a comprehensive pension plan, and, most important of all, launching the world's only fully public health-insurance plan for doctors and hospitals. When sovereignty emerged as a major political force in Quebec in the 1970s, it was clear that only the Liberals could contain the centrifugal forces straining the federation. Pierre Trudeau confronted and defeated René Lévesque, while expanding the bilingual and multicultural foundations of the country and patriating the Constitution, enshrining a bill of rights that would further transform the federation.

Although, in the ultimate political irony, it was a Conservative government that negotiated the Free Trade Agreement with the United States, the Liberals under Jean Chrétien returned to form when they returned to power, endorsing the expansion of the free-trade agreement to include Mexico, embracing (hypocritically) the tax reforms that were the other signal achievement of the Brian Mulroney government, while correctly diagnosing and curing the fiscal crisis created by two decades of deficits.

Finally, successive federal Liberal governments helped build the cosmopolitan, diverse urban wonders that are Canada's gift to the world. Liberal immigration policies brought people from here, there, and everywhere. Bilingualism and multiculturalism ensured that new arrivals could be confident their culture would be respected, provided only that they adhere to the customs and values enshrined in Canadian laws and the Canadian Constitution. Liberal social policies ensured that these new arrivals would immerse themselves in a society that had evolved beyond tolerance to the blessed state of indifference toward skin colour, religion, and sexuality. The Liberal Party created the modern, urban Canada that the Conservative Party simply does not understand.

A century and a half after Confederation, the Liberals remain the only political party able to command major representation in the electorally all-important provinces of Quebec and Ontario. As a fillip, they remain strong as well in Atlantic Canada. If the party is starved for support in much of the West, well, 'twas almost ever thus. The Conservatives' continuing incomprehension of Quebec, the latent Ludditism that infects the grass roots of that party, not to mention its chronic internal contradictions and inability to gauge, let alone ride before, political winds, promises to ensure Liberal dominance throughout the foreseeable future, whatever the vagaries of this election or that. The Liberals governed for better than 70 per cent of the twentieth century. The only question in the twenty-first century is whether they will beat their record.

And this is a tragedy for Canada. For the Liberals of 2005 are ridden with political cancer. The disease has not only attacked their own party, it has metastasized to the bureaucracy, and threatens to sicken the entire body politic. The Liberals are tired, spent, and casually corrupt. As currently constituted, their hegemony

47

represents the single biggest threat to the continued health of this country. Canada's weaknesses are weaknesses fostered by Liberal error, arrogance, and misdirection. The federal government's declining legitimacy reflects the declining legitimacy of the Liberal Party.

That which ails the Liberal Party ails Canada itself.

Most Canadians know in their bones that the sponsorship scandal in Quebec is about far more than simply alleged abuse by a small handful of officials. Jean Chrétien, panicked by his near-loss of the country in the 1995 referendum, ordered up a government program to flood Quebec with the Canadian flag, as if a sudden plethora of Maple Leaves would awaken Quebeckers to the blessings of federalism. The program was quickly perverted into a cash-for-contracts scheme: evidence at the Gomery inquiry into the fiasco suggested that advertising executives were pressured to kick back millions of dollars in cash donations and free services to the Liberal Party and senior executives in it – an accommodation some of these businessmen were all too happy to make, given the millions more in money-for-nothing profits that they earned through the sponsorship deals.

To be fair, there is no reason to believe that Chrétien himself approved, or even knew of, the abuses being committed in Quebec in the party's name. It appears the scam was limited to a few bureaucrats, politicians, party fundraisers, and advertising executives. But that it should ever have taken root at all speaks to the culture of entitlement that infects the Liberal Party, especially in Quebec, and the implicit assumption by the bureaucracy that the party is the government and the government, the party.

The scandal is both symptom and symbol of the malaise within the Liberal Party. Within any healthy, multi-party democracy, an abuse of process and power so grave should have certainly led to the government's swift defeat, and good riddance to it. That Paul Martin has been able to cling to power – albeit via a minority government – speaks to the desperate weakness of the alternatives. The irony is that, on top of everything else, the scandal spoke to the disintegration of the bond that once existed between the party and its central bastion of support: Quebec.

Government advertising has traditionally been among the most obscene abuses of liberal democracy. Parties of all stripes at both the federal and provincial level have used taxpayers' dollars to promote the party in power through thinly veiled propaganda masquerading as information. If there is one immediate, emphatic reform that all citizens should demand of their governments, it is to eliminate patronage and partisan politicking in the awarding of government advertising contracts. Dalton McGuinty's Ontario Liberals have embarked on exactly such reforms at the provincial level. But within the federal Liberal Party, the mere thought of surrendering such a valuable patronage tool is enough to make a political operative swoon.

The sponsorship program turned out to be the epitome of Liberal patronage politics triumphing over sound public policy. Only this time, they went too far. A $250-billion program not only failed to produce a single demonstrable benefit, it left the federalist cause in Quebec dangerously discredited, reviving the Parti Québécois and the danger of a successful referendum on separation.

On top of everything else, the sponsorship scandal highlighted the corrosive effect that too many years of Liberal government was having on the federal public service. Senior bureaucrats, political advisers, and at least one cabinet minister co-operated to launch and exploit the ill-conceived program, without the normal checks and balances that a properly functioning mandarinate would insist upon from its political masters. The incestuous relationship that had developed between the bureaucracy and the Liberal Party, as revealed by the sponsorship mess, was distressingly par for the course. It also offered further evidence of serious problems within the federal public service.

There are few top-quality people in the most important posts; it can take months to replace a deputy minister; institutional memory is noticeably failing. Too many senior bureaucrats are marking time till retirement – "retired in place" – while the brightest and best of younger workers are reluctant to commit themselves to such a rigid, hierarchical organization. In fairness, those who lament the loss of the "golden age" of the federal public service forget that the service was almost exclusively male, white, and elitist in the extreme. The actual calibre of men and women in the senior ranks of the Ottawa mandarinate today is probably neither better nor worse than it was a generation ago. Nonetheless, evidence of sclerosis is in plain view, and efforts at renewal have proved, thus far, tentative and largely ineffectual. At the lead-up to the first ministers health summit in September 2004, for example, provincial politicians were genuinely dismayed by the lack of information or coherent analysis coming out of Ottawa. Federal politicians were similarly alarmed. The Department of Health lacked the skills and resources to develop a comprehensive national picture of the state of the health-care system, identify its weaknesses, and propose remedies. The job had simply gotten beyond them.

Consider one simple, but telling, example of the substitution within the public service of process over performance. The federal public service has always placed a premium on bilingualism, while accepting that only a minority of the country is or will ever be fluent in both official languages. French-language services are rarely needed in Calgary, and the Employment Insurance office in Jonquière does its work almost exclusively in French. In Ottawa, most officers communicate in French and English, recognizing that in some work situations, English is likely to be the only language that everyone in the room understands.

But a misplaced determination by the Chrétien government to elevate the level of bilingualism within the senior ranks of the public service led to a coercive program of enforced bilingualism training. Mere working knowledge of both languages was no longer sufficient for public servants; instead full proficiency was the goal.

The new regulations led to hundreds of public servants leaving their jobs for up to a year, in a grim, and sometimes futile, attempt to achieve the new proficiency. The loss to productivity in the federal public service from senior managers forced out of their jobs for months at a time, if not permanently, was incalculable. The loss to the country, from excluding the overwhelming majority of its citizens who are not fluent in both languages from the most important positions within the public service, is similarly impossible to gauge. But anyone who believes it is well and good to confine the federal public service, especially in its upper reaches, to the lucky few who grew up in the "bilingual belt" on either side of the Quebec border, or who were blessed with the opportunity and capacity to enter French or English immersion programs at a young age, is someone who believes in the primacy of form over function, of keeping up appearances over getting the job done.

In imposing this latest intrusion on the bureaucracy, the Liberals have once again signalled their determination to persist with what could be called a certain idea of Canada, a Canada crafted in the imaginations of post–Second World War planners, a Canada that was never fully realized, that has in some cases slipped away from, and in other cases surpassed, that ideal. Canada doesn't want to be what the Liberals want it to be any more. The inability of the Liberals to recognize this and adapt produces an endless, debilitating friction between the federal government and the Canadian people that enervates the nation.

We see this manifested in the chronic warfare between the provinces, who are responsible for delivering social policy, and Ottawa, which seeks to control it through its spending power. We see it in the criminal neglect of the armed forces under Liberal command. We see it in the hypocrisy and confusion attending our foreign policy. We see it in the latent anti-Americanism that infects elements of the Liberal Party and impairs relations with our all-important neighbour.

We see it in the decay and decline of the Liberal Party itself.

The sponsorship scandal was not simply a case of Liberals running amok in Quebec. It was a manifestation of the ongoing civil war within the upper reaches of the party, one that consumes its leadership and weakens its ability to act in the national interest.

In the last years of Pierre Trudeau's reign, a band of young Liberals chafed at the secretive and elitist barons who managed the machinery. These young rebels included David Herle and Terrie O'Leary. Later allies would include Richard Mahoney, Tim Murphy, and Scott Reid. They fought against the power of the backrooms; they backed outsider John Turner against the party hierarchy's chosen successor, Jean Chrétien; they defended Turner against attempted coups by Chrétien forces after Turner lost the 1984 election; they supported Paul Martin against Chrétien in the 1990 leadership contest; and they plotted Chrétien's over-throw, when it became clear the prime minister wasn't prepared to cede power on Martin's own terms.

Today, the Liberal Party remains riven with faction. The prime minister, presiding over a minority government, must keep one eye cocked for restive backbenchers who threaten to vote against their party's own legislative agenda, humiliating the administration. Leadership aspirants such as Martin Cauchon, Frank McKenna, John Manley, and Joe Volpe are for the moment quiescent, but everyone knows that, whatever the results of the next federal election, the jockeying to replace the aging leader will begin the day after the vote. Meanwhile, the sponsorship scandal continues to divide the party between the Chrétien wing, which is enraged at being depicted by its own leadership as corrupt ward-heelers, and the Martin wing, which lays the sponsorship mess squarely at Chrétien's door, and blames him and his supporters for almost destroying the party.

Consumed by internal strife, terrified of losing their grip on power, the Liberals continue to push outdated policies and pri-orities that are at direct odds with the best interests of the country. The Canada of Louis St. Laurent, of Lester Pearson, of Pierre Trudeau, of Jean Chrétien, is a Canada bound by shared social commitments, by east-west bonds of culture, communication, and responsibility. Since Canada's vast geography and scattered settlement patterns do not lend themselves to an organic expres-sion of these bonds, the Liberals consider it the job of the federal government to manufacture them: through the social safety net, through such cultural institutions as the Canada Council and the CBC, through vehicles to enhance national communications (the CRTC) and transportation (VIA Rail).

These policies, even when they seemed most relevant, were always questionable or incomplete. Today, they are anachronistic. Canada always was and has increasingly become a nation of disparate regions far more oriented north-south, both economically and culturally, than east-west. British Columbia pursues a destiny manifestly different from that of Alberta, let alone New Brunswick. Federal Liberal efforts to break down the country's internal borders through so-called national standards in social, cultural, and communications policy are doomed to failure, simply because the populations of the regions are indifferent to that goal. Many of them are also hostile to the principle tool used to achieve that goal: redistribution. It can be said without exaggeration that the primary function of the federal government today is to redistribute wealth. It is redistributed vertically through progressive taxation, which takes from the better-off and gives to the less-well-off through the mechanism of the welfare state. Ottawa pursues the same policy horizontally, taking from the wealthier provinces and shovelling the funds to the poorer provinces through equalization and economic development programs. These policies are not only unfair – in that there are limits to the obligation of those who accumulate wealth to hand over that wealth to those who have failed to accumulate it – they are also inefficient, in that capital is transferred from the most productive and successful regions to the least, with no tangible, lasting economic benefit to show for it. Yet the Liberals under Paul Martin continue to pursue their Pearsonian ideals with vigour.

Why? Because, apart from wealth redistribution, Liberals are unable to think of a reason for Ottawa to exist.

Such a blinkered conception of the role of the federal government within Confederation approaches the tragic, both for the Liberal Party and the country. Because of its obsessions with domestic social policy, especially as expressed through redistributive programs, the Liberals not only impair the fair and efficient working of the economy, they denigrate and neglect the real purpose of the federal government, which is to defend the nation from its enemies, maintain the peace, secure the borders, and represent Canada before the world.

Worst of all, they institutionalize and worsen the very regional disparities that the federal government is sworn to ameliorate. The Liberal Party of Canada has created a country of solitudes, each indifferent toward, or resentful of, the others. And that is where we must turn our attention next.

CHAPTER TWO

FOUR SOLITUDES

Very shortly after Confederation, Nova Scotia almost left it, and with good reason. A lot of Nova Scotians thought the union had been a huge mistake. The largest colony of the Maritimes was thriving. A reciprocity agreement with the United States, coupled with robust shipbuilding and merchant shipping industries, had made it prosperous. Halifax was a financial and cultural hub of British North America. Why surrender all of this, for the sake of union with some distant inland cousins? Charles Tupper, the political leader of the province and a staunch supporter of Confederation, was so afraid of what the voters would do if given the chance that he refused to hold elections until after the British North America Act came into effect. He was right.

When Tupper finally called an election in September 1867, a furious citizenry drove him from office, installing in his place Joseph Howe, the firebrand opponent of union.

But Howe turned out to be simply one of a long string of politicians bested by the political genius of Sir John A. Macdonald. Canada's first prime minister sweetened the pot by increasing federal transfers to Nova Scotia – infuriating the premiers of the other provinces, who had to subsidize the bribe against their will – while convincing Howe that the new union was a *fait accompli*. With a few dollops of patronage in the right places, the separatist premier and his supporters accepted the new arrangement. Confederation was secured, and no one has been truly happy since.

Hugh MacLennan derived the title of his 1945 novel *Two Solitudes* from the writings of Rilke: "Love consists in this, that two solitudes protect, and touch, and greet each other."[1] If only. This is a foul-tempered federation, steeped in the ancient resentments of the conquered French, in Maritime remembrance of prosperity past, in an outsized Western inferiority complex. Maybe it's inevitable that in a thinly populated land, whose disparate outposts of settlement are separated by hundreds, even thousands, of kilometres of bush, mountain, and prairie, citizens should approach each other as strangers and potential antagonists. Whatever the reason, Canada has evolved into at least four solitudes: Atlantic Canada, Quebec, Ontario, and the West. Even this is highly simplistic. Newfoundland and Labrador differ markedly in their history and culture from the Maritimes. (For that matter, Labrador differs markedly from Newfoundland.) More than mere mountains separate Calgary from Vancouver, while Winnipeg isn't entirely sure it is in the West, or wants to be. And then there is the North, with its own culturally and racially distinct communities.

But to keep from going mad, let's look upon Canada as a political union of four regions: the Atlantic East; the French Centre; the English Centre; and the Prairie and Pacific West. Each is, in its own way, distinct. You would think that the job of the central government in such a scattered federation would be to draw these communities together. But while there have been some successes, Ottawa has accomplished little beyond making everyone, everywhere equally mad at Ottawa. Too much more of this, and we could talk ourselves out of a country. But before we can prescribe a cure, we must understand the malady that has convinced each of Canada's four regions that the other three are out to get it. And let's start with the region that a lot of people don't even think of as a region at all: Ontario.

Ontario can be a bit much.

Confederation, as the smarter historians have observed, was a divorce as well as a marriage. Upper Canada – young, English, Protestant, prosperous, full of pioneer spirit and imperial ambitions to colonize the West – had run out of patience with French, Catholic Lower Canada, which was already two centuries old and set in its ways. In 1841, London had ordered the two colonies to federate in a single Province of Canada; the British North America Act of 1867 was partly an attempt to fix that mistake by creating two new provinces: Ontario and Quebec. For the next three decades, Ontario was the bad boy of Confederation, using its influence in Parliament to procure policies that served its interests, defying that Parliament whenever the federal power tried to constrain the aggressive, ambitious province. Ontario and Ottawa fought over border issues, control of natural resources, regulating the insurance business, nationalization of the emerging electricity sector, who got to name Queen's Counsels. Time after time, Prime Minister Macdonald tried to rein in the obstreperous province that, even more than Quebec, challenged the federal power for primacy. Time after time, the Judicial Committee of the Privy Council in London sided with Ontario premier Oliver Mowat – the only politician who regularly bested Macdonald – leaving Ontario in control of the vast lands stretching from the French River to just beyond Lake of the Woods; securing provincial control over natural resources; and affirming the unchallenged sovereignty of Queen's Park in the fields of its jurisdiction. "What luck Mowat has had with the P.C.!" Macdonald wrote in despair.[2] His successor, the wary Wilfrid Laurier, decided to leave well enough alone, effectively surrendering the federal power to disallow offensive provincial legislation: Ottawa had learned that taking on Imperial Ontario was a losing proposition.

As often as not, however, the two got along. Ontario politicians supported federal efforts to push Confederation westward, securing new markets for Ontario's manufactured goods. And Ontario fervently supported the National Policy, first enunciated by Macdonald and entrenched by his successors, which erected prohibitive tariffs to exclude American manufacturers from the Canadian market, forcing consumers in other provinces to purchase their plows – and later their refrigerators – from Ontario factories. Because the National Policy worked for Ontario, Ontario decided it was a virtue. Tightening the bonds that linked east to west, be it through tariffs, railroads, or a public broadcaster, was both patriotic and good for business. It ensured that even the most far-flung regions of the federation would look toward the

Centre – for manufactured goods, for bank loans, for the news, for political leadership – whether they wanted to or not. Over the years, and through the crucible of two world wars, tensions between Toronto and Ottawa eased, as the interests of the one harmonized with the interests of the other. Ontario became so synonymous with Confederation itself that some observers were moved to wonder: Does Ontario exist?

And then came 1984.

Brian Mulroney simply didn't understand the way the system worked. Federal governments were supposed to consist of Ontario and Quebec MPs acting in the national interest. The national interest was the interest of the Centre, where most of the people lived. The provinces, it had to be said, were increasingly failing to do their part. They obstructed Pierre Trudeau's efforts to bring home the Constitution and create a charter of rights; Quebeckers elected a sovereigntist government that claimed Quebec wasn't part of Canada at all, much less at the centre of it; and Albertans simply refused to understand the cool logic of the 1980 National Energy Program, which sought to nationalize the oil-and-gas sector, subsidize oil prices, and protect industrial (principally Ontario) jobs. But however much provincial governments might howl, Parliament was supposed to be based on rep. by pop., and Ontario had 40 per cent of the pop.

Yet, although 32 per cent of Mulroney's caucus after his humongous 1984 landslide consisted of MPs from Ontario, 27 per cent of his seats came from the West, and a further 27 per cent came from Quebec. Temperamentally, Mulroney's was a government of Quebec and Western nationalists, implicitly allied against the English Centre. Such a shaky coalition could never last long, and the administration ultimately foundered on its internal contradictions, leading to the rise of regionally based protest parties, the Reform and the Bloc Québécois. But none of that happened until after the Mulroney government's single greatest achievement: a Free Trade Agreement with the United States.

In the end, free trade was good for Ontario. The province's branch-plant economy, protected from real competition by tariff walls and subsidized energy, was growing steadily less competitive. Free trade replaced all those dull-witted CEO's of Acme (Canada) Inc. – whose principle duty it was to travel once a year to Head Office in the United States for instructions – with entrepreneurs able and willing to compete in the continental and even global arena. By 2004, Ontario manufacturers were sending $494 million a day in exports to the United States, compared to $114 million in 1987; trade at the Detroit/Windsor gateway alone had surpassed $120 billion a year.[3] As with all markets everywhere, the elimination of tariffs directed resources to the most efficient and cost-effective parts of the economies. Shoe manufacturers might suffer, but communications, computers, and other high-tech industries thrived.

But at the time the Mulroney government first proposed free trade, Ontario politicians could see nothing on the horizon but lost jobs. Besides, what did the federal government think it was doing, negotiating such an enormous economic reform without Ontario's consent? Liberal premier David Peterson fought tenaciously to scupper the deal, campaigning against Mulroney in the 1988 federal election, warning that unfettered competition would turn Canada's industrial heartland into a Bruce Springsteen song. But Mulroney had Quebec and the West in his pocket, and despite losing twenty-one seats in Ontario, retained enough of a majority to ratify the treaty.

In the short term, Peterson was right: the loss of tariff protection, coupled with an oncoming recession, the determination of the Bank of Canada to squeeze inflation out of the economy through high interest rates, and the Ontario Liberal government's disastrous decision to expand welfare-state programs and increase taxes devastated the Ontario economy. Unemployment soared to 11 per cent. Dozens of factories closed, now that Acme (Canada) Inc.'s Canadian market could easily be serviced from the plant in Milwaukee. At the worst of it, in 1993, 607,000 people were out of work, and 660,000 on welfare. Ontario had lost its sense of certainty, of confidence, of self.

It took the better part of a decade to set things right, but by 1999, 200,000 new made-in-Ontario jobs had been created, personal and corporate taxes had been trimmed to competitive levels, unemployment was down to 6.3 per cent, and the welfare rolls had been slashed by 181,000. The economic engine of the country was more powerful and dominant than ever, with more than 5 million people clustered in and around Toronto; new automotive and auto-parts plants had opened or were under construction; groundbreaking high-tech industries bolstered the economies of Ottawa and the Kitchener-Cambridge-Guelph triangle. The growth was often badly managed: not only did infrastructure fail to keep up with urban expansion, but weak-willed politicians and planners allowed Ontario to become exceedingly ugly, as countless thousands of acres of pristine farmland and rolling countryside were replaced with cookie-cutter communities devoid of architectural imagination. But the province was rich again, and that was all that mattered.

The scars of the 1990s, in conjunction with the bursting of the high-tech bubble at the turn of the century, reminded

Ontarians that the provincial economy was always under threat, that its lifeblood was trade, and that jobs had to be earned, fought for, and protected by increased productivity. A wary province, bloodied by restructuring but strengthened by the very competition that failed to kill it, approached the twenty-first century cautiously optimistic of its ability to preserve and enhance one of the most enviable standards of living in the world.

In the midst of all this, Ontario turned into a region. With the National Policy replaced by the Free Trade Agreement, the old, artificial east-west bonds ceased to have any economic meaning. British Columbia could look to Cascadia and the Pacific Rim as the natural market for its natural resources. Offshore investment fuelled Vancouver's real-estate bonanza, and the tourists came from Japan and Hong Kong, not Toronto or Saskatoon. Oil-rich Alberta swaggered like the Texan it wanted to become; the Maritimes, after more than a century of isolation and stagnation, took its first, tentative steps to reintegration with the New England market it has been so rudely and forcibly separated from. And Ontario became what it has always been meant to be: an integrated partner in the industrial engine of the Great Lakes region. More than ever, Ontario's interests were the interests of the continental auto, aviation, communications, and financial services sector, with the province's economy bolstered rather than sustained by the agricultural produce, wood products, and minerals industries. The power failure of August 2003, which originated in Ohio and quickly cascaded across the Northeast, blacking out Ontario and giving children in cities their first view of stars, reminded anyone who needed reminding that Canada's industrial heartland was intimately and physically connected to its American counterpart.

Question: If the rest of Canada no longer buys from Ontario, why is Ontario subsidizing the rest of Canada? NDP premier Bob Rae first raised this embarrassing interrogative in the early 1990s. Rae was struggling to rein in the province's alarming deficit, reduce unemployment, and relieve the burden of the welfare rolls. (He went about it all wrong, but that's no never mind.) Yet Ontario dollars were steadily flowing out of the province: in equalization payments to the poorer regions; in economic development assistance that seemed mostly to be about getting federal politicians re-elected in their rural ridings; in clawbacks that deprived Ontario of the very federal assistance that its citizens' tax dollars were supposed to provide. The NDP calculated that 5.5 per cent of provincial gross domestic product was being drained away in regional development assistance of one kind or another. That had been fine, when the money went to help New Brunswickers pay for the widgets from Acme (Canada) Inc. But with free trade in, and Acme out, Ontario no longer looked to the East and the West as natural markets. The principle of equalization sounded noble – ensuring that all Canadians received basic standards of service at reasonable levels of taxation – but what was in it for Ontario?

This was a bit rich, the rest of the country might say. As long as it benefited Ontario, the province trumpeted the virtues of an internal economic union. All the other stuff, all the nation-building, all the grand vision of driving on two good lanes from Halifax to Vancouver, all the National Dreams of subsidies to books and magazines, all that Terribly Important to the Nation programming on the CBC, had been about convincing the hinterlands that it was worth it to pay 20 per cent more for a television than they had to. As soon as free trade made it possible for

people to buy their televisions directly from the United States –
well, Taiwan, actually – Ontario wanted to know where its money
was going. Yes, it was brazen, but individuals and communities
invariably act in their perceived self-interest, and it was no longer
in Ontario's interest to prop up the Canada of Pierre Berton.

The wars that Mike Harris, Rae's Conservative successor,
fought with Prime Minister Jean Chrétien reached new heights
of ludicrousness, as both sides waged television advertising wars
against each other, with each billing the same taxpayer for the cost.
But Harris and his successor, Ernie Eves, hammered the principle home: The province would continue to support equalization
grants out of a sense of *noblesse oblige*, but the *oblige* ended there.
Ontario would no longer acquiesce in regional skewing of federal
assistance, because it was Ontario taxpayers who were getting
skewed. Dalton McGuinty, who came to power in 2003 vowing
to smooth the waters between Queen's Park and Parliament Hill,
was instead by 2005 waging a political jihad of his own, declaring that Ontario taxpayers sent $23 billion more to Ottawa than
they received back in federal transfers, and demanding that the
gap had to narrow or else.

Let's just say it. Economically, Canada doesn't matter to
Ontario any more. The ties that bind the province with 40 per
cent of the country's population and economy to the rest of this
land are remnants of a time past. Besides, those ties are a joke.
The national transportation system is a myth: Ottawa long ago
abandoned any pretense of responsibility for the Trans-Canada
Highway; VIA Rail, which is mostly a gaggle of isolated regional
lines, wastes $170 million a year in federal subsidies getting 4
million passengers to their destination two hours late; the airport
system has been largely off-loaded to the private sector. And so

has the national communications system: private corporations established the cellphone network; the Internet is a private sphere that even the Stalinist Canadian Radio-television and Telecommunications Commission admitted was impossible to regulate. Federal ambitions to subsidize broadband Internet service to remote regions foundered when taxpayers realized their dollars would be spent on making it easier to download porn in Labrador. Satellite dishes, digital cable, and specialty channels are steadily eroding the federal government's communications policy and further marginalizing the CBC. And someday soon, Ontario taxpayers are going to ask why their dollars are being used to subsidize Canadian books, radio CanCon, and Telefilm Canada, when our authors, singers, and filmmakers define success by six- and seven-figure international deals.

The gall of it! While it suited Ontario, the province was the patriotic heartland of the country. Now, it asks the rest of Canada: What have you done for us, lately?

Actually, it's not quite that bad. Most citizens don't base their beliefs and attitudes around strict calculations of profit and loss. Whenever Ontarians are polled, they continue to lead the country in their commitment to Confederation and their determination to make it work. There is no Ontario separatism. No one wants to build firewalls around *that* province. Nonetheless, successive Ontario governments, of all political stripes, have come to question the horizontal transfers of wealth from the richest regions of the country to the poorest. The traumas of the early 1990s, and the crash of the dotcoms less than a decade later, reminded Ontarians that their taxes are needed at home. Resistance to having those resources bleed east and west will only increase as the economic challenges multiply over the coming years. And yet the very raison d'être of the federal government is to transfer wealth. If it can't take from the rich in Alberta, Ontario, B.C., and Saskatchewan, and give it to everyone else, then what's a federal government to do?

How else will it be able to keep Atlantic Canada in thrall?

Pity poor Mabel Gallant. She and her husband owned a few small businesses on Prince Edward Island. But it was hard to find workers. In Atlantic Canada, calculating Employment Insurance benefits is an advanced science that an astonishing number of otherwise not-terribly-well-educated workers have mastered to an alarming degree. How many weeks you work, and how much you make, determines how many weeks of pogey you qualify for, and how much you receive. Upsetting the balance by taking a part-time job, simply because one is available, could prove financially ruinous. For that reason, the Maritimes suffers from a pronounced labour shortage, at least in the area of part-time, low-paying work. To compensate, the Gallants did what everyone knows everyone does: they hired the workers, but kept them off the books. This time, though, someone ratted, the feds pounced, and in the autumn of 2002, Mabel Gallant was sentenced to sixty-eight days in jail.

Her incarceration enraged the *Journal Pioneer*: "It is appalling in the extreme," the Summerside newspaper thundered in an editorial, "that in this rich, opulent country, the poorest of the poor, the unemployed, the sick, seniors, veterans and students struggling to get an education so they can be productive members of society, seem to be hounded and harassed to pay back the small pittance they need to get by, while billions are wasted on a federal gun registry and GST fraud."

Sure, what Mabel had done was against the law, "but it was done so a small business could get employees when they needed them, and not penalize a family on assistance, who no doubt needed a pay cheque and a bit of support from the EI system . . . Gallant displayed a humane and compassionate understanding for people over a system that is seriously flawed. And she is paying for it. Big time."[4]

Imagine: a local newspaper defends the right – why, it's almost the duty – of local businesses to break federal laws, because Employment Insurance, which is already more generous in the Maritimes than in other parts of the country, still isn't sufficient to help people make ends meet. Prosecution of such businesses – no mention, by the way, of what happened to those who broke the laws by working under the table – is nothing more than harassment, in the eyes of the *Journal Pioneer*.

When talking about Atlantic Canada, the natural question to ask is, who's to blame? A century and a half ago, the Maritime colonies were at least as wealthy as their Upper Canadian counterpart, at least as culturally vibrant, with a future every bit as bright. Yes, its pioneer days were long past, but the region had close ties to its New England neighbours, its seafaring citizenry were far more cosmopolitan than the dirt farmers of the Thames Valley, and there was no reason whatsoever to believe that Halifax would languish in the shadow of Toronto, any more than Boston was fated to be eclipsed by Chicago.

Today, the region is kept alive only because the rest of Canada transfers wealth through equalization grants and other props. Forty per cent of Prince Edward Island's provincial budget consists of federal transfers. Unemployment in New Brunswick has averaged 3 per cent above the national average over the past ten years. Newfoundland and Labrador in 2004 posted a deficit of $840 million on a budget of $5 billion – which, when you think about it, is a pretty good definition of "bankrupt."

So who *is* to blame? Maybe no one. Maybe the region's soil was too poor, its climate too foul, its population centres too far removed from the industrial heart of the continent, for Atlantic Canada ever to have thrived. But no, that simply doesn't work. There is no necessary correlation between physical assets and cultural and economic wealth. Japan is virtually without resources, and yet has risen to become the world's second largest economy. There may be geographical reasons why southern Italy is poorer than northern Italy, but analysts are far more likely to point to vicious circles and virtuous cycles that propelled one region forward and held the other back. Most poignant of all, Iceland labours under all of the disadvantages of Newfoundland, and yet that island nation enjoys one of the world's highest standards of living. As for Newfoundland, well, it's better to avert one's gaze.

So let's go looking for scapegoats. Ontario is a good place to start. As previously discussed, the National Policy cut Atlantic Canada off from its natural markets, forcing it into economic dependency on the Centre. Stagnation followed. Quebec can take a bow as well. Its influence helped convince the federal government to develop the St. Lawrence Seaway, turning Montreal into a major port and diminishing Halifax's single most important physical asset: its harbour.

The federal government is certainly to blame. Confronted with the economic decline of the region, Ottawa pursued policies that quickly turned it into a de facto colony, administered from afar. The annual economic transfers were often directed to ridings that favoured the incumbent Liberal cabinet minister, rather than to areas where the money was most needed. Federal mismanagement of the fishery led to its collapse and to the near extinction of the northern cod, one of the greatest environmental and economic failures to beset a modern democratic government. For the same reason that it allowed the cod stocks to be destroyed – a chronic inability to say "no" – Ottawa colluded with provincial governments through relaxed Employment Insurance rules and grants to squander valuable capital, by permitting, and even encouraging, people to remain in isolated communities that, with each advancing year, were less able to provide steady jobs, much less the necessary infrastructure.

And the region's inhabitants have themselves to blame, for allowing their own slide. Too many Atlantic Canadians are comfortable with a life of churlish dependence on federal handouts, defiantly defending their cultural heritage by blaming the very hand that feeds them (even if with cause), and blindly, blithely carrying on with what every single citizen should consider an intolerable status quo, sighing resignedly when anyone with the gumption packs up their bags and leaves. We should all be ashamed of ourselves, for letting it come to this.

There is a resource that trumps all other resources. It is more valuable than diamonds or gold and more difficult to mine. It takes longer to nurture and harvest than a replanted forest. Guarantees of return on investment can seem as tenuous as a wheat field in spring. Yet the riches for those economies that can harness and exploit this resource surpass the most lucrative oil deposit. This resource is us: human skill, enterprise, knowledge. Atlantic Canada has been eclipsed, not because the cod disappeared, but because an entire society banked on cod, and lumber, and coal.

Consider, again, Iceland. For virtually all of the second millennium, this barren island in the North Atlantic was subject to neglect, periodic depredations by raiding parties, and volcanic eruption. So isolated were the Icelanders that even today they speak Old Norse, and so ethnically homogeneous are they that the population of 288,000 is a prized laboratory for genetic research.

In 1944, Iceland declared its independence from Denmark. Given its location, its lack of any meaningful resources other than fish (quick: name a prosperous modern economy based on fish), and its history of colonial dependence, Iceland's prospects seemed bleak.

And yet, the country had tremendous inner potential. Its people were fiercely independent of mind. The first general assembly, *Althingi*, convened in 930 and met yearly to pass laws and judgments. With independence, the island moved quickly to establish itself as a valuable member of the Western Alliance, while fiercely protecting the all-important fishery, successfully taking on the Royal Navy in defence of the island's right to unilaterally extend the boundary of its coastal waters. But despite its heavy reliance on the fishery, the Icelanders were also passionate self-improvers – for example, Icelanders read more books per capita than any other people in Europe – and their efforts soon paid off. Today, Iceland's economy boasts real economic annual growth of 5 per cent, well above the average of the rest of the industrialized world. While fishing continues to account for about 20 per cent of gross domestic product, financial services, communications, and tourism now make up about two-thirds of the domestic economy. The country's efforts to exploit geothermal and hydroelectric energy sources have made it less dependent on imported oil, and the low energy costs have attracted heavy industry. Icelanders are highly educated, routinely leaving the island for a first or second post-secondary degree, but because of the strong local economy – unemployment sits at just over 3 per cent – and their deep attachment to their land, most of them come back. Despite its tiny population – less than half that of Newfoundland's – Iceland boasts a national university, a national museum, a fine symphony orchestra, an opera and ballet company, a broadcasting network, and its own central bank and stock exchange.

Newfoundland, by contrast, elected to join Confederation in 1949 (although there are still those who insist the vote was rigged). Since then, Ottawa has mismanaged the fishery, the Newfoundland government was hornswoggled in its negotiations for hydroelectric development at Churchill Falls, and statist attempts at jump-starting the economy have ranged from the merely incompetent (the Come by Chance refinery) to hilarious (cucumbers?).[5] The government has exhausted its meagre resources trying to keep uneconomic fishing villages alive, rather than concentrating the population in larger centres, which contributes to an unemployment rate of 16 per cent and an outflow of human capital so devastating that the population of the province has declined by 10 per cent over the past decade. Newfoundland and Labrador has failed to preserve and improve the only resource that mattered, its human resource, and it has paid the price. The federal government, in its economic development strategies, its mismanagement of offshore natural resources, and its paternalistic (and ultimately profitable) trade in human talent in exchange for financial subsidies has left Newfoundland bankrupt, despondent, and resentful. And this from a province that has oil off its shore and nickel in its ground.

Atlantic Canadians who consider the sad comparison of Iceland and Newfoundland and conclude from it that independence might well have served the region better than Confederation have a point. But they miss a larger point. Yes, Iceland prospered in part because it kept control of its natural resources. But it prospered equally, and ultimately more, by developing its human potential: by capitalizing on its historic sense of self, its pride in its culture, its centuries-old traditions of literature and painting; by fostering a proud and educated population willing to sacrifice and able to succeed. Atlantic Canadians, too, are proud of their culture, but it has become, for them, a museum – a memory of happier times, a proud testament of ancient ties that bind. Cape Bretoners celebrate the Auld Alliance between Scotland and France, as though it were of even the remotest relevance today. For Atlantic Canada, cultural memory is a crutch rather than a catalyst.

As previously mentioned, even as Atlantic Canadians watch their brightest and best going down the road, they make little meaningful effort to replace them with the one community that could revive and revitalize the local economy: immigrants. Seven per cent of Halifax's population consists of immigrants; in St. John's the figure is 3 per cent. Yet 18 per cent of the national population is foreign-born, including 44 per cent of Toronto's population. Twenty-two per cent of British Columbia's population is foreign-born. In Nova Scotia, it's 4 per cent; in New Brunswick and Prince Edward Island, it's 3 per cent. In Newfoundland, it's 1.5 per cent.[6]

Atlantic Canadians argue back with good reason that immigrants don't come to the region because the economy isn't strong enough to sustain them. (Some argue, nonsensically, that the analysis itself is racist, that saying "Atlantic Canada is too white" is the same as saying "Atlantic Canada is too black" or "Atlantic Canada has too many Jews." The argument is garbage; we're talking about the link between immigration and economic development. Most immigrants are non-white. It's as simple as that.) Yes, more immigrants would come to the region if there were more jobs. But immigrants themselves are job-creators; they bring entrepreneurial energy, marketable skills, and a general attitude of optimism and future possibilities. And, of course, they expand the size of the market. The uncomfortable truth is, Atlantic Canadians do not go out of their way to attract immigrants. The people retain the old elitist, exclusionary attitudes that label anyone who cannot trace their lineage in the region for several generations as being "from away." The very phrase says it all. And immigrants, of course, are the epitome of "from away."

Many Atlantic Canadians recognize and accept some or all of this diagnosis. They have set about analyzing and implementing solutions. The University of Prince Edward Island, for example, has made remarkable strides, improving the quality of its faculty and resources, which helped it land the National Research Council's new nutriscience centre,[7] while Summerside is home to a nascent aerospace industry that employs eight hundred people. The elites of the island are working hard to improve education and create meaningful jobs.

But the Atlantic Canadian solitude is the most dispiriting of all: its people see themselves as isolated, when isolation is largely a self-perception; they blame others as the perpetrators of their economic misery rather than looking to themselves to alleviate it; they celebrate and defend a stagnant culture rather than searching for ways to infuse that culture with new vitality. They are programmed to fail, and at this, at least, they succeed. Unless and until it can break this cycle of dependency, resentment, and decline, the Atlantic coast will remain rich in heritage and poor in prospects.

The first mistake we often make when talking about the West is to assume there is one. "The West" is anything but homogeneous. New Brunswick, Nova Scotia, Prince Edward Island, and Newfoundland, despite their differing histories, possess sufficient common attributes of culture and economy to make it possible to speak of Atlantic Canada as a single region without doing fatal violence to the truth. But what is Manitoba to British Columbia, or Vancouver to Winnipeg? What do the Prairies have in common with the Rocky Mountains? How does the long tradition of NDP governments in three of the four Western provinces jive with Alberta, which has elected only conservative governments of one variety or another for as long as anyone can remember?

Westerners look everywhere except at each other. British Columbia is firmly entrenched as part of the eastern perimeter of the Pacific Rim. If Toronto, Montreal, New York, London, and Paris retain common elements of a North Atlantic civilization a millennium old, Vancouver with each passing year becomes more firmly attached to the Eastern hemisphere, making Hong Kong feel closer to home than Ottawa. Alberta and Saskatchewan gaze south, though with differing degrees of approval, at the conservative heartland of the American Midwest, while Manitoba casts furtive, resentful, and envious glances at Ontario and the American Northeast, and sighs at what Chicago became and it did not. Given their disparate histories, orientation, and outlook, it's hard to speak of the West at all.

In truth, the only thing about the West that makes it the West is its obsessive awareness of not being in the East. For Canada, this is a profound distinction, analogous to the dichotomy between the north and the south of England, or between the old slave and free states of the United States. In some ways, the difference is even more pronounced in Canada. Arguably, northern and southern England are converging, as the former finally parts with its outdated industrial and mining past and integrates with the high-tech and financial services economy of the south. The American polar divide has been mitigated by the emergence of strong, modern southern and western economies, leaving the Northeast wondering why no one listens to it any more.

In Canada, however, the West feels intensely and self-consciously marginalized. In part, that marginalization is environmentally determined; Canada jogs to the north as its border slices through the Great Lakes, leaving Western Canada considerably farther north than Eastern Canada. Calgary is farther north than Hearst, a remote town in what Ontario considers its far north. Most Ontarians would never consider moving to Hearst, (getting them to venture to wintry Ottawa can be a considerable challenge), if for no other reason than the winters are too long, summers too short, and the mosquitoes too many. And yet the climate of Calgary (chinooks notwithstanding), Regina, and Winnipeg is easily as severe. Climate will always be an impediment to Prairie progress, because only the hardiest of souls will want to live there.

History conspired with geography to increase the West's sense of otherness. The four eastern provinces that created Confederation did so of their own accord. Manitoba, Saskatchewan, and Alberta, however, were granted provincial status by a beneficent federal government. Prior to that they had been territories, dependencies in law and in fact. They were, to be honest about it, colonies, and were seen as colonies, especially by the business and political elites of imperial Ontario, who viewed the West as a valuable source of raw goods and agricultural produce that would feed Laurentian stomachs and Laurentian industries, whose products could then be sold back to the colonists, who could always take out another loan from the Royal Bank if they couldn't afford to pay.

An Albertan nationalist – it seems the only thing to call him – will talk about the pernicious federal refusal to transfer control of natural resources to the province prior to 1930 with all the passion and sense of personal affront of a Serb recalling the Battle of Sarajevo.

Like that Serb, Albertan nationalists have a very selective memory. Although Manitoba developed before Alberta and Saskatchewan, most of the Prairie settler populations arrived around the turn of the twentieth century; all three provinces depended largely on prairie farming to sustain their economies; all found their economies going into decline, as agriculture waned in importance. (Winnipeg was particularly hard hit by the opening in 1914 of the Panama Canal, which allowed the three westernmost provinces to reorient their economies to the Pacific and reduced Winnipeg's importance as a regional centre.) To this day, Saskatchewan and Manitoba struggle to define a future beyond one of outmigration and relative decline.

Alberta seemed fit to share Saskatchewan and Manitoba's fate, which was why in the 1930s that province experimented with populist agrarian reform in the same way that the other Prairie provinces did. (In Alberta's case, it was the Social Credit movement of Bible Bill Ablehart.) But on February 13, 1947, they struck oil at Leduc. Petroleum replaced agriculture as the main-stay of the Alberta economy, transforming its society. Unlike the two provinces to the east, which were obsessed with the equitable distribution of scarce resources, and British Columbia to the west, which polarized into a pseudo-European confrontation between workers and capitalists, Alberta evolved – some would say devolved – into an agglomeration of materialist conservatives, bent on enjoying their new-found wealth and determined to preserve it. They developed, in effect, the political culture of a province of wealthy farmers.

Albertans suffer from the same amnesia as Ontario's pioneer settlers, who stumbled onto some of the richest farmland in North America and then, when it made them prosperous, decided that Divine favour and innate virtue were the cause of their bountiful harvests. Alberta has no provincial sales tax and no debt. It spends more per capita on health care than any other province. Its students routinely score at or very near the top in international tests, due in part to a first-rate education system. But rather than give thanks for their endless good fortune, many Albertans chafe at what they consider intolerable interference by Eastern interests intent on dominating their province and siphoning their wealth. That resentment is in part justified: Eastern financial and political interests did retard development in the early decades; federal policies did force Alberta to sell discounted gas to feed Ontario industries in the 1970s; the National Energy Program of 1980 was as insensitive as it was ill-conceived. Still, Albertans and their talk of firewalls can ruin the sunniest day.

The provinces of Manitoba and Saskatchewan are far from the struggling dependencies of Atlantic Canada; farming continues to underpin their economies, though those farms are every year fewer, larger, and more automated. Their mineral and forest industries also buttress their economies, while their cities serve as vital entrepots for their region. Winnipeg is so dominant in Manitoba that 60 per cent of the population lives there. Saskatchewan's petroleum reserves, though not so lavish as Alberta's, are sufficient to keep its books balanced and even, when oil prices are high enough, to enjoy the status of "have" province. Manitoba's economy, though not blessed with oil, muddles along. But their precarious economies and stagnant or declining populations leave both provinces, and both populations, unwilling or unable to challenge the East politically or economically, much as they might like to. Colonies they were; politically weak provinces they remain.

British Columbia's political genesis is unique to the West. It entered Confederation in 1871 of its own accord, at least nominally. But union was actually a desperate move by the former colony's political leaders, aimed at reversing the decline that set in with the wane of the first gold rushes. Their cap-in-hand arrival in Confederation, coupled with the delays in completing the promised transcontinental railway, left British Columbians feeling permanently ambivalent about the Canadian experiment. A provincial economy that repeatedly soared and crashed with the rise and fall of its forestry and mining fortunes accentuated that chip-on-the-shoulder attitude.

Nonetheless, British Columbia's resource wealth, though subject to boom and bust, enjoys a long-term sustainability; the products of its mines and forests will always find willing markets to the south and west. Its temperate climate ensures that Vancouver Island, the lower mainland, and the Okanagan region will always be welcome destinations for retirees or anyone in search of the good life. And speaking of the good life, Vancouver is one of the most exciting cities on earth, with bold new architecture accentuating its magnificent setting, accompanied by startling real-estate prices and shops, restaurants, and other diversions to accommodate those who can afford them. Vancouver remains the city outside the centre most likely to challenge the dominance of Toronto and Montreal. This leaves British Columbia – the one jurisdiction that culturally, geographically, and economically is the most distinct from the Centre – relatively indifferent, but by no means hostile, toward it. Much of the time, Victoria's principle concern in federal-provincial relations is distinguishing itself from the rest of the West, insisting on a separate voice. When Jean Chrétien, chastened by the near loss of Canada in the 1995 referendum, passed legislation acknowledging the distinctiveness of Quebec society, while giving four vetoes over constitutional reform – one to Atlantic Canada, one to Quebec, one to Ontario, and one to the West – the howls came, to the prime minister's considerable surprise, from British Columbia. B.C. was a Pacific province, its politicians and people argued; its interests were not Prairie interests and, with a population of 4 million, it deserved a veto of its own. And it got one.

In reality, British Columbia's human and natural resources ensure that it needs little from the rest of the country. Provided the federal government is sensitive to its distinct interests within the Pacific Rim, the province can be left pretty much to its own devices, which is how the people there prefer it.

Which brings us back to Alberta. Someone once pointed out that there may be no city in Canada with more Canadian flags draped from its buildings than Calgary. This is important. For

Calgarians, and Albertans in general, are perhaps the most intensely patriotic people in this federation. They *want* to believe in Canada. It's just that this particular version of Canada doesn't entirely appeal.

Had Alberta not won the natural-resource lottery by striking oil, its situation would be as precarious as Manitoba's. But Albertans have wealth – more wealth than power, in fact. And it infuriates them.

The dynamics of Confederation dictated that the Atlantic Canadian provinces would receive a disproportionate share of federal resources and representation. It was the necessary compromise to get the Maritimes to enter into a Confederation that was mostly about realigning powers between Ontario and Quebec. The price of that accommodation was paid by the West, which is chronically underrepresented both within the House of Commons and the Senate. While for Manitobans and Saskatchewanians this is an annoyance, for Albertans – or at least for that minority of them who are politically engaged – underrepresentation in Ottawa is a wound that never heals.

This political offence is compounded, immeasurably, by the different paths of development followed by America and Canada, which has worked to Alberta's disadvantage. This is not the place to analyze why the North American interior differs politically from its coasts; suffice it to say there is a general acceptance, borne out at each election, that the American states of the Pacific West share a liberal political point of view with the Atlantic Northeast and the Great Lakes centre, although they are the product of very different cultures. So too, the cultures of Ontario, Quebec, and Atlantic Canada are politically and intellectually

liberal – concerned with securing collective benefits and mitigating the differences between economic winners and losers
through redistribution. British Columbia, though it suffers from
political bipolar disorder, alternating between social democratic
and libertarian ideologies, displays at least a respectable liberal
tinge, which is why Liberal and NDP candidates traditionally do
well, at least in the lower mainland and on Vancouver Island.

The Midwest of the continent, however, is of a more economically libertarian and socially conservative bent. These are the
red states: the bedrock of Republican America, where the right
to bear arms is absolute and the rite of gay marriage shall be forever
proscribed. The difference between America and Canada in this
respect is profound, and the reasons for that profound difference
are demographic. While soil, climate, and resources permitted
substantial settlement in the Midwest, the Prairie provinces could
sustain only a much smaller population relative to its Eastern
counterpart. Further, the Midwest was able to ally itself politically
with the South – both east and west – to rival and, increasingly,
surpass its liberal counterpart in the West and Northeast. But there
is no counterpart to the South in Canada. Meanwhile the economic fragility of Saskatchewan and Manitoba bred a pronounced
collective-benefit strain in their political cultures, reflected in the
strength of the New Democratic Party in both provinces. NDP
governments were in power in Saskatchewan for twenty-four of
thirty-four years between 1971 and 2005, while they have controlled Manitoba for better than two-thirds of the past three and
a half decades. The two eastern Prairie provinces may display
signs of social conservatism, but in most respects they are at least
as liberal as their Ontario counterparts.

This leaves Alberta as odd man out: the province that has had only conservative government of one sort or another since 1935, the province that boasts the same roughneck oil culture as Texas, with Calgary as affluent and as conservative as Denver, the province where the religious right is a permanent and prominent fact of political life, the province – probably the only province – that would have voted for George W. Bush. And yet, while social conservatism and economic neo-conservatism wax ever-stronger in the United States – matching the growth of the Old South, the Southwest, the Mississippi watershed, and the western plains – Alberta remains a marginal player, with only twenty-four of 308 seats in Parliament, and no hope of ever sending to Ottawa a majority government dominated by its interests and concerns.

It leaves Albertans seething. It pushed them to spin off their own political party, the Alberta-dominated Reform Party, during the debacle of Meech Lake in the late 1980s. When Reform failed to get its interests properly addressed in the House of Commons, several of the province's leading political voices – Stephen Harper was one of them – called for the creation of a firewall, as they called it, around Alberta, with Calgary (the real capital of the province) exercising all of the rights and powers demanded by Quebec, including its own police force and a separate income tax.

Easterners dismiss Albertan protest as the parochial mewling of an ethnically unified and politically immature province that can't even master the art of multi-party politics. They ignore the fact that Calgary, which is politically far to the right of Edmonton, has a population almost as ethnically diverse as Toronto. Something about Alberta makes people Albertan, no matter where they come from. The problem for Alberta – and it is a problem for all of Canada, as well – is that its political culture cannot find expression at the national level, leaving the people of the province rich and frustrated, always a dangerous combination.

It's understandable that Canadians in the rest of the country sometimes wonder whether Quebec deserves so much attention. After all, its history is one of unrelenting decline.

New France was once the dominant colony in the northern half of North America. Even after the British conquest of 1763, it remained much larger than the Maritime colonies or the near-empty lands to its west. When the rebellious Americans sent an expedition under the generalship of Benedict Arnold to conquer Canada in 1775, it was to Quebec that they made their bedraggled and futile way. Even after the war, as loyal American settlers, retired British troops, and new arrivals from England swelled the population of Atlantic and Upper Canada, Quebec remained for decades the richest, most populous, and most powerful colony in British North America. At Confederation, although Ontario was now slightly more populous, Montreal was still the largest and most powerful city in the fledgling dominion, and Quebec politicians secured a permanent place for French as one Canada's two founding languages and cultures, along with permanent constitutional guarantees to protect Quebec culture, language, and political influence.

But already, it was evident to keen observers that Quebec's day of dominance had passed. In the late nineteenth century, thousands of Quebeckers left their homeland for Ontario and New England, in search of better land and better jobs. Through the two world wars Quebec was a sullen bystander, protesting federal involvement in what it saw as British imperial wars, and threatening to secede if its citizens were conscripted. The province remained quasi-feudal, under the dominance of the Catholic Church and the Union Nationale, while the rest of North America continued its march of economic progress and social liberation. Financial power shifted west to Toronto, which in the 1960s surpassed Montreal as Canada's first city. The rise to power of the Parti Québécois in 1976 prompted another exodus of workers and businesses. By the turn of the millennium, Quebec's population had fallen to only one-quarter of the Canadian total. Its industrial base was fragile, its taxes and debt were high, and its population teetered on the brink of absolute decline.

Under the circumstances, a newly arrived immigrant to Toronto, an Albertan oil worker, or a Vancouver stockbroker today might reasonably wonder why Quebec is always in the news, why its nationalist belligerence must be endlessly accommodated, why its two referendums on sovereignty were such national crises, why its persistent, prickly demands dominate federal politics, why practically everyone in the public service seems to be francophone.

And yet, as Lawrence Martin, a columnist for the *Globe and Mail*, has observed, French Canada has shaped English Canada more than English Canada may understand, or would like to admit. In many ways, the values of Canada are the values of Quebec.

In its efforts to respond to the restiveness of Quebec society that accompanied the Quiet Revolution in the 1960s, the federal government placed an increasing premium on incorporating French interests in Ottawa. As a result of, and on top of, all the appeasements – the Royal Commission on Bilingualism and

Biculturalism, the tortured efforts to patriate a Constitution that could accommodate the French fact, Pierre Trudeau's Herculean (and ultimately failed) attempts to strengthen bilingualism and the central government – Ottawa became a town dominated by Quebec thought, Quebec values, Quebec priorities. Cheddar was eclipsed by brie. Since 1968, no Canadian prime minister has been elected from any province other than Quebec, with the short-lived exception of Joe Clark's 1979 administration. Francophone cabinet ministers have held senior ranks in every cabinet, while the public service has become increasingly Québécois: one-third of the federal public service is francophone, compared to one-fifth in the 1960s.[8] Since the vast majority of Canadians who have easily embraced bilingualism live close to either the Quebec–Ontario or Quebec–New Brunswick border, these border bilinguals, along with their culture and thought, dominate the culture and thought of Ottawa.

As a result, Quebec values and priorities have subconsciously infused federal-government decision-making. And as Quebec society went through its social revolution – transforming itself from a hierarchical theocracy into an ultra-modern secular society – it transmitted its revolution to the rest of the country. It was a Quebec political leader who liberalized the marriage laws and legalized homosexuality; it was in response to Quebec indifference and resentment that almost all vestiges of Canada's monarchical ties were swept out of sight; it was Quebec that led Canada in the drive to legalize abortion, to end capital punishment, to expand same-sex benefits and rights. It was Québécois justice minister Martin Cauchon who fought passionately within cabinet to decriminalize marijuana possession, and who in time introduced the first version of the bill. It was the corporatist mentality of Quebec (more pronounced than in Ontario and light years from Alberta) that kept Canada clinging to, and even expanding, its welfare-state apparatus long after both the United States and Great Britain had embarked on programs of government downsizing, deregulation, and tax-cutting.

To be sure, that influence has, in some respects, waned. The demonstrable (and Lord, how it was demonstrated) folly of stifling enterprise and preserving statist programs and economic directions, while permitting deficits to accumulate when resources no longer matched demands, pushed the federal government to switch from Franco-driven to Anglo-driven economic priorities in the 1990s. In eliminating the federal deficit while slashing program spending and, ultimately, delivering $100 billion in tax cuts, Finance Minister Paul Martin (who was born in Windsor, Ontario, but adopted Quebec as his home) mimicked the conservative revolutions of Ralph Klein and Mike Harris, of Ronald Reagan and Margaret Thatcher.

Nonetheless, the French pull remains powerful. True to its pacifist form, Quebec society was far more opposed to Canadian participation in the second Iraq War than was the rest of the country, which was either divided (Ontario) or actively supportive (the West)[9]. Canada stayed out. Support for same-sex marriage was stronger in Quebec than in any other part of the country (in the West, sentiment was generally opposed). Quebec public opinion was largely hostile to participation in the American ballistic missile defence program; the Martin government moved from support for that program to anguished indecision to ultimate rejection (spurred in part by opposition from the Quebec caucus). For two generations now, Quebec has shaped the national agenda, with no end in sight.

Sadly for Quebec, the exchange has been largely one-sided. While English Canada has inherited French cultural secularism, while the rest of the country has learned – through gritted teeth, but they've learned – to accept one rule for Quebec and another for everyone else, while federal governments have either covertly or openly embraced asymmetrical federalism (which is a fancy political term for "giving Quebec whatever it wants"), Quebec has learned nothing from the rest of Canada, or at least has pretended not to. While English Canadian economic policy over the past fifteen years has focused on lowering taxes, deregulating the economy, and fostering entrepreneurship, Quebec has only partially and reluctantly weakened its corporatist ties – ties that substituted a secular bureaucracy for that of the Church; ties that emphasize close, and often incestuous, relations between government and dominant industries. While English Canada has embraced a global economic vision, emphasizing low tariffs and knowledge-based industries, Quebec throws up non-tariff barriers against Ontario workers and clutches its language laws to its chest even though they demonstrably impair competitiveness. While half of all immigrants flood to Toronto, hidebound regulations and a creaky economy ensure that Quebec receives only 17 per cent of newcomers, when it should be taking in at least a quarter.[10]

The results, frankly, are suicidal. The province is still paying the price for a generation of separatist rhetoric and policies, which drove almost a million people out of Quebec between 1976 and 2000. The language barriers that Quebec raises to immigrants, coupled with the lowest birth rate in Canada, have put the Quebec population on track to go into absolute decline in the next decade. How long will Canada remain bilingual, how much energy will it be prepared to expend accommodating the French fact, when that fact drops below 20 per cent of total population? Below 15 per cent? How will the Quebec government protect Quebec culture without the tax dollars necessary for all those subsidies? Where will the tax dollars come from?

The miracle of Canada is not that two different cultures have survived together for going on 140 years. The miracle is that the two cultures were French and English, and have still survived. Because talking about the past is out of fashion, most Canadians don't realize that, for much of modern history, France and Great Britain were at war, locked in a mortal contest, not simply between two opposing armies and navies, but between two starkly opposing views on the nature of the state. The France of the Bourbons, the revolutionaries, and Napoleon sought to impose on Europe a system of government based on corporatist values, on rule by bureaucracy, on the strength of the collective, on deference to an enlightened and absolutist leadership, be it the Church, the Crown, the Committee, the Emperor, or the president. In contrast, the British Empire found its strength by protecting the rights and welfare of the individual, by constraining the excesses of royal or bureaucratic tyranny, by promoting free trade, and by tolerating diversity of religion and independent thought. By 1763, that contest of ideas and arms had already been settled in North America, although it took until 1815 for the French to surrender the fight in Europe. From that time on, France was a weakening, ultimately secondary power, while the English-speaking peoples went on to bestride the globe.

Europe still grapples with the legacy of this contest. Jacques Chirac opposed American intervention in Iraq, not simply because he believed the war foolhardy and immoral (who knows if he even did?)[11] but because America was once again having its way in a region that, in colonial times, was within the French sphere of influence. Tony Blair allied himself to George Bush (as did John Howard of Australia) because the Anglosphere (as it is now called) had to stick together. Canada stayed out of that war in part because a French-Canadian prime minister bowed to francophone opposition to the war and ignored Ontario ambivalence and Western support.

In Canada, French and English cultures have been forced together in a political union that in Europe would be unthinkable. France and Great Britain may both belong to the European Union, but so does virtually every other Tom, Dick, and Poland. In Canada, however, the legacy of French North America and English North America must make common cause within a single nation state, even though both inherited and preserve separate and differing traditions. And this is why, since the English haven't had a truly bad day since 1066, English Canadians often have difficulty comprehending French Canadians: their easily wounded pride; their fierce determination to retain their autonomy; their obsession with culture, even at the cost of economic growth. (The English have never found the one to be in conflict with the other.)

French Canada will forever be in, but not of, the rest of Canada. The waves of Asian and Latin American new arrivals no more comprehend its obsession with identity than did the Anglo-Saxons before them. Even francophone immigrants who arrive in Montreal as a condition of their settlement often flee as quickly as they can. (Quebec, nonetheless, gets to enjoy the federal funding, but that's another story.)

And yet for the *pure laine* of Quebec, the priorities of its government and the preservation of its culture are worth whatever sacrifice. They are what makes Quebecois music, literature, and cinema so vibrant and so successful. They are what makes Montreal so much more appealing a city than Toronto, especially on a Saturday night. They are what makes so-called federalist premiers only a soupçon less autonomist than their sovereigntist opponents. Quebec, although Quebeckers are loath to admit it, enjoys all the cultural strengths and weaknesses of its French heritage. Its culture thrives, and its economy totters, in rough synchronicity with the Mother Country. And just like the Mother Country, it struggles to preserve its heritage, its independence, and its ever-waning influence in the midst of an English sea.

All in all, it seems a miracle that the country is still intact. And yet we carry on, and not only survive but thrive. Each of the regions, and regions within regions, struggles through its impediments – learning to cope, searching for ways to surmount obstacles, fumbling for a voice and a vocabulary, seeking also a common language with which to greet the other solitudes. Each has reason to honour its past and celebrate its present. Each has reason to hope for a better future. Each must, to some extent, find its own way. But in other ways, this gaggle of solitudes must work cooperatively, acting for all the world as though Canada were really a country.

We could go on like this indefinitely, and the evidence outside the window suggests that life for most Canadians would still be just fine. But in politics, stasis is never an option. Irritants must either be addressed, or they will fester; strengths must be reinforced, or they might fail. We're never going to be able to fully fix Canada – no country on earth has fully succeeded in eliminating its internal tensions – but we have to find ways of making it work better. If we don't, our political dysfunctions might reach a state where they begin to actively impair the quality of Canadian life. So let us turn from problems, which are always dreary, to solutions.

CHAPTER THREE

MIGRATIONS

I n surveys, Canadians almost invariably identify health care as
their single greatest policy concern. They're wrong. Improving the health-care system, while important, is not crucial to
Canadian success and prosperity in the coming years. All countries struggle to manage their health systems and contain costs,
and all fail. Despite the wide variety of systems employed – a
mostly private one in the United States; a mostly public one in
Canada; a mix of public and private throughout the rest of the
developed world – health outcomes and overall longevity are
largely unaffected. The state can make the quality of your life
better or worse, but neither socialism nor the market can do much
about it when your time finally comes.

Nor is education, vital though it is, our most important priority. Or the fight against poverty. Or the sorry state of Canada's military. Or the shambles of our foreign policy. Or our approach to the environment.

All of these concerns pall before the overriding issue of people moving about.

Two great global migrations are underway, both of them potentially virtuous, both of them of vital importance to Canadians. The first migration is from poorer countries to richer countries. The second is from the countryside to cities. These migrations are universal and continuous; how each country manages them will determine the winners and losers among nations in the twenty-first century. The good news is that Canada is handling both migrations more successfully than virtually any other country, and good on us. The bad news is that our success is in part accidental and still incomplete. Rather than exploiting our competitive advantage, in some respects our governments seem perversely determined to mess things up. Canada's long-term health, wealth, peace, and order will depend, more than anything else, on how successfully our population and our political leaders target and treat the challenges of the twin migrations.

Canada is a settler country. That is, our population is almost entirely derived from people who came here from other places, long or not-so-long ago. The first immigrants might have come across the land bridge that once connected what is now Siberia to Alaska somewhere around 12,000 B.C., give or take. These settlers have inhabited the North and South American continents for so many millennia that we refer to them as indigenous.

The major waves of European settlement to what is now Canada began in the seventeenth century, accelerated in the eighteenth and nineteenth, and became a veritable torrent in the twentieth. Up until about forty years ago, the mother country for most Canadians was one in Europe. Today, Canada's immigrant pools are found in Asia, Latin America, and Africa. European immigration accounts for only 20 per cent of new arrivals, and many of those are Third World immigrants arriving here via a European country. The reason for this shift is simple: After sixty years of peace and prosperity, white Europeans are no longer motivated to migrate. Life is pretty good at home.

Settler countries are profoundly different from traditional nation states because settler cultures lack a shared past. It took the better part of a millennium, accompanied by migrations, wars, revolutions, evolution, and assorted bouts of rape and pillage, before the English began to think of themselves as English; the Russians as Russian; the Chinese as Chinese. But once the idea took hold, it did so with a vengeance. The nation state – a sovereign polity whose borders roughly correspond to a self-identified homogeneous cultural grouping – is a powerful entity. "All my life," Charles de Gaulle loved to say, "I have had a certain idea of France."[1] So intense was that identification that de Gaulle actually believed he physically embodied the sovereignty of France in those years when part of his country was overrun by Nazi Germany, with the rest governed by a bastard collaborationist regime. More extraordinary still, other governments accepted the almost transubstantial notion of de Gaulle as the literal personification of France, even if a weary Winston Churchill was said to confess that "the greatest cross I have to bear is the Cross of Lorraine."[2] Nation states are like that: Some of them may be so ethnically distinct that their people largely share the same hair and eye colour (Denmark, for instance). Others may be composed of several related ethnicities. (The Italians of Sicily differ considerably from the Italians of Piedmont.) Regardless, they hold this certain idea of who they are. Sometimes they hold that certain idea in their head for centuries, even if they lack a government to speak on their unified behalf. Germans were Germans long before a German state finally and belatedly gave expression to that fact – with fell consequences, as it turned out.

Settler nations are not like that so much. True, they can have a very strong sense of national self. Australians are very Australian, and New Zealanders no less New Zealandish. The United States of America, though it plays host to many ethnicities (not all of whom are particularly well integrated into the mainstream of American society) has an intensely strong sense of national self, based on its revolutionary ideological past. Many of the settler cultures of Latin America and the Caribbean ceased to attract much in the way of immigration after the eighteenth century, and now neither act nor feel like settler countries at all. In fact, for better or worse, Canada is unique in the way its waves of immigration shaped, and have been shaped by, its identity.

Simply put, and to repeat, this country was confronted with the unalterable fact of two nations – French and British – cohabiting in the same political space. In order to accommodate that fact, Confederation created a loose and flexible federal union that ensured the two cultures would enjoy considerable autonomy, principally through the powers exercised by their provincial governments, but also through linguistic and educational rights enshrined in the Constitution itself. In the 1960s, when the strain of accommodating the two cultures nonetheless threatened to become intolerable, federal politicians more or less unconsciously decided the answer to the problem was to swamp both cultures in a sea of immigrants who shared little or nothing in common with either. To what degree multiculturalism was an accident and to what extent deliberate is a matter of debate; to what extent, if any, new arrivals in Quebec diluted the sovereigntists' fervour sufficiently to produce No results in two referendums is so delicate a topic that when, on the night of the 1995 referendum, separatist premier Jacques Parizeau attributed the narrow defeat of his cause to "money and the ethnic vote," he was immediately forced to resign.

Parizeau's resignation was a classic example of the ingrained political correctness that has dominated Canadian discourse, to the chagrin of libertarian critics, since the first days of Confederation. The truth is, freedom of expression is limited in Canada in a way it is not limited in the United States. That is because Canada was not founded purely on democratic principles, but also as a way to accommodate conflicting cultures. Americans cherish the freedoms enshrined in their Constitution and Bill of Rights so intensely, and guard them so jealously, that even the insanity of mass possession of handguns is tolerated. The Canadian Constitution was founded on a desire to pacify two polities who were perpetually on the verge of divorce due to irreconcilable differences. In consequence, Canada has developed an entrenched culture of polite speech, of knowing that there are certain things – even though they might be partly true – that one just cannot say, of accepting necessary compromises that are theoretically in conflict with a secular liberal democracy – publicly funded Roman Catholic schools, for example – but that are necessary if everyone is to get along. It is why Canada has a law against hate crimes and Americans do not; why Canadian libel laws are so much stricter than their American counterpart; why the Canadian

Radio-television and Telecommunications Commission dictates much more than does the Federal Communications Commission who gets a broadcasting licence and what they must program. Every example is a travesty of liberty, but in the beginning such compromises were necessary, and today they have become a positive virtue, making it easier for people of every creed and culture to come here and live in relative harmony, bound by Canada's strict and implacable dictates of politeness.

So accommodating was the Canadian mosaic to fresh waves of immigrants from evermore exotic lands, that English and French Europeans are becoming a minority in what used to be their own land. And a good thing, too. For Canadian multicultural lack-of-identity uniquely positions this country to succeed in a century when many traditional nation states may start to fail.

Most Canadians are probably only dimly aware, if they are aware at all, of the emerging demographic wave of depopulation. In this sense, they are like the Englishmen in the early 1800s who failed to grasp the social implications of the canals, factories, and railways that were beginning to transform the landscape, or the Europeans and North Americans in the early 1900s who failed to grasp the explosive and destructive potential of the revolutionary new ideas galvanizing political theory, the social sciences, and the arts. For as industrialization was to the nineteenth century, and ideology was to the twentieth, so a globally declining population will be to the twenty-first.

Already you may be saying to yourself, "This can't be so." Throughout the last half of the twentieth century, experts at the United Nations Population Fund and elsewhere warned of a population explosion. The baby boom that followed the Second World War, along with improved medical and social conditions in the Third World, have already combined to swell the ranks of humanity from 2.5 billion in 1950 to 6.4 billion today. UN projections have the global total reaching 9 billion by 2050. What kind of depopulation is that?

But the truth is that the latest UN projections[3] are below previous estimates, which had the population reaching 9.3 billion in 2050. Far more important, the UN projections now have the global population levelling off or even declining in the second half of the century. Already, the annual increase has declined from a peak of 82 million new people a year in the 1990s to 76 million today. Average family size has declined from six children per woman in 1960 to three today. And even these forecasts are considered unrealistically conservative by many demographers. The UN's own "low variant" scenario would see humanity topping out at less than 8 billion around 2040 and starting to decline by 2050.

What we do know for sure is this: The population of the developed world has already plateaued, and in many countries – including Germany, Japan, Russia, Spain, and Italy – may already have started to decline. For more than two decades, most developed countries have failed to maintain the Total Fertility Rate of 2.1 births per woman needed to sustain equilibrium. In Italy and Spain, the fertility rate has dropped as low as 1.2 births per woman of childbearing age. Unless these figures are reversed, Japan could lose half of its population this century; Germany could lose a fifth of its current total over the next forty years. Russia is already losing an estimated 750,000 people a year.[4]

Yet this is not the half of it. In recent years, fertility rates in the developing world have also plummeted. China's strict birth-control policies have been too successful by half. That country's population is expected to enter into a steep decline by around 2020; by mid-century the world's most populous country could be shedding about a quarter of its citizenry with each passing generation. Other Third World countries, using less draconian policies, have also defused their population bombs. India is approaching the 2.1 fertility rate, as are the Philippines. Thailand has already dropped below it. Mexico and most of Latin America are at or below the replacement rate. Only in the Islamic world and Africa are birth rates still well above replacement levels, although they are steadily dropping in the former as well. And in Africa's tragic case, HIV/AIDS could lead to population decline even if fertility rates do not drop.

The reasons for depopulation are many and sometimes conflicting. (In Russia, depopulation could be the product of increasing poverty; in other areas, it could be the result of increasing affluence.) But two causes stand out. The first is continuing global urbanization. Simply put, it makes economic sense (at least, on the surface) to have many children if you are a farmer, for they can help you to farm. But once you move to the city, children are an economic liability. Second, in most parts of the world women are gaining greater personal autonomy. It appears to be a universal phenomenon that once women gain sovereignty over their own bodies, they choose to have fewer children.

Whatever the cause, depopulation will have an epochal impact on the social and economic life of humanity. If your population is stagnant or in decline, immigration is the only remedy. In Europe and Japan, however, a strong sense of cultural individuality militates against wide-open immigration policies. It is inconceivable, at least under present circumstances, that Germany or Japan could bring in the hundreds of thousands of immigrants annually that would be needed to prevent or reverse their population decline. Yet without those immigrants, the future of such countries is bleak. Even without depopulation, most developed countries are bracing for the consequences of an aging society: the result of the post-war baby boom that was followed by a rapid baby bust. With more older people, and fewer young ones, pension plans are strained, health-care costs threaten to overwhelm personal and government budgets, and consumer spending collapses (along with property values and attendant personal savings) because there are fewer people to buy houses and home furnishings, the big-ticket items that drive the consumer economy. Add to this the accelerating factor of depopulation, and your population not only ages but soon begins to diminish, magnifying the problem. Already, some economists suspect that depopulation may be contributing to the chronically sluggish performance of the Japanese and European economies.

Settler cultures are far better positioned than mother countries to respond to the problems presented by depopulation. But while Australia and New Zealand both consider themselves multicultural societies, both also continue to struggle with a monocultural European heritage and a fear of being swamped by the "yellow peril." The United States alone, among developed countries, retains a fertility rate close to the replacement line, thanks to a higher-than-average number of births among black and Hispanic Americans (although birth rates among African Americans are dropping sharply, probably due to rising affluence within the community). And Canada, although its fertility rate is only at 1.5, imports twice as many immigrants per capita as the United States. For these reasons, Canada and the United States are uniquely positioned to ride out the impending demographic wave.

Given the importance of depopulation as an economic and social force, what should Canada be doing to exploit the competitive advantage afforded by its open-door immigration policies? First, we need to review existing policies, in order to better understand how they can be modified or improved.

Immigration to Canada has greatly increased in recent years. In the 1980s, an average of 125,000 people arrived here annually, down a bit from previous decades. In the 1990s, that number almost doubled, to 220,000 a year. It is the declared goal of Citizenship and Immigration Canada, and of the Liberal Party, to increase annual immigration levels to 1 per cent of the existing population, or around 310,000 people a year – far more, on a per capita basis, than any other member of the G8 group. Almost 11 per cent of Canada's new arrivals come from China, followed by India and the Philippines. About three-quarters of all immigrants belong to what is currently called a visible minority – although the term itself is anachronistic, since Europeans are becoming a minority in Canadian society. Because people generally prefer living among their own kind, and because finding a job is the highest priority, 80 per cent of Canada's immigrants locate in one of the country's five largest cities. An astonishing 43 per cent of all immigrants to Canada settle immediately in Toronto, while Vancouver accounts for 18 per cent and Montreal for 12, with Calgary and Ottawa each taking around 4 per cent.[5]

About 60 per cent of the immigrants allowed into Canada each year are chosen because they have the education and job skills that are in short supply. About a quarter make it in because they have a close relative already here, while about 12 per cent are refugees granted asylum. Forty-six per cent of all immigrants have a university degree, while another 13 per cent have post-secondary diplomas or certificates. Those in the skilled-worker category are on average better educated than the indigenous population. Contrary to popular belief, immigrants are disproportionately possessed of so-called useful educations, such as science, engineering, or the skilled trades. Twenty-seven per cent of the workforce in the manufacturing sector is foreign-born, 18 per cent of the workers in the construction industry were born outside the country; the same is true of 25 per cent of corporate managers. Seventy per cent of the growth in Canada's labour force and population was provided by immigrants. Twenty-five years from now, thanks to this country's low birth rate, all labour force and population growth, if we have any, will be immigrant-driven.

This last statistic is the most important of all. Immigrants are vital to Canada, not simply because they help to infill sectors of the economy where there are labour shortages. They are vital because they represent the very future of the economy itself. Within a decade or less, *all* sectors of the Canadian economy will experience labour shortages. They are already emerging in places where such a thing was once thought impossible. In Quebec, for example, 44 per cent of the public-service workforce is expected to retire over the next ten years.[6] Whereas only a decade ago Ph.D. graduates despaired of finding a tenure-track position at a good university, administrations at even the best schools today are struggling to recruit qualified faculty to replace retiring professors. The nursing and teaching professions are already having difficulty finding people to fill jobs. Shortages in the skilled trades have been chronic for years, and are repeatedly cited as a reason for delays in construction. Churches are closing for lack of ministers. With each passing year, these shortages will worsen and expand. Help Wanted signs will proliferate. Workers will be asked to put in extra hours, and mandatory retirement will be replaced by incentives to keep workers on the job as long as possible. Look around any office. How many people are due to retire within the next fifteen years? How many people have been hired in the last fifteen years? Who is going to replace all those grey-haired workers?

Clearly, Canada's historic predisposition toward accepting large numbers of immigrants will work in our favour over the coming years, as competition for young, skilled workers increases among developed countries, many of which will also face entrenched resistance from native-born citizens worried about cultural dilution. This country's open acceptance of peoples from all parts of the world, its reputation for diversity and tolerance, and its pool of recent immigrants who themselves serve as recruiters for friends and family, will work to our advantage, bolstering our workforce and our population, improving our productivity, and providing fresh sources of capital, entrepreneurial spirit, and creativity. Yet, perversely, there are influential voices within Canadian society who seek to restrict the flow of immigrants. And the federal and provincial governments actually obstruct the very policies they created to promote immigration. If Canada is to make the most of the advantage afforded by its open-door immigration policy, then these voices of doom must be contradicted and these flawed policies corrected.

A number of academics and policy analysts have raised a red flag over increasing poverty among recent immigrants. Statistics Canada reports that new arrivals to Canada in the late 1980s and the 1990s are not doing as well as those who arrived in the 1970s. Naturally, you say, the earlier arrivals have had longer to adjust. But immigrants from the 1970s, on the tenth anniversary of their arrival, were making on average as much as their native-born counterparts and were less likely to be unemployed. Immigrants who arrived in the past fifteen years or so, however, are not meeting that standard. Their average incomes are only 80 per cent of the national average after ten years of residency. Unemployment rates among immigrants who have been here for five years or less are about 50 per cent higher than the national average.[7] This deterioration has occurred despite a deliberate shift by the federal government to reduce the percentage of family-class immigrants (who are less likely to have the education and job skills required for rapid integration into Canada's workforce) from 47 per cent of all immigrants in 1985 to 27 per cent in 2000, while the percentage of new arrivals who were refugees fell from a high of 28 per cent of all immigrants in 1980 to 13 per cent in 2000. Meanwhile, the economic class of immigrants has increased from 35 per cent in 1985 to 59 per cent in 2000.[8] The Liberals in April 2005 tripled the number of parents and grandparents allowed to reunite with family members already living in Canada, in an effort to shore up ethnic support for the party. But the broad pattern of preferring economic to family migrants still holds.

The numbers are clearly worrying. Even though the federal government has intentionally tightened immigration rules in favour of highly educated and skilled workers, at the expense of family relations and refugees, the economic performance of recent immigrants has declined. This has led numerous newspaper columnists (who are, granted, prone to hysteria), the C.D. Howe Institute (a sensibly conservative think-tank), and especially the Fraser Institute (to the right of the C.D. Howe) to argue for limits to future immigration. Martin Collacott, a former diplomat and senior fellow at the Fraser Institute, has made it a personal crusade to convince Canadians and the federal government to shut off the immigration tap. "We are doing no favour to many immigrants by allowing them to come here if their economic prospects are seriously limited," he wrote in a 2002 policy paper. "Sheer numbers and their concentration in relatively few areas could, moreover, lead to a reduction in the level of acceptance by Canadians that would affect not only new immigrants but many of those who have already arrived. It is important, therefore, that instead of concentrating on larger numbers, we look at the quality of the newcomers, and ways of ensuring that those who do come have a reasonable opportunity to be successful in their new land."[9]

Such criticisms are based on a short-sighted concern about unemployment levels among immigrants – and, in Collacott's case, complaints that the Liberal Party fosters high immigration levels in order to recruit voters – and play to xenophobic fears within the population that strangers are swamping the country and contributing to poverty, urban decline, and The End of Everything as We Know It. But these Cassandras threaten Canada's long-term prospects for prosperity. Newcomers to Canada from China and India are bound to do less well, initially, than those from European countries. There is greater suspicion among employers of their educational qualifications. Their English or French may not be as good as that of Europeans. There are cultural obstacles posed by migration from a Third World state that don't exist for immigrants from developed societies. Nonetheless, these obstacles need to be overcome. The truth is that the available pool of immigrants from the United States and Europe is far too small to meet Canada's emerging labour needs. China, India, and other large Third World societies are the best source of future immigrants. If the lag time before these new arrivals reach the national average in affluence is longer than it was, say, for Italian immigrants in the 1940s and 50s, then so be it. It can be reduced by improved language and skills training. But the brutal truth is that, with every passing year, the competition for skilled immigrants will increase. As developing countries such as India and China become more modern, and as their own populations level off and then start to decline, the pool of potential emigrants will shrink. It would be an act of rank folly to turn off the immigration spigot now, at the very moment when this vital human resource is most needed.

Perversely, federal and provincial policies sometimes conspire to defeat this country's own immigration goals. Though it seems hard to believe, 12 per cent of the immigrants who arrived in Canada in the 1990s with specialized skills in health care had emigrated from this country by the year 2000.[10] They either went to a different country or returned to their country of origin. Why? Because restrictive regulations prevented them from practising their profession in Canada, even though the Canadian government had admitted them as immigrants precisely because of the shortage of doctors, nurses, and other health-care workers. Professional colleges are often reluctant to accredit foreign workers unless they can prove they are able to meet Canadian standards. That requires money for training and testing that provincial governments fail to provide. Frustrated, workers leave for more hospitable climes, while politicians furrow their brows and wonder what to do about the worsening shortage of doctors and nurses. One Statistics Canada study reported that 60 per cent of skilled immigrants to Canada were forced to find work outside their area of expertise.[11]

If immigration is to supplant native births as the source of population growth, then immigrants should be young. Not only are they more adaptable, they are more likely to have children of their own. However, only two-thirds of all immigrants to Canada in the 1990s were of working age (twenty-five to sixty-four), and the rest were much more likely to be over sixty-four than under twenty-four. The federal government should skew its immigration policy in favour of younger workers. This could be expensive, since Canada, rather than the country of origin, will be responsible for educating and training young new arrivals. But since their education is often not recognized here as valid anyway, it would be in Canada's long-term interest to provide the necessary training.[12]

The government of Quebec is pursuing an immigration policy that is not only bad for Quebec, but bad for the rest of Canada. Under an agreement negotiated in the early 1990s between Brian Mulroney and Robert Bourassa, the Quebec government gets to choose those immigrants who come to Quebec under the economic class. This alone was a terrible mistake. Although immigration is constitutionally a shared jurisdiction, the provinces effectively ceded to Ottawa responsibility for deciding which and how many new arrivals to select. Ottawa should never have ceded that power to Quebec City. That said, the Quebec government should be obsessively interested in immigration. After all, with a birth rate below the Canadian average, and after a full generation of outmigration due largely to the self-inflicted separatist wounds from which the province has repeatedly suffered, Quebec's population is at risk of going into decline within a decade, further weakening its economy and placing at risk its culture. The Liberal government of Jean Charest is aware of the problem, which is why his government announced in 2004 that Quebec would seek to substantially increase immigration to the province over the coming years. But the Charest government also introduced obnoxious legislation that would allow the Quebec government to impose quotas that in effect limit the number of people who would come to the province from places outside the francophone experience.

This is madness. The brutal truth is that many of the countries of the Francophonie are among the poorest in the world. By letting language trump all else, Quebec is closing its doors to Chinese and Latin American immigrants, and opening them to new arrivals from Haiti and French Africa. Language aside, an immigrant from Taipei or Santiago is far more likely to possess the education and job skills that will ensure their smooth transition into the Canadian economy and society than one from Port au Prince or Abidjan. Worse, the rest of Canada will pay for the consequences of Quebec's cultural xenophobia. Immigrants who come to Quebec often decide to leave the province, frustrated by restrictive language laws and poor economic prospects. Toronto, Calgary, and Vancouver are the cities most likely to receive the migrating migrants. But federal funding for training and integration of immigrants remains in Quebec, a sweet deal for the Quebec government and a raw deal for everyone else. Quota-based immigration policies that bring ill-educated immigrants with few appropriate job skills to Montreal, who then head down the 401 to Toronto in search of better times, only exacerbate an already difficult situation.

These are only a few, and not even the most egregious, of the follies and contradictions that plague Canada's immigration policy. The $975 head tax levied on all new arrivals is a pernicious revenue tool that needs to be dispensed with. Thanks to an admirable but excessive concern for fairness, thirty-six thousand refugee claimants whose applications were refused continue to live and work in Canada, undermining confidence in the immigration and refugee process and increasing the chances that criminal or terrorist elements could infiltrate Canadian society, which in turn undermines American confidence in Canada's ability to secure its borders from terrorist threat. Laudably, the Canadian and American governments signed a Safe Third Country Agreement, which went into effect in 2005, in which refugees coming to Canada from the United States (and usually originating from Latin America) have to remain in the United States while their applications are assessed. (Similarly, refugee claimants arriving in the United States via Canada must return to Canada.) The agreement should slow the flow of so-called economic refugees, who are in reality simply immigrants trying to jump the queue. Nonetheless, the federal government must streamline and tighten its refugee program, with swifter judging of cases and fewer avenues for appeal. Every time the media reveals another case of an illegal arrival with a dubious past who is able to exploit the creaky and over-cautious refugee adjudication system year after year, only to disappear the day after the final order for deportation, or who fails to be deported and commits a crime, or who then sneaks back into the country, only to cause more mischief, the citizens' faith in the fairness and efficiency of the system is dealt another blow.

Finally, staff shortages at Citizenship and Immigration, coupled with insufficient funds, cripple federal efforts to meet existing immigrant quotas, let alone increase those quotas to the avowed goal of 310,000 new arrivals a year. Immigration totals have actually dropped slightly this decade, from a high of 256,731 in 1993 to 221,352 in 2003. If we want our pension plans to remain funded and our offices and factories staffed, rules will have to be simplified and funds increased. As a practical goal, the federal government should set and meet the target of increasing immigration levels by ten thousand people a year each year for the next decade.

Despite its flaws and internal contradictions, however, Canada's immigration policies remain essentially enlightened. As populations decline and conditions in developing countries improve, the world will become an immigrant's market, with countries competing to lure and retain the brightest and the best from around the globe. Thanks to wise decisions by political leaders and public officials over the past four decades, Canada is better positioned than any other country to compete in the immigration game. Multiculturalism turned out to be not only the right thing to do, but the smart thing as well. It will be the all-important key to Canada's prosperity in the twenty-first century.

What do Russell Baker, Frederick Banting, Pierre Berton, Robert Borden, Emily Carr, Bill Clinton, Hume Cronyn, Clarence Darrow, Thomas Edison, Dwight Eisenhower, Edna Ferber, Herbert Hoover, Lyndon Johnson, Robert MacNeil, L.M. Montgomery, Edward R. Murrow, Ronald Reagan, Donald Sutherland, James Thurber, and Harry Truman have in common? All of these distinguished figures of the twentieth century were born in small towns or provincial cities of Canada or the United States. Although this is a most arbitrary list, a remarkable number of important Americans and Canadians were born in rural or remote parts of their respective countries. Often with little money or education, they migrated to larger centres, where, by dint of hard work and exceptional ability, they rose to the peaks of politics, science, journalism, and the arts. Collectively, they forged a myth of men and women who rose to greatness from humble roots, shaped by common-sense values that they transcended but never abandoned.

Except, of course, it's not quite as simple as that. Leaving aside the question of to what extent Donald Sutherland's magnificent gifts as an actor were shaped by his upbringing in Saint John, N.B., the truth of the matter is that many great figures of twentieth-century North America came from rural roots because much of the population of the late 1800s and early 1900s lived in rural areas. It would be much harder to assemble a list of great names who dominated the closing decades of the last century or the first decade of this one who hailed from farms, small towns, or even provincial cities, since with each passing decade, Canada and the United States became more and more urban. In Canada, urban-ization has reached staggering levels: 55 per cent of the Canadian population can be found in either Greater Toronto, Montreal, Vancouver, Ottawa–Gatineau, the Calgary–Edmonton corridor (though statisticians who nonchalantly disregard the three hundred kilometres between those two cities should be compelled to drive Highway 2 in January), Quebec City, Winnipeg, or Hamilton. Add the smaller cities of the B.C. interior, Saskatoon, Regina, Southwestern Ontario, Moncton, Fredericton, Halifax, and St. John's and a few others dotted here and there, and you have accounted for 80 per cent of Canada's population, making this among the world's most urban nations. And the trend is accelerating. Between 1981 and 2001, one-third of Canada's 2,607 individual communities lost populations. That statistic would sound alarming, were it not for the fact that these villages and towns now represent only 9 per cent of Canada's population. Almost without exception, they were located in regions that depended on agriculture or resource extraction.[13] That's why all the images of the Rocky Mountains, Prairie wheat fields, and sea-bound coasts that typically accompany the national anthem on late-night television are so galling: the overwhelming majority of Canadians, if placed in a canoe, would tip it over.

This is all to the good, for rural life – despite its relentless mythologization – is overrated. First of all, it is often not economically viable. Even in the Third World, agricultural practices have become so efficient that only a tiny fraction of the people now tilling the soil are actually needed, which is why countries such as China are experiencing massive and rapid urbanization. Today, only 4 per cent of the Canadian population makes its living from agriculture. If it weren't for federal subsidies, that number would probably be even less.

Similarly, fewer people than ever are required to fell trees or extract nickel, thanks to improved technology. Some respectable cities were built on resource extraction, with Sudbury, Ontario, being perhaps the leader of the pack. But a more common tale is one of boom and bust, as towns were thrown up around mines and then slowly abandoned as the vein was exhausted. The Alberta tar sands may keep Lloydminster going for a few more decades, but the long-term prospects of Kelowna, B.C. – a thriving city on the shores of Okanagan Lake based on viticulture, tourism, and retirement – are probably more encouraging.

The migration, then, to Canada's large cities is largely virtuous. Some environmentalists fret over the increasing pollution caused by overcrowding, but the potential for erosion and soil degradation from a badly managed farm is far greater. Properly handled – though we have yet to properly handle it – per capita pollution from urbanites should be much lower than from rural dwellers. Productivity is higher when a whole lot of skilled and well-educated workers live in close proximity to the offices and (to a diminishing extent) factories that drive the modern economy. And though it is an article of faith, we have centuries of accumulated evidence to justify the belief that artistic and entrepreneurial activity thrive from having lots of people inhabit a small space cheek by jowl. Jazz didn't come from the Prairies, nor a treatment for diabetes from a Newfoundland outport. Things happen in cities. Not much happens outside them.

Most important of all, if Canada is a tolerant nation, that tolerance derives from its intensely urban character. People worry that cities create ghettoes, but there is no ghetto to match the ghetto of small-town Saskatchewan, where almost everybody who isn't aboriginal is white. Civic leaders need to guard against circumstances that can lead to racial tensions in Vancouver, Montreal, or Toronto, but nothing that takes place in an inner-city schoolyard begins to match the casual racism, sexism, and homophobia that go without saying in the Central Ontario counties and districts between the Ottawa River and Georgian Bay. This country's hard-earned reputation for diversity and tolerance comes out of the Canadian urban tradition, shaped by elites – business, political, and artistic – who may have been born in the sticks, but who got to the cities as soon as they had enough money for the bus ticket. There will always be poets in small towns, painters on farms, utopian activists who have fled the smell and cramp of the city for the idyllic village. The Internet has made it possible to buy and sell stocks a thousand kilometres from the nearest stock exchange, to write and edit books from a rambling house deep in the Ottawa Valley, to run a small business out of a Newfoundland outport. The very technologies born out of and perfected in cities have made it possible to live a twenty-first-century life in a nineteenth-century environment, and some people will always be drawn to that prospect. But the limits of telecommuting have already been proven. Creativity, discovery, action, value flow from the interaction of disparate personalities in close proximity, often when they face that most urban of all creations: the deadline. Canada's future lies in its cities, and because so many Canadians live in cities, and because those cities are so wonderful, Canada's future is bright.

But as anyone who lives in a city, or who reads a newspaper, knows, our cities are troubled. Now, before we go another sentence, let's add to this one very large caveat: our cities are not nearly so troubled as their worst critics claim they are. If things were truly spiralling out of control, then crime would be on the increase. But in fact violent crime has been steadily decreasing across Canada for several decades. No, we are not more virtuous. The demographic bulges described above have reduced the number of young men, comparative to other age cohorts. There is nothing worse for a society, *nothing*, than too many young men with too little to do and no convenient war to ship them off to. In 1966, 49 per cent of Canadians were under the age of twenty-five. Today that figure is 32 per cent. That is why the crime rate has fallen, although slightly tougher law-enforcement policies may have had something to do with it as well. What matters is there is less crime than there once was. Nothing erodes the quality of urban life more than a diminished sense of security, but our cities are more secure than they have been in decades.

Nor are our downtowns collapsing, as some critics warn. In 1996, former United Way chair Anne Golden headed up a task force that, among other things, sought to prevent the "hollowing out" of downtown Toronto, which was (and is) beset by high taxes, increasing homelessness, and declining public transit. Yet over the past ten years, property values in downtown Toronto have increased by an average of 58 per cent. In Vancouver the figure is 23 per cent. Even Montreal is finally catching the wave. Property values over the past decade have skyrocketed by 70 per cent.[14] There is an unmistakable buzz about Montreal, these days: construction cranes in the downtown, new shops on St. Catherine Street, and a spring in the step of Montrealers that confidently predicts that Canada's first great city is back.

Neither do we lack for monuments, those great urban construction projects that probably are not the most efficient way to spend a taxpayer's dollar but without which a city – or a nation – has no sense of forward momentum. Toronto has its new opera and ballet house, along with Daniel Libeskind's bold new extension to the Royal Ontario Museum. Winnipeg is anticipating a new museum dedicated to human rights, Vancouver is preparing to host the Olympics, Montreal recently opened its new Grande Bibliothèque, and Ottawa finally has a war museum appropriate to the subject.

Nonetheless, there *are* problems. Some of them are literally concrete; others are more human in dimension. Our cities are congested. Neither the construction of freeways nor the expansion of public transit have kept pace with increases in population. Between 1950 and 1980, Toronto constructed 56.25 kilometres of subway. Thanks to its skilful integration with above-ground buses and streetcars, the Toronto Transit Commission had earned the reputation of being one of the world's most efficient and effective transit systems. But since 1980, the TTC has added only fifteen kilometres of new subway track and only seventy-two kilometres of streetcar track. In 1990, the city's bus network encompassed 68,756 miles. By 2001, that had dropped to 61,993 miles. The subways are visibly deteriorating, and a seat is a hopeless quest during rush hour. Since 1990, fares have increased from $1.20 to $2.50; if the 1990 fare was adjusted for inflation, riders would still be paying only $1.60.[15] When it comes to public transit, Toronto is the sick man of Canada.

The population of Greater Vancouver has grown by 68 per cent between 1981 and 2003. Yet no new vehicular bridge has been built or significantly upgraded since 1985.[16] Not surprisingly, traffic jams in the city are now among the worst in Canada. The trip along Granville Street from the airport to the downtown can wear at the soul. In Winnipeg, everything from playground equipment to sewer pipes is deteriorating, with the cost to bring everything up to an acceptable level estimated at more than $1 billion.[17] Meanwhile, Halifax continues to dump its raw sewage directly into the ocean. It's a disgrace, but not a singular one; Victoria does exactly the same thing.

Many regions seem to simply have given up on sensible urban planning. The sprawl in Toronto reaches in a virtually unbroken stretch now from Stoney Creek in the southwest to Milton in the west, the Holland Marsh in the north, and the newly fabricated municipality of Clarington in the east. Calgary now sprawls over 702 square kilometres, more than the *combined* size of Ottawa, Amsterdam, and Brussels, each of which has about the same population as Calgary.[18] Despite repeated attempts at rejuvenation – the most ambitious being the commercial and recreation redevelopment of the Forks – Winnipeg's downtown suffers from some of the worst design mistakes in all of Canada. It's bad enough that someone actually decided to seal off the famous intersection of Portage and Main from pedestrian traffic. The real atrocity is that years have gone by, and still no one has fixed it. Ottawa and Gatineau stubbornly refuse to synchronize their planning priorities and transit systems, which may be one reason why a metropolitan area of a million people still relies almost exclusively on bus service.

The single greatest problem that Canada's cities face may be the spectre of homelessness. According to the 2001 census, 2,570 people in Toronto slept in shelters. In Vancouver, the figure is 630; in Montreal, 1,785. In Winnipeg, the spectre is compounded by the racial component: many of the indigents of that city are indigenous, stoking fears of an emerging racial underclass.

Homelessness degrades all who come in contact with it. It dehumanizes people who must live Third World lives in First World cities. It shames and angers the more fortunate who must endure repeated pleas for money, plus the occasional curse or threat. It contributes to vandalism, litter, filth, and the general decline of that all-important urban space: the neighbourhood sidewalk. Dirty, messy, graffiti-ridden streets and storefronts are the early warning signs of a neighbourhood in jeopardy. Homelessness, combined with deteriorating streets, increases fears of crime and lack of personal safety; these fears may be unfounded but simply having them is sufficient to cheapen the quality of life.

As potholes deepen, sidewalks crumble, and bums abound, a growing number of voices have called on the federal government to take action. This, on the face of it, is illogical. Under the Canadian Constitution, municipalities are "creatures of the provinces," as the saying goes. They exist at the pleasure of provincial governments, which can create, amalgamate, or disband them at their will. They receive whatever taxing powers they enjoy –

principally property-tax levies, plus various user and licence fees – from their provincial masters, who also provide them with direct grants. If Greater Toronto is bursting at the seams and fraying at the edges, then it is the responsibility of Queen's Park to provide the remedies. If Vancouver is sinking beneath the weight of its burgeoning population, then it is Victoria's responsibility to come to its aid.

Nonetheless, hungry sheep look up to Ottawa to be fed. Partly, that is because Ottawa has served as shepherd in the past. In the 1960s, the federal government decided that it had the power, the money, and the responsibility to intervene in a host of provincial responsibilities, from health care to education to cities. The mandarinate and political elites of the time believed that the federal power would wither unless it involved itself in the lives of its citizens. Besides, thanks to a series of agreements negotiated during and shortly after the Second World War, the provincial governments had ceded much of the tax room that they had formerly occupied to Ottawa. Rather than restoring the balance once peace and good times had arrived, Ottawa decided instead to help the provinces out, in part by providing direct grants to citizens, in part by negotiating federal–provincial agreements in which Ottawa would establish and help fund national standards in programs that provincial governments would deliver. In this way arrived medicare, and the Canada Student Loans program, and the great subsidized housing projects of the 1960s and 70s.

After more than twenty years of accumulated deficits, however, the federal government decided enough was enough. Ottawa cut back its funding for health care, welfare, and other social services. It also got out of the subsidized housing game. Provincial governments, which were also struggling to bring back balanced budgets, also downloaded some or all of the responsibility for sub-sidized housing, public transit, roads, and general infrastructure repair to municipal governments, while cutting their grants. No wonder that, a decade later, cities were looking tattered and beleaguered. Yet now that the nation's finances are in order, urban activists are focusing most of their attention on Ottawa, rather than the provincial capitals, in their demands for greater financial assistance. The reason is simple: the federal government still has almost all of the taxing authority it had after the Second World War (apart from a small portion transferred to the provinces in the late 1970s). That is why provincial governments continue to struggle to keep their budgets balanced, even as the federal gov-ernment hauls in mega-billion-dollar surpluses. It is why Toronto mayor David Miller has repeatedly called on Paul Martin to rescue his city; why former Winnipeg mayor Glen Murray pro-posed a New Deal for cities that would have shifted a portion of sales and income taxes to municipalities. It is why the *Toronto Star* proposed its own New Deal for cities (read Toronto) that, in essence, consisted of a massive transfer of federal tax dollars to city (read Toronto) coffers.

In fact, increasing federal transfers to cities was a bad idea, and the Martin government's botched and mismanaged cities agenda – one of the worst policy fiascos of that policy-obsessed govern-ment – proved why. Simply put, the federal government is not responsible for cities. This does not mean it does not influence their character. As we have seen, federal immigration policies over the past forty years have powerfully transformed the shape of urban Canada. And certainly the federal government is – or should be – responsible for funding the language and skills train-ing of landed immigrants, for helping them find housing, and for easing as much as possible the consequences of federal immigration polices on provincial governments and cities. But direct intervention in city finances is another, and quite extra-constitutional, thing altogether. As provincial governments bitterly attest, federal–provincial shared-cost programs are splendid ideas that federal politicians enthusiastically embrace. Health care for everyone. Housing for everyone. Daycare for everyone. The problem is, federal funding invariably dissipates over time, as Ottawa chases after whatever shiny new policy bauble catches its eye. The expectations and the costs, however, remain, leaving cash-strapped provincial governments to fund the hospitals, apartment blocks, and daycare centres that Ottawa helped build but is no longer willing to help run. For that reason, the Martin government found provincial premiers distinctly wary about entering into any grand shared-cost program to renew urban infrastructure. They knew this bag all too well, since they'd been left holding it often enough.

Recognizing that provincial co-operation was unlikely to be forthcoming, the prime minister's advisers came up with another tactic: Ottawa would give the cities half of the revenue from the gasoline excise tax. The money, to be phased in over a number of years, would be used by cities to rejuvenate their infrastructure. The money could go to upgrading transit, improving sewage disposal, modernizing water mains, repairing or replacing bridges, whatever the city felt was its top priority. Months before he became prime minister, Paul Martin had already promised the rescue, even as his senior advisers bent their minds to working out a coherent policy.

But it was not to be. The needs of Canada's cities may be paramount, but the collective power of the hinterland is greater.

The reason can be found in what is perhaps the greatest flaw in the Canadian parliamentary system: its protection of small provinces and rural ridings at the expense of cities. In 1915, the federal government promised the government of Prince Edward Island that it would never have fewer seats in Parliament than it would have in the Senate, where it is constitutionally guaranteed four seats. Another febrile promise by the federal government, in 1985, that no province would lose seats as a result of parliamentary redistribution, means that Newfoundland and Labrador is guaranteed seven seats. Although seats are redistributed periodically in the House of Commons to reflect population shifts, the skew in favour of Atlantic Canada cannot be corrected without enormously increasing the size of the House of Commons, and most Canadians believe there are enough politicians in Ottawa as it is. Thanks to this imbalance, as previously mentioned, urban ridings often have several times as many voters as rural ones. To compound the skew, separate commissions set the riding boundaries for each province, and they invariably overrepresent rural areas and under-represent urban ones. (The reason given is that rural ridings would be so geographically large as to be unmanageable for candidates or for the elected member of Parliament to navigate.) As a result, rural and small-town communities in all parts of Canada have a disproportionately large voice in federal political counsels (and in provincial legislatures, as well), while cities have relatively little clout, despite being home to most of the population and the engines of most of the economy.

It was hardly surprising, then, that Paul Martin, under attack from small-town and small-city mayors, and from MPs in his own caucus, backed off his cities agenda. Instead, once the Martin government began negotiating with municipalities – the first, with those of British Columbia, was signed in April 2005, with most other provinces falling into line in the following months – the gas tax was transferred on a mostly per-capita basis: everybody got a little, while no one got a lot. Rural municipal politicians rightfully argued that their communities had needs, too. Indeed they do, but the consequence of the shift in Martin policy was that taxpayers from cities once again saw their dollars siphoned to prop up and preserve smaller municipalities, which is precisely (and perversely) the exact opposite of the original cities agenda.

Nonetheless, the needs of the cities remain, and grow, and provincial governments continue to struggle to find the resources to meet them. There are two concrete steps the federal government could take to rejuvenate Canada's beleaguered urban spaces. The first would be to cancel the gasoline tax rebate (though any existing agreements should be honoured until they expire), recognizing that it is a policy failure, and instead to permanently transfer the equivalent portion of the federal government's taxing powers to the provinces. In essence, the federal government would take a bit less from you in income tax each year, and your provincial government would take a bit more. In exchange for this permanent fiscal windfall, the provincial governments would have to agree to spend the new tax revenue on municipalities, without cutting existing grants, for a five-year period. This solution is not ideal, since rural provinces would not benefit as much as the large provinces with the big cities that matter. But at least all provinces would benefit, and Ottawa would be rid of the temptation to meddle.

The second concrete step that Ottawa could take to improve city living would be to fight the scourge of homelessness. At its root, people sleep on the street because provincial and federal governments abandoned their responsibilities, both to them and to the larger community. While exact figures are difficult to compile, conventional wisdom holds that about half of the homeless are people with serious psychological problems or mental disabilities. (Although simply being homeless suggests a mental or social dysfunction of some kind.) Many of these street people were discharged from provincial institutions in a well-intentioned effort to help them live out their lives within the community. Well-intentioned, but cheap, because governments failed to provide the housing and treatment necessary for that integration. As a result, too many of the mentally ill or disabled ended up on the street. Compounding the problem, courts and government relaxed the laws on vagrancy, making it harder for police to crack down on panhandlers or to compel people sleeping outside to move into municipal shelters. It was academic anyway, for many nights all the shelter beds are full.

Nonetheless, the public spaces belong to the public. The sidewalks are *our* sidewalks, and all of us, including the homeless woman, the pedestrian, and the shopkeeper, have a right to traverse them without hindrance. We have a right as well to expect, and to insist, that people sleep with a roof over their heads, whether they want that roof or not. Ottawa could further transfer a portion of its taxing power to permit provincial governments to fund subsidized housing, treatment programs for the mentally ill or disabled, or shelters for the homeless, as they saw fit. It could also reform the criminal code to give police greater powers to deter panhandling and to move street-sleepers to shelters. Some will criticize such policies as heartless, but nothing is more heartless than allowing those who live on the street to stay there, and nothing more seriously jeopardizes the life and health of inner cities. Similar policies in American cities, especially New York, have contributed to the revival of downtown streets and neighbourhoods. Canadians have tended to be smug about the superior quality of our downtowns. But ask yourself this: Why do you almost never see a beggar in Manhattan any more?

One further migration could profoundly influence the shape of Canada's cities in the coming decades. An influx is underway of aboriginal Canadians from reserves and rural areas into urban centres. Far too many of these new arrivals lack the education and training needed to prosper in a twenty-first-century urban environment. And unlike other groups in Canadian society, aboriginal Canadians have a fertility rate comparable to that of Third World societies. Yet, perhaps out of a sense of resignation, or for fear of causing offence, Canadians are reluctant to openly discuss, let alone address, the challenges facing native Canadians. Unless that silence is broken, and those challenges faced and overcome, Canada risks creating a large, poor, angry, urban aboriginal underclass.

When discussing aboriginal issues, the most important first step is not to succumb to the assumption of stasis. According to that assumption, Canada's Indians, Inuit, and Métis populations mostly live in isolated and unproductive parts of the country, where they abuse their bodies with alcohol and chemicals, while their elders misspend gazillions of federal dollars, much of it on protracted and fruitless legal battles over treaty rights and land claims. Those who leave the reserves invariably end up living in urban slums or on the street. The only solution – well, frankly, there is no solution.

This is nonsense. While Canada's aboriginal populations[19] are in flux, the overall quality of their lives is improving, despite relentless media reports to the contrary. Pockets of despair remain, and cultural assumptions both within and outside the aboriginal community are sometimes a drag on progress, but progress is steady and real. And for those problems that remain, solutions are readily at hand.

Sometimes, what looks like bad news is really good news in disguise. Consider life expectancy, for example. Everyone knows that Native Canadians have a reduced life expectancy. And yes, Canadian aboriginal males have a life expectancy 7.4 years lower than that of the general population. But in the 1970s, the figure was eleven years.[20] Clean water and improved housing on reserves have brought dramatic gains in the general health of First Nations populations. There is more to be done, but much has been done already.

Fertility rates offer another example of hidden good news. "Everyone knows" that aboriginal women have more children than non-aboriginal women, which contributes to urban ghettoization and to large, poor, dysfunctional families on reserves. In Saskatchewan, some observers predict that high Indian birth rates, coupled with a trickling exodus of the settler population to other provinces, could result in a majority aboriginal population in that province by the end of this century.

Even if that were a bad future, it is also an unlikely one. Aboriginal birth rates are falling like a stone. Forty years ago, they were pegged at 6.1 for First Nations women and 9.1 for Inuit women. By the 1980s, they were 3.1 and 4.1 respectively. Today, the estimated fertility rate among First Nations women is about 2.45, not far from the 2.1 replacement rate, and not that far above the 1.5 of the general population.[21] A generation from now, if birth rates continue to decline and immigration continues to increase, the aboriginal population could be diminishing as a share of the overall population.

As well, "everybody knows" that aboriginal cultures do not value education, at least of the European variety, which contributes to their low incomes. Schools on reserves are too small and ill-equipped to provide a decent educational experience. Provincial governments are reluctant to accept the marks of students educated on reserve, and are equally unwilling to invest the money needed to bring those schools up to the provincial standard. (Each level of government claims it's the other level's responsibility.) The abuses of the residential schools program and a general fear that the public education system – with its secular, pluralist values – is itself a form of cultural genocide, makes aboriginal parents less likely to insist that their children attend school. All of this is true, except that it does not account for the fact that over the past forty years, the number of aboriginals enrolled in post-secondary education has increased from 200 to 27,000. The number of First Nations in the legal profession has increased from 110 in 1981 to 1,370 in 2001 and from 30 aboriginal doctors in 1981 to 210 doctors in 2001.[22]

Granted, in the autumn of 2004, Auditor General Sheila Fraser warned that the estimated time it would take to close the gap in high-school completion rates between First Nations students and the general population had increased over the past four years from an estimated twenty-seven years to an estimated twenty-eight years. While seven out of ten non-aboriginal Canadians complete high school, the figure for First Nations Canadians is four in ten. But while these numbers are deeply worrying, the A.G. also pointed out that the gap *was* starting to narrow, and pointed to innovative programs in some provinces that were helping to narrow it further.

Finally, "everyone knows" that the First Nations reserve system is a cultural catastrophe, rampant with unemployment, alcoholism, spousal and child abuse – a miniature system of semi-voluntary apartheid operating within a country that likes to consider itself the most culturally egalitarian in the world. Tragically, some First Nations reserves fit that stereotype with depressing accuracy. But many others do not. The Sarcee Indian Reserve, on the edge of Calgary, now renamed the Tsuu T'ina First Nation, already boasts twenty-one commercial enterprises, fine schools and health-care facilities, a busy arena, and a residential neighbourhood known as Redwood Meadows. In 2004, the Tsuu T'ina approved an ambitious development plan featuring a casino, big-box stores, an industrial park, and an ambitious eco-tourism project. Wal-Mart is building stores on two reserves in British Columbia. The Tyendinaga Reserve, on the Bay of Quinte, boasts a welfare rate of 2 per cent, a third of that of surrounding Hastings County,[23] or that the Wahta Mohawk of Bala, Ontario, in the heart of Muskoka's cottage country, operate Ontario's largest cranberry farm.

The truth is that, where reserves are located near urban centres or on usable land, aboriginal populations are about as successful as anyone else at providing jobs, housing, and quality of life for their population. The reserves that reinforce the stereotype tend to be in remote, isolated areas where any group of people, if plunked down there, would soon find themselves in trouble. About what you'd expect.

Nonetheless, overall rates of alcoholism, infant mortality (in the Northwest Territories, it is three times that of the population as a whole),[24] mental-health disease (one off-reserve native in eight reported having a major depressive episode within the last year, according to a Statistics Canada study; only one person in fourteen reported the same condition among non-natives),[25] crime (aboriginals are three times as likely to die a violent death as non-natives),[26] tobacco-related diseases, domestic violence, and poverty remain alarmingly high within Canada's aboriginal population. Unless they come down steadily over time, Canada will have failed as a society to meet its most pressing internal challenge. But how?

Money is not the problem: the federal government alone spends $7 billion a year on supporting First Nations families – about $46,000 per family of four. Nor is there a lack of information: aboriginal issues have been the subject of an exhaustive Royal Commission; there are federal and provincial departments of native affairs; Statistics Canada has studied demographics extensively; both Paul Martin and Jean Chrétien made improving the lives of native Canadians major priorities; natives are ably represented by tribal and national leaderships. There are a great many people who make a living talking about how to make life better for native Canadians.

But two major obstacles stand in the way: process and culture. The process for negotiating land claims and for determining self-government for native peoples is proceeding at an excruciatingly slow pace. More than 120 land-claim treaties remain under negotiation, giving joy to lawyers and no one else.[27]

First Nations claim most of the Crown land in Canada, saying that where they did not specifically cede it, it belongs to them. They see themselves as sovereign peoples who never surrendered that sovereignty, and who should, at the least, enjoy all of the rights and responsibilities of provincial governments, which are also sovereign in the spheres of their jurisdiction. The federal and provincial governments share responsibility over Crown land, complicating negotiations. The courts, in general, insist that the federal government respect native claims and negotiate with native governments in search of a fair settlement based on rights that were never extinguished.

Where disputes remain, all sides need to recognize the rights and responsibilities of the other sides, especially the right of native communities to share in the rents from resource extraction. Further, individual claims need to ensure that First Nations have the land, resources, and autonomy necessary to govern themselves well and to make a reasonable living off their land. In exchange, the First Nations leaders need to surrender the notion of ever taking back all of the land that was taken from them. History has moved on. What matters now is looking after the future needs of the band populations, not waging some mythical struggle to reclaim a lost birthright. All sides need to get real.

More important even than settling land claims, federal and provincial governments working with band councils need to make a concerted effort to improve the quality of aboriginal education. Reserve schools need the resources to provide an education equal to that of all provincial schools. If that means a much lower teacher–pupil ratio, so be it. If reserve schools can't match their off–reserve equivalents, then on–reserve families should be given vouchers enabling them to send their children to the public or private school of their choice. Education is the single most important tool in breaking the aboriginal cycle of poverty. Failure is simply not an acceptable outcome. Period.

In this respect, native leaders need to get off some of their high horses, and exorcize the cult of victimization in which so many of them delight to wallow. Educational standards among natives are below average not simply because education is not valued highly in a culture that continues to see itself as rooted to the land. Education is looked upon in part with active suspicion, as a form of cultural expropriation that imposes European values and norms on native culture. Maybe it does, but the fact remains that there is only one way to multiply; the truths of geological and biological evolution are implacable, however much they might contradict tribal lore; and if you want to be able to make your way in the world, a good education is an essential asset. Far too often federal education funds intended for reserve schools are diverted to other uses, often to put relatives of band council members on the payroll for no good reason. To pretend to the young that they can have a good life simply by living off the land and the taxpayer is its own, pernicious form of parental abuse. The horrors that occurred in residential schools in past generations were unconscionable. But they have ended − though the process for providing financial compensation has degenerated into one of pay-them-off-whatever-the-cost − and there were abuses in non-native schools as well. None of that is any reason to diminish the vital necessity of providing each and every aboriginal Canadian with the best possible education.

Third, aboriginal society needs to accept that there are elements of non-native culture that natives would do well to adapt. The aboriginal tradition of governing by consensus is admirable, except when it leads to inaction in the face of pressing needs. Awarding property titles to the land occupied by natives on reserves would confer the right and responsibility to manage homes, build and increase equity, and permit investments in upgrades that would do more to improve native housing than would a host of government initiatives. The idea of collective ownership may be traditional, but it is also Marxist, and it won't work in twenty-first-century Canada any better than it did in the twentieth-century Soviet Union. (Has it never occurred to native leaders that their inability to provide and maintain functional housing is identical to the same problem that plagued the U.S.S.R., and that the absence of private property was the common denominator?) Finally, bands living in remote, isolated, and chronically poor reserves need to ask themselves: What are we doing here? Why are we staying? Hasn't the time come to leave? After all, more than half of First Nations Canadians now live off-reserve.

That last statistic may be the most compelling of all. Aboriginal Canada may be in the process of slowly disappearing, despite the best efforts of its leadership and various levels of government to buttress it. After all, as previously observed, aboriginal birth rates are steadily declining. Aboriginal populations may be becoming increasingly dominant in the Prairies, but that is only because Europeans are leaving and not enough new immigrants are arriving. The real solution lies in providing an economic and social environment in Winnipeg, Saskatoon, and Regina that will attract Asian, Latino, and African new arrivals.

If that solution is achieved, then natives there will do what natives are doing everywhere: they will marry non-natives. Already, aboriginal bloodlines are becoming so mixed that Assembly of First Nations chief Phil Fontaine has called for a rewriting of the Indian Act to loosen the definition of what is a status Indian. Otherwise, he fears that by the middle of this century "legislative extinction" will result from Indians marrying non-Indians.[28] But that, of course, is the whole point of the Canadian experiment. The assumption behind multiculturalism is that when a broad range of cultures intermingle and intermarry, society as a whole is enriched. Canada will be defined by the future that awaits the daughter of a Haitian mother and a Croat father, who marries the son of Japanese and Egyptian parents. Within that matrix, it is inevitable that a Cree boy will fall in love with a Guatemalan girl. Their children will be enriched by both cultures, but both cultures will recede in dominance as a result.

This may be the ultimate fate of migrating, urbanizing aboriginal Canada. If so, it will be neither a blessing nor a curse. It will simply be. The ultimate solution to ending the aboriginal disadvantage within Canada might lie in integration – not as a matter of policy, but as a matter of destiny. There will always be a native Canada. The Inuit will continue to inhabit the North. Reserves will continue to house aboriginal populations and preserve aboriginal culture. But as the rural recedes in importance in Canadian life, the importance of rural indigenous populations will inevitably recede as well. They will become a small minority within the larger aboriginal culture, which itself will be increasingly urban, cosmopolitan, and, yes, diluted. It's the future for all of us, WASP and Mohawk alike. The alternative is to permit the evolution of a segregated aboriginal society within our urban spaces, which in turn will descend into a racially defined urban underclass. And that, whatever the cost, must never be allowed to happen.

CHAPTER FOUR

A
NEW
SOCIAL
CHARTER

National governments have four big jobs: security, finances, foreign policy, and social policy. For most citizens, social policy trumps the rest. Pundits and analysts might pore over foreign-policy or defence reviews, politicians will vie to trumpet the latest government scandal or blacken the Opposition's image, but it doesn't matter to most Canadians, nor should it. Each of us lives a life surrounded by family and friends, preoccupied with work and wages, most likely comforted by religion and governed by the changeless cycles of growth, fulfillment, and passing. Governments can profoundly influence the quality of that life. They can make it easy or hard for parents to nurture their young and live in the community of their choice. They can make work a means toward privately fulfilled ends or frustrate that fulfillment through punitive or rapacious taxation. They can compel employers to deal humanely with their workers or let the rules of contract be red of tooth and claw. Governments can encourage each citizen to maximize their potential, or limit potential to promote equality. Governments can reaffirm and celebrate shared values, or protect the rights of each individual to seek a personal definition of truth and justice. Government, in other words, can make life better or make it worse. This is why politics matters.

The first half of the twentieth century must be marked as one of the most horrific in human history, comparable to the collapse of Rome, the Black Death, the Thirty Years War. Tens of millions of people died in wars of unimaginable brutality; tens of millions more died through state-imposed starvation, extermination, or forced relocation. In the twentieth century, for the majority of the human population, the greatest non-natural risk to your life came from your own government. But whether through exhaustion or fear, the second half of the twentieth century witnessed the exact opposite: For perhaps the first time since the *Pax Romana*, no great power went to war with any other great power for more than fifty years. In consequence, at least in the developed world, politicians and bureaucrats were able to apply ideas first articulated in the nineteenth century to a world now more or less at peace. Governments established new baselines of responsibility. It became the duty of the state to house, clothe, and feed anyone who could not do so on their own; to care, either directly or indirectly, for the health and education of every citizen; to regulate commerce in order to protect workers and the environment; to foster and support the unique culture of its people.

Although there were differences in the details, over thirty years, stretching roughly from 1950 to 1980, the industrialized nations of the world developed the infrastructure of what became known as the welfare state. Every state regulated its economy, employing variations of the counter-cyclical economic theories espoused by John Maynard Keynes, which partially succeeded in mitigating the human cost of capitalism's endless cycle of boom and bust. Every state took steps to ensure universal access to health services, education, insurance against unemployment. For those who fell into, or were trapped in, poverty, every state provided the equivalent of a guaranteed annual income. All that, and old-age pensions too.

Unfortunately, Keynesian economic theory revealed a stubborn tendency to create unsustainable inflation, erratic interest rates, and, worst of all, entrenched deficits. In reaction, governments scaled back the more luxurious entitlements, abandoned the excesses of regulation and nationalization, reduced taxes, and handed monetary policy over to central banks, where there were people who knew what they were doing. In most countries, the remedies worked, although there was much pain attached.

When Konrad Adenauer became the first chancellor of West Germany after the Second World War, his campaign slogan was: "No experiments." The twenty-first century is starting out, and may well end up, as a no-experiments century. It would be nice to conjure up fiery visions of Utopias yet to come, but we have lived with the consequences of ideology and the forced imposition of other men's nirvanas. The watchword in the twenty-first century will be *balance*. Balance between humankind and nature; between work and leisure; between the citizen and the state. Knowledge will continue to expand, though perhaps not so exponentially as in the past two centuries, and new gadgets will make life and communication simpler. But no one is willing to wage war for the sake of an idea, or to impose that idea on all humanity against its will. Well, actually, there are still a few who are. We call them terrorists.

In the absence of experiments, governments and citizens are left with the challenge of perfecting, or at least managing, the various balancing acts that, added together, comprise the social contract. We need to find ways to encourage growth while mitigating its side effects. We need to weigh the benefits of social services – health care, education, housing, poor relief, child care – against the economic costs and personal affront of income redistribution. We need to maximize opportunity for the poorer regions of Canada without undermining success simply to reinforce failure. And we need to start by recognizing that there is one chronic social-policy challenge left unmet, without which all other challenges will go unfulfilled. We need to confront the challenge of rescuing our health-care system. And yes, believe it or not, in spite of all that you've heard, it can be done.

On a fine July day in 2004, Ralph Klein said the unthinkable. The premier of Alberta was meeting with his provincial counterparts at a resort and conference centre at Niagara-on-the-Lake. Of course, the issue was health care. Of course, the premiers all wanted more federal money. But Klein wanted something else as well. He wanted people to start thinking outside the box, and the box in this case was the sacred tabernacle of medicare.

"In society today, you can go piddle [money] away at the casino down here," the premier told reporters, pointing in the general direction of Niagara Falls. "You can buy a new car. You can buy a new house, you can buy clothes for your wife; you can buy clothes for yourself. You can do anything in the world. The only thing you can't do in this country is spend money on your own health care. I think it's wrong. That's my personal thought."[1]

Klein was asking the unaskable question: If I work hard, and make some extra money, why will the State allow me to spend that money on a plasma-screen TV, but prohibit me from helping my mother get cataract surgery? The answer lies in the unique and perverse way health care in Canada has evolved.

Tommy Douglas is considered the hero of medicare. He introduced the concept to Saskatchewan in 1959, and saw it taken up by the Liberal government of Prime Minister Lester Pearson in 1965. For this, Douglas is revered as the greatest Canadian who ever lived – or so said voters to a CBC show. But what voters of all kinds forget is that Douglas was a populist, grassroots social-ist, a Baptist minister steeped in the culture of British class warfare and Depression-era social gospel. Douglas's ideas on medicare were anchored in the prairie populism that celebrates the little guy against the Big Interests, and in the industrial socialism that dictated that the state should directly control the main levers of the economy. As such, his government was unwilling to intro-duce a system of publicly funded health care to buttress or even partially supplant private care. Oh no, for Tommy Douglas, nothing less than full nationalization of hospital and doctors' services would suffice. Doctors could continue to operate as inde-pendent professionals; hospitals could carry on as non-profit cor-porations – to this extent, to be fair, Douglas's reforms were less radical than the British prototype, the National Health Service, on which Canadian medicare was based. But while Britain and other European countries tolerated a parallel private health sector,

Douglas opted for full nationalization. Private delivery, supplemental charges, or any kind of direct costs to patients were to be discouraged. Medicare was to be the ultimate command-and-control mechanism, in which state planners would assess future demand, and then train the workers and build the facilities to meet that demand. It was this populist ethos of socialist evangelism that the Liberals adopted when they expanded the program nationwide. They could have drawn back. They could have said that Saskatchewan's experiment, while noble, went too far. Like every country in Europe, plus Japan, Australia, and New Zealand, Canada could have built in a private-sector safety valve. But no, when it came to the commanding heights of the health industry, Canada adopted the tenets of Prairie socialism. There are still people in this country who think that was a good thing.

If history has taught us anything, it is that the state is not competent to manage any industrial sector, be it automobiles or airlines or health services. Civil servants making mediocre salaries are somehow expected to divine future demand and adjust supply accordingly, with funds provided by politicians. But the civil servants aren't that smart – if they were, they'd be making seven figures working for a pharmaceutical – and you'll be shocked to hear that politicians too often manipulate the system for partisan gain. Things were manageable in the 1970s, when the demographics skewed toward younger and healthier citizens, thanks to the Baby Boom, and in the 1980s, because federal and provincial governments were prepared to run deficits to ensure that supply more or less kept up with demand. But in the 1990s, the system began to totter, and today it is on the brink of collapse. Politicians – determined to balance budgets and constrain taxes, and bolstered by faulty analyses from bureaucrats who assured them, among other things, that there was a glut of doctors – slashed funding. Today, there is a chronic shortage of doctors, as well as nurses and other health-care workers, although the civil servants who reassured those politicians a decade ago are still there, and still earning their bonuses, while the politicians have largely escaped incarceration. But patients wait weeks or months for cancer treatments and heart operations; the wait for hip replacements or cataract surgery can stretch into years. After a plethora of studies and a Royal Commission – perversely chaired by *another* former Saskatchewan socialist premier, Roy Romanow – Prime Minister Paul Martin sat down with the premiers in September 2004, and worked out a deal in which the provinces would get more money, while Ottawa would coordinate efforts to develop and report on national standards. As of this writing, there has been no evidence of meaningful progress toward reducing those waiting lists. Instead, across the country, premiers and health ministers continue to alternate between threatening and cajoling doctors and hospital administrators, in an effort to control health costs, which continue to increase at about twice the rate of inflation and which now account for up to half of all provincial spending.

Ralph Klein understood, perhaps intuitively, something that no other Canadian politician dared to openly confront. Klein knew that the first duty of a liberal democracy is to satisfy the needs of the middle class. Liberal democratic governments[2] can abuse and offend the wealthy; the rich are punitively taxed because there aren't enough of them to vote a government in or out. (Although, if pushed too far, they can transfer their capital elsewhere, a major check on democratic abuse of elites.) The poor don't matter because they don't vote and are smaller in number than the middling classes. The legitimacy of the Canadian government rests on that broad mass of citizens making somewhere between $25,000 and $75,000 a year, give or take, who constitute a majority of the workforce, create and consume most of the national wealth, and vote governments in or out of office. If they lose confidence in a particular political party, that party is in a lot of trouble. If they were ever to lose confidence in the system itself, the system would be in a lot of trouble. Klein believed that middle-class support for medicare is eroding, and people were prepared to consider private-sector alternatives. Studies and polls consistently report that he was right, that public impatience with a health-care system that consumes vast resources and delivers a mediocre product is steadily growing.[3] The Supreme Court of Canada echoed that sentiment in June 2005, when it ruled that the delivery of health care in Quebec had deteriorated to the point of imperilling the citizen's constitutional right to security of person, opening the door (at least a crack) to parallel private care. Faced with this public and judicial mutiny, the apex of the Canadian political policy establishment is fighting back.

The intellectual elites who dominate Canada's universities (at least in the humanities and social sciences) and media came to the conclusion, somewhere in the 1970s, that medicare is more than a commodity. It is even more than a public good, such as education or public utilities that require state regulation or even control to ensure equitable distribution. Health care, they decided, is the answer to a question they had been asking themselves, but were unable to resolve satisfactorily. What is it to be Canadian?

There is no question more tiresome than the question of national identity. First of all, almost no answer could encompass both French and English Canada. Second, culture and identity are forged horizontally, through the interaction of individual citizens – be it on a hockey rink or in a book club – and not imposed vertically by the state. Cultural elites may think that the CPR and the CBC shaped the Canadian identity, but the truth is that a railroad is just a railroad, and the national broadcaster was never as popular as its private-sector rivals, and now draws only 6 per cent of the national audience.[4] For at least half a century, the editors of the *Toronto Star* and the inhabitants of the common rooms of the University of Toronto have flailed about in search of a definitive expression of what it means to be a Canadian. They have never come close. In despair they have concluded that to be Canadian is to support medicare.

Medicare (even though the name is borrowed from the United States) crystallizes the difference between Canadian and American societies, goes this argument. The United States, far more than any other developed society, relies on the private sector to provide medical services to the middle class. (American Medicare, a $505-billion system, is available to the poor and elderly.) For once, rather than borrowing from European and American models, Canada has gone further than any of them in creating a truly socialized medical system, with no private delivery at all. (There are many exceptions to this statement,[5] but this idea is what drives the cultural-nationalism argument.) By defining health care as a universal right rather than a public/private service, Canadians are demonstrating their national sense of compassion, fairness, and equity. It also demonstrates Canadian practicality, for our nationalized medicare system consumes less of our gross domestic product on a percentage basis than the Americans' largely private system.[6] For this reason, goes this argument, any intrusion by the private sector into Canadian medicare is not only

inequitable, it is inherently treasonous, diluting the political manifestation of the national essence.

This is bosh, and dangerous bosh at that. Permitting a social
policy to run amok simply to compensate for a demonstrable
lack of patriotism among the broader public is madness. Equally,
stifling debate over the efficient delivery of a public good by
invoking the credo of social justice only succeeds in perpetuat-
ing bad policy, while ultimately undermining the very social
bonds that medicare is intended to promote. The question is not
whether introducing private elements in the health-care system
will weaken the bonds of Canadian society. The question is, how
do we keep the middle class satisfied with the quality of health
care they are receiving, at the (very high) level of taxes they are
paying? Politically and socially, that is the question that must be
answered before all others. That's the question Ralph Klein asked.

The Klein government failed to provide a compelling answer
to the premier's question. Reform proposals issued in the summer
of 2005 consisted of mostly namby-pamby measures, accompanied by promises of further, endless consultations. But now that
the Supreme Court has opened the door to experimentation,
Alberta is likely to be the province where the first system-shaking
reforms occur, whoever is premier. For one thing, the province
is rich enough: The Alberta government, debt-and-deficit free,
could afford whatever financial penalties Ottawa might impose
if some prime minister, content to write off any hope of his party's
ever winning a seat in that province for a generation, should cut
funding to the province on the grounds that its government has
violated the sacred precepts of the Canada Health Act.[7]

For another, Albertans would be more likely to rally to a
defiant, health-reforming premier than would voters in other

provinces. That isn't because Albertans are enamoured of private care: polls show that they are as committed to medicare as citizens in other parts of the country. But Alberta displays a political homogeneity unique to Canada (although it shares certain similarities with Quebec). Its citizenry are more culturally conservative, affluent, and independent-minded, and Alberta continues to nurse its ancient grudge against the hucksters, sharpies, and fat cats who run the show from Toronto, Montreal, and Ottawa. Provided Albertans could be assured that privatizing reforms would be accommodated within a majority-public system that continued to provide quality care for all who needed it, regardless of income, they might well be willing to risk experiment, especially if that experiment were clothed in the political rhetoric of rebellion against the Centre.

What might such an experiment entail? A sharp reduction in the number of listed services, which would focus only on major traumas and illnesses. The imposition of modest user fees, to limit exploitation of the system by the hypochondriacs among us (or at least to make them pay for their obsession). An invitation to for-profit companies to compete for contracts to deliver publicly funded services. (Who cares who owns the bed, as long as there's a patient in it?) These are only first steps, designed to increase efficiency within the state system. But as Mikhail Gorbachev of Russia discovered, attempting to reform a command-and-control economy invariably leads to broader deregulation, whether you want it to or not. In the case of Canadian health care, that could include permitting the private sector to provide, and charge for, surgeries that the public system has difficulty providing efficiently, such as hip replacements. It could include private clinics that allow patients to obtain tests more quickly, if they are willing to pay. It might even lead to private delivery of high-cost and exotic treatments that the public sector is not prepared to shoulder. Some people might take out private health-insurance policies, to ensure access to these private services. The goal would not be to reduce health spending: public pressure to protect the public system would see to that. But it might help to slow escalating health-care costs, which are already taking up a larger portion of government budgets each year, and which are expected to skyrocket in the next decade, when the Boomers start to get Really Sick.

What would happen to medicare in the rest of the country, were Alberta to go it alone? The impact would be both good and bad. Already, the Province With All the Oil is straining health-care systems in other provinces. Alberta pays its health-care professionals better, and aggressively recruits them from other jurisdictions. Those jurisdictions include such places as Brandon and Corner Brook. Governments in poorer provinces are hard-pressed to keep their health professionals at home, when richer provinces offer better facilities and better pay. Partially privatizing the system in Alberta would only increase those pressures, placing the poorer-off provinces at a further competitive disadvantage.

(On the other hand, critics of privatization insist that businesses are attracted to Canada because they are not required to pay the exorbitant costs of providing health insurance for their employees. If this is true, they should welcome the Alberta experiment, which would drive investment out of that province and create jobs in other parts of the country.)

Nonetheless, all provincial governments should welcome any privatizing moves by Alberta. One of the great strengths of Confederation is that individual provinces can serve as guinea pigs. Quebec pioneered old-age pensions and created its own child-care system. Saskatchewan was the birthplace of medicare. British Columbia gave us the citizens assembly. (More on this later.) Saskatchewan pioneered the concept of publicly owned automobile insurance (go figure). The West led the way in reforming (read "toughening") school curriculums. In each case, other provinces and the federal government could watch experiments unfold, ultimately deciding whether to copy, modify, or avoid the reform. Critics complain of a patchwork system of policies across the country; most of them, however, are bureaucrats pining for the pleasing symmetry of a uniform regulatory structure. The rest of us seem content to accept the confusion, knowing that circumstances alter cases, and that what works for one neighbourhood doesn't necessarily work for another.

In the meantime, the Canadian health system continues to privatize across the country, despite the best efforts of some politicians to contain it. At last count, there were thirty-three private MRI clinics in Canada, providing impatient patients with immediate tests that doctors can then use to prescribe treatments. (In Newfoundland, where there is no private MRI clinic, it can take more than two years to get a test.) The Liberal government of Premier Dalton McGuinty, in Ontario, delisted a variety of medical procedures in 2004 (including chiropractic treatments and eye exams), despite its avowed determination to preserve medicare as we know it. An estimated 30 per cent of all health-related services in Canada are provided by the private sector, up from 25 per cent in 1975. People simply won't wait six or eight weeks for a test to find out whether they have cancer; they won't languish at home for months, hoping that their heart holds out until the scheduled operation. People want to be able to walk, to see. They do not consider surgeries that make that possible non-essential. As the latest efforts by state bureaucracies fail to seriously reduce waiting lists, or to provide anything more than ephemeral relief, demand for private-sector alternatives will continue to grow, provincial governments everywhere will be encouraged – or forced – to experiment, and a federal government that attempts to yoke those governments to the strictures of the Canada Health Act will only reveal, once again, its own impotence. That is how this country will fix health care: piecemeal, no doubt, and incrementally, province by province, but steadily adding a parallel private sector to compete with, supplement, and sharpen the public system that most of the middle class will still use most of the time.

The great, unspoken price of a universal public health-care system is its opportunity cost – that is, the cost of government investments that were not made because health expenditures drained those dollars away, or of tax dollars that could have stayed in taxpayers' pockets, but for the needs of state medicine. Perhaps the greatest opportunity cost of all is the price that Canada's post-secondary education system has paid, in order to feed the health-care beast.

That education is vitally important to citizens and society is a "yeah-yeah" assertion. It is so true, has been accepted for so long, that every time this truism is repeated the listener goes "Yeah, yeah, but so what?" Well, here's what: Canadian governments have let their education systems steadily run down, as the price for sustaining public health care. In a country that should be aspiring for excellence in this one thing above all, we struggle to preserve mediocrity.

Canada actually has two fully nationalized fields of social policy. We talk a great deal about the health-care sector, while virtually ignoring the post-secondary sector. With a couple of insignificant exceptions,[8] the Canadian university sector is entirely public. Our universities are non-profit institutions, just like hospitals, that receive much of their funding from government grants and corporate and private donations, also just like hospitals. The only difference is that, whereas hospitals are prohibited from charging user fees for their services, user fees are accepted at the university level in the form of tuition. (That's some user fee, mutters the university student, who may well face a debt of twenty-five thousand dollars upon completion of a four-year undergraduate course.) At the diploma-granting college level, the private sector is more fully involved, usually in the form of business schools. Still, even here, the public sector dominates. Ontario, for example, has 153,000 students at public colleges, and approximately 35,000 at private career colleges.[9] Given the spread of private, for-profit health clinics across the country (despite governments' far-from-best efforts to curtail them), post-secondary education could now be seen as a more fully public service than medicare.

Just as with health care, the American education system is far different from the Canadian system. Private universities, although generally non-profit corporations, charge their students whatever the market will bear (with bursaries for qualified students from low-income families), receiving little or no direct government funding, while state and federal governments support a network of public universities for those who can't make it into the elite private schools. Given the Canadian preference for publicly funded universities, and the American reliance on a private-public mix, given the dominance of conservative Republican governments at the state and federal level over the past generation, and given the yeah-yeah nature of the education argument, you would expect to see ever-greater American reliance on private funding for post-secondary education. In fact, exactly the opposite has occurred. Between 1980 and 2005, American government funding of post-secondary education increased by 25 per cent. In Canada, over the same period, it *decreased* by 20 per cent.[10] To make up the shortfall, most provincial governments have allowed universities to increase their tuition fees, which have tripled, overall, since 1990, even after adjusting for inflation. Despite that added source of revenue, Canada's universities and colleges remain grossly underfunded, and students are being saddled with extraordinary levels of debt. This is compounded by an emerging shortage of graduate students and an incipient mass retirement of aging academics, even as all parties unanimously agree that research and development, now more than ever, drive the knowledge-based economies of the advanced industrial states. No wonder, in an international ranking of the world's top five hundred universities, Canada's finest university, the University of Toronto, came in 24th. Not only did the Americans dominate the top twenty (only Cambridge, Oxford, and Tokyo universities were also named), but most of the American schools on the list were public universities. Proud holders of Canadian degrees should know that, within the top one hundred, the University of British Columbia ranked 36th and McGill University ranked 62nd, while McMaster University was tied with the University of Freiburg for 88th spot. If you hold a degree from another school, it might be best not to mention it.[11]

Such mediocrity cannot be tolerated in a society and economy dependent on advanced research and skilled workers. This, above all, is why Canadian governments must rein in health spending and redirect resources to post-secondary education. Yet, as with everything else, simply increasing funding won't do anything except increase salaries for professors and other workers in the field. Other innovations are needed. Since students pay an ever-increasing portion of post-secondary education costs, they should have the maximum amount of choice in determining how their money is spent. Simply put, universities need to become more competitive. That might mean encouraging a private university sector, in which charters are granted to either non-profit foundations or for-profit companies seeking to establish new post-secondary institutions. These are likely to be niche schools devoted to providing degrees or diplomas in specialized areas where public universities are failing to meet the grade. Public universities should also be encouraged to specialize in areas of their expertise: not every university currently offers a law degree; not every one needs to offer a degree in philosophy, either. Governments should encourage universities to compete more openly against each other for students, which could reduce wasteful or shameful practices such as guaranteed tenure (which simply rewards unproductive academics), or enormous class sizes, which degrades the quality of undergraduate education. Finally, governments should continue the process already underway that encourages businesses to enter into partnerships with universities and colleges for research and for job training, while all post-secondary schools should demonstrate, as a condition of continued public funding, that they are making every effort to expand the corporate and private contributions to their endowment funds. Beyond and above all this, however, Canadians must commit themselves and their governments to making post-secondary education the highest governmental priority of the coming decade. Our success in improving the quality of post-secondary education in Canada will determine both our competitive future and quality of life.

At the elementary and secondary level, the story is more mixed. Education funding in most provinces has not kept pace with increases in health-care funding. Nonetheless, there is a solid understanding by provincial politicians that educating the young is one of the most vital tasks a government performs, and as a result the education sector has generally been less affected by spending cutbacks than have other government departments. Further, most provincial governments launched major and much-needed reforms of their education systems in the 1990s, which have started to bear fruit in this decade. All governments moved away from the feel-good, child-centred, learn-at-your-own-pace, social-engineering-in-disguise curriculum that led to a genera-tion of confident but illiterate graduates. Instead, they toughened their curriculums and instituted province-wide standardized testing. The bravest among the premiers also took steps to curtail the powers of teachers' unions and the school boards that had become their pawns. In Ontario, under the premiership of Mike Harris, the war between a reform-minded government and the entrenched interests of the teachers' unions led to year after year of strife and strikes. But the reforms that mattered most – a new and stronger curriculum accompanied by standardized testing and increased teacher training – were pushed through, and by the early 2000s, Ontario students were showing marked improvement in their test scores.[12]

In fact, in international comparisons, Canadian students don't do all that badly. In a recent study of students from forty-one coun-tries conducted by the Organization for Economic Co-operation and Development, Canadian fifteen-year-olds ranked among the best in the world in mathematics and reading. In math, only students from Hong Kong and Finland scored better, while Japan, Korea, the Netherlands, Belgium, and Switzerland performed as well. Alberta, British Columbia, and Quebec students equalled the best in the world, although students in Atlantic Canada fared significantly worse (but still above the OECD mean). In reading, only Finnish students scored better than their Canadian counterparts, while in science Canada ranked behind Finland, Japan, Hong Kong, and Korea.[13]

This is hardly grounds for complacency. Close observers of recent comparative international tests worry that Canadian scores are stagnant, relative to other jurisdictions, and might even be starting to slip. More important, test scores measure only the performance of students in the public education system; they ignore early-childhood and adult education programs, both of which are essential if Canada is to produce a workforce that is both knowledgeable and adaptable. After all, the one thing we can say with certainty in what *New York Times* columnist Thomas Friedman calls the "flat world" of global innovation and integration, is that whatever skills you possess today will be hopelessly antiquated ten years from now. Or five. Or two. Or already. Provincial governments have, as yet, had little success in creating seamlessly integrated educational streams that offer lifetime learning in essential skills. The most that can be said is that they do a relatively good job of providing basic education from ages five through eighteen.

In comparing elementary/secondary and post-secondary education in Canada, an interesting phenomenon emerges. According to the Canadian Constitution, social policy is supposed to be strictly the domain of the provincial governments. But because

Ottawa has the lion's share of the taxing power, and because politicians of all stripes consider social policy the most important game in town, the federal government has repeatedly intervened in the provinces' jurisdictions. Two areas where they intervened most heavily were post-secondary education and health care.[14] In both these areas of shared federal-provincial jurisdiction, funding is inadequate, quality is poor, and prospects are worrying, at best. Part of the reason for that may be the buck-passing that each level of government indulges in when confronted by failure and declining standards. But since provincial governments are far more accountable for their elementary and secondary school systems, provincial politicians take care to ensure those systems are adequately funded and properly run. Another reason may be the federal penchant for ensuring uniformity of standards across the country. For example, in 2000 the federal government launched an ambitious program to endow two thousand research chairs. The National Research Chairs are awarded using a complex formula that, in essence, is based on previous research grants to the university. (The more you received in the past, the more you qualify for.) And, of course, it wouldn't be a federal program without a special equalization component, which ensures that smaller schools that would otherwise not qualify for a research chair get one anyway.

One hesitates to criticize a government program dedicated to improving funding for post-secondary education, but the questions remain: Would the $900 million that has been set aside for the National Research Chairs be more efficiently spent if provincial governments had the money? Shouldn't the provinces be given the money directly, to spend as they see fit, provided the money goes toward university research?

Consider one further example. Critics argue that the load students are being asked to bear is becoming excessive. According to Statistics Canada, university graduates who relied on student loans typically graduated with a debt of $21,500, while for college graduates the cost was $12,360. These figures are behind calls for tuition-fee reduction. Those calls are ill-advised. There is no reliable evidence that tuition fees deter qualified students from attending university. Besides, the sad truth is, any tuition cuts would disproportionately benefit upper-income families, whose children make up the vast majority of students in university. After all, 51 per cent of university graduates and 47 per cent of college graduates have no student debt at all. Since most summer jobs aren't that lucrative, these students probably relied on parental contributions. Any reduction in tuition costs would simply be a tax break for those affluent parents.

The goal must surely be to ensure that universities raise as much tuition money as possible to fund research and teaching programs, while ensuring that able students from poorer families have the resources to complete a university or college degree. However, the various permutations of federal and provincial student-loan programs are cumbersome and arbitrary, depriving this student of assistance while that one is generously rewarded. One strongly favoured solution is known as the income-contingent loan (ICL), an idea that has been around for at least fifteen years. Under such a program, a student's post-secondary education expenses would be fully funded, up to whatever was considered a reasonable amount. Upon graduation, the student would pay back the loan over time, with the individual payment based on the student's earned income after graduation. A doctor would be expected to pay back the loan relatively quickly. Those few brave souls who took their B.A. in one of the Humanities, and who then went to work for an environmental group at slightly more than minimum wage, would pay less each month and have longer to pay. The advantage of the income-contingent loan program is that it allows each student to choose his or her education path, regardless of parental income, without imposing punitive costs immediately upon graduation, when earning potential is at its lowest ebb. Critics maintain the system still forces poorer students to pay back more debt with more interest over time, but for those critics the only solution is to reduce tuition fees to the point where anyone can afford them, which is a ludicrous misreading of government priorities and resources. See health care, above.

Yet the federal Liberal government of Paul Martin has pursued exactly the opposite course. Rather than co-operating with any province interested in merging provincial and federal loan schemes to create an income-contingent loan system – in Ontario, for example, former premier Bob Rae released a report in February 2005 that recommended income-contingent loans and deregulated tuition[15] – the prime minister agreed in April 2005, as part of a deal with the NDP to sustain his minority government, to throw $1.5 billion at reducing university tuition. Political desperation, coupled with crude misreading of the challenges facing post-secondary education, produced this nightmarish policy. So, while Australia has already adopted ICLs and Great Britain has announced plans to do the same, Canada continues to pursue a fragmented policy of subsidized tuition and chronic underfunding. At the very least, Ottawa should be working with provinces to target student aid to those students most genuinely in need, through means-tested grants and bursaries. But then, such students are not the daughters and sons of the middle class. And the middle class has to be kept happy.

The best policy of all would be for the federal government to hand the $1.7 billion in the Canada Student Loans program over to the provinces directly, letting each government experiment with the funding mix that works best for its universities, colleges, and students. If provincial governments took exclusive responsibility for post-secondary education, in the way that they take exclusive responsibility for elementary and secondary education, then perhaps one day Canadian university students would be able to read and calculate as well as a Finn.[16]

The argument can be expanded across the social-policy sphere. In welfare and subsidized housing, as well as health care and education, the federal government has intruded on areas of provincial jurisdiction, ultimately with baleful results. Federal programs propose generous national standards, with cash to help provinces meet them. Under pressure from citizens eager for expanded services, provincial politicians reluctantly agree, only to find years later that Ottawa is reducing its funding commitments, leaving the provinces to struggle along with all the obligations, but far fewer of the resources that attended the original program. And they invariably take the political heat when welfare funding is cut back or subsidized-housing programs are scrapped. The same, sad cycle is about to be repeated, as Ottawa boldly and foolishly launches itself into the field of child care. In April 2005, as part of a pre-election spending spree, Paul Martin reached an agreement in principle with the premiers of Saskatchewan and Manitoba to implement the first stages of what is intended to be a national child-care program, based on the four principles of QUAD: quality, universally inclusive, accessible, and developmental. (The Canada Health Act comes to daycare.) Nova Scotia followed suit in May. Though other provinces balked, at least initially, at the restrictive conditions of the program, it was clear that Ottawa had cemented a further addition to a welfare state that socialist critics had claimed was being dismantled.

The Liberal government's latest social-development program boasts all the worst features of its predecessors. First, it is illegitimate in principle, since child care is social policy and social policy is a provincial jurisdiction. Second, it is discriminatory, since it provides a subsidy for families who choose to place their children in daycare, effectively penalizing parents who choose to raise their children at home by having only one spouse at work. (Fully half of all families outside of Quebec, which already has a state-subsidized child-care system, continue to raise their children with one spouse remaining at home.)[17] Third, it is expensive, with a five-year federal commitment of $5 billion that is certain to rise over time. Fourth, it is ineffective, since any substantial increase in state funding for daycare will be at least partially eaten up in pay raises for daycare workers. (Daycare workers are, by any measure of fairness, seriously underpaid, since they often make little more than minimum wage despite having diplomas or degrees in their field. Nonetheless, market forces are market forces, and labour supply seems to meet demand.) Daycare workers will benefit, but how many actual new spaces will be created is uncertain. Fifth, it is dangerous, at least for provincial governments, who administer the programs and who will be left holding the funding bag when, inevitably, the federal government begins to scale back its commitment. Sixth, it is statist, since the same advocates who promote subsidized daycare also oppose for-profit delivery of the service, claiming that the profit incentive leads to poor-quality delivery. Finally, it is deceitful. Middle-class families, while they would welcome a tax break on daycare, have demonstrated that they have the means to provide daycare for their children. Working-class families, however, often do not. (The very poor are already entitled to daycare subsidies.) They are more likely to leave the child with a parent or grandparent, who may not read enough to the child or provide other forms of stimulation that will maximize the child's learning potential. The sooner the state can get that child out of the home, goes this reasoning, and into an enriched, non-profit learning environment, the better the chances that child will do well in school, earn a good income, and pay taxes rather than consume services. You'll never find a politician or a policy analyst who will tell you this on the record, but it is the unspoken underlying assumption behind state-sponsored daycare.

Provincial governments should have rejected the federal initiative entirely, for all the reasons above. But parents are a powerful lobby, as are daycare workers and child-care activists. The program will go ahead, with some form of cash grant for Quebec, which already runs a program that is generally seen as the model for the national initiative. The smart provincial governments will use the money to expand junior kindergarten, making the national child-care program in effect an extension of the public education system. This will still lead to the unwelcome intrusion of the federal government in education, but it will be better than wasting taxpayers' money on unionized, non-profit daycare spaces that will cost billions, penalize stay-at-home parents, and never meet demand, leaving those who don't have the right connections inexplicably but inevitably at the back of the queue.

Here is one good argument in favour of federal-provincial shared-cost social programs. The provinces: as constituted, they don't make any sense. We have ten provinces, but only one of them, Alberta, has a population roughly equal to 10 per cent of the country's population of 32 million, though British Columbia comes close, with a population of 4.2 million. The rest are either grossly oversized (Ontario and Quebec) or undersized (everyone else). This disparity in size leads to illogical demarcations. After all, as one federal bureaucrat observed, the only reason that there is a New Brunswick regional office of the Canadian Red Cross, and a Nova Scotia regional office, and a Prince Edward Island regional office, is that New Brunswick, Nova Scotia, and Prince Edward Island are all provinces. Public-policy planners have long pined for the amalgamation of these three provinces, and there are even some febrile souls who have advocated the union of Saskatchewan and Alberta. (Saskatchewan and Manitoba would actually make more sense, but why yoke yourself to a have-not province, when you could cash in on amalgamation with a wealthy one?) But parochial pride will prevent amalgamations from ever happening. And that's fine; politics is local and the residents of the small provinces know and are comfortable with their own local history and culture. Nonetheless, the vast disparity in the size of provinces leads to equal disparities in the quality of service delivery. Simply put, some provincial ministries aren't very sophisticated, and service delivery, if left entirely in their hands, would deteriorate quickly. Apparently, equalization programs aren't enough; regional development assistance isn't enough. Only direct federal aid, along with the professional advice and assistance on which smaller jurisdictions depend, will ensure that health care, education, and now daycare programs are properly administered.

For that reason, any sensible analysis of federal-provincial social policy must acknowledge the wisdom of asymmetricality. This cumbersome word, and the idea behind it, have been kicking around since at least the days of the failed Meech Lake and Charlottetown accords, but many Canadians were introduced to the concept in the September 2004 health-care agreement reached between Prime Minister Paul Martin and the provincial and territorial premiers.[18] In principle (whether it ever comes to be in practice is another matter), all provincial governments received a significant infusion of federal funds – the last, best attempt to rescue the status quo. In return, each province agreed to report nationally on its progress in reducing waiting lists and improving standards, based on a common reporting mechanism. Quebec, which already has its own reporting mechanism and which would never accept such an intrusion by the federal government into its domain, agreed to share its information with the provincial and federal governments, in effect co-operating without being seen to co-operate. This asymmetrical solution satisfied the goal of establishing national standards in service delivery, while preserving Quebec's autonomy in the constitutional sphere of its jurisdiction. What mattered in the agreement, however, was not the Quebec accommodation; what mattered was that all provinces were entitled to take advantage of an asymmetrical agreement, if they chose. In future agreements, such as child care, we might well see this provincial government agreeing to use federal child-care funding in one way, and that government using it in another way. We might even see agreements in the future in which national programs are really federal programs for small and poor provinces, with more-competent jurisdictions simply receiving the appropriate cash transfer.

In federal-provincial negotiations, larger provinces often unwittingly tread on the needs and sensibilities of the smaller provinces. From time to time the premier of a large province will argue, for example, that the ultimate solution to the tangled mess of social policy is for the federal government to transfer tax points to the provinces. An arcane concept with a complex history, tax-point transfers in fact date back to the dark days of the Second World War, when the federal government "rented" from the provinces much of their taxing authority, for the simple good reason that Ottawa needed to control all national resources in its to-the-death struggle against German and Japanese militarism. However, as previously noted, after the war Ottawa kept the "rented" taxing authority, on the grounds that the federal power needed the resources to coordinate the enormous national development programs underway: the St. Lawrence Seaway, the national roads system, the TransCanada Pipeline, the new network of airports, Cold War defence. But social needs – housing, health care, education – also exploded, and the provincial governments no longer had the revenue base to provide for those needs. That is the reason that the provincial governments are perpetually starved for funds, and forced to rely on federal grants to carry out what should be their responsibilities. In the late 1970s, Pierre Trudeau agreed to transfer some of those tax points, as they were now called, back to the provinces, but the federal mandarinate quickly concluded that such transfer undermined the legitimacy of the federal government, weakening its ability to influence social policy. They resolved never to succumb to such provincial pressure again, and steeled their political masters against temptation. Nonetheless, tax-point transfers are the only sensible solution to what is now referred to as the fiscal imbalance, in which the federal government raises the bulk of tax revenues, and currently enjoys the enormous surpluses that result, while provincial governments must beg for federal grants to deliver mandated services while avoiding deficits (a task not all of them successfully manage).

The problem with transferring tax points is that some provinces would benefit more from the process than others. Provinces such as Ontario, Quebec, Alberta, and British Columbia, with solid industrial sectors and relatively affluent populations, provide a tax base large enough to permit them to deliver services at the highest level. All they need is a more secure revenue source, by getting their taxing powers back. Atlantic Canada, the territories, and, to a lesser extent, Manitoba and Saskatchewan would not benefit so handsomely from transferred tax points, because their own tax base is relatively weak and unstable, and because they need federal assistance to manage complex programs. Any permanent solution to the fiscal imbalance, therefore, would have to be asymmetrical, with some provinces choosing to receive the transferred tax points, and others choosing to stay with the status quo. Negotiations, needless to say, would be complex, but in Canada, negotiations always are. It's the nature of the place.

There are, as well, aspects of Canada's fiscal and economic policies that strongly influence the social order. The Liberal government's decision in the mid-1990s to balance the federal deficit come flood or perdition placed serious strains on the health, education, and welfare matrix, as cuts to provincial grants left those governments struggling to provide basic services while also eliminating deficits of their own. Parts of the welfare state – in particular welfare rates that in some cases exceeded the minimum wage – were dismantled; the health system went into a spiral of decline from which it has not yet emerged, while class sizes increased and tuition fees soared. Nonetheless, eliminating the deficit and reducing the debt-to-GDP ratio was itself a social policy. Compound interest is implacable; thanks to escalating, accumulating deficits, the federal government was on the brink of insolvency in 1994, and some provincial governments weren't far behind. Ontario, in particular, was running a deficit that approached 20 per cent of the total budget. Deficits had to be brought under control, or interest payments would soon have eliminated the government's capacity to fund any other program at all. The ongoing, if duplicitous,[19] campaign to pay down as much as possible of the accumulated federal debt in this decade – the goal is to bring the federal debt from a high of 68 per cent of GDP in 1995 to 25 per cent of GDP in 2014 – is also social policy in disguise. An aging society will bring unprecedented demands to bear on governments in the next decade, as tax revenues from a shrinking workforce dwindle, while health and pension demands from a bloated cohort of retirees strain services to the limits. Canada has gone further than any other industrialized nation to prepare for this threat, by refinancing the Canada Pension Plan to place it on a sounder footing, and by steadily reducing the federal debt. This foresight is something of which the Liberal government can be justly proud.[20]

However, fiscal policies also act as social policies in other, less beneficent, ways. As previously discussed, Canada is increasingly dividing into two nations. *The Economist* described it thus: "Today, the most visible cleavage in Canada is not between French-speaking Quebec and the English-speaking rest, but between five large urban areas (dynamic, successful, with many immigrants but with strained public services) and the rest (mainly rural, declining economies with high unemployment, kept alive by federal aid)."[21]

One of the principle tools by which the federal government continues to prop up the declining economies of rural Canada is through Employment Insurance. There are two kinds of EI: one for workers who don't expect to lose their jobs, and one for those who do. For most Canadians, EI is there in case our plant suddenly closes or the boss develops a hate-on for us. After years of contributions, the fund is there to tide us over until we find another job. With unemployment rates in recent years hovering around 7 or 8 per cent, another job should not be all that hard to come by, though we may have to reduce expectations for a while.

But as we have already seen, for workers in marginal, resource-based regions, especially Atlantic Canada, EI is a permanent source of income. In order to keep people from migrating – and in order to secure votes in elections – successive Liberal governments have used EI to subsidize wages for seasonal, resource-based workers in Atlantic Canada. In many cases, as few as fourteen weeks of work will entitle you to an EI stipend for the rest of the year. And it is notoriously true – though rarely spoken – that workers will stay at a job only until they are "stamped up" and then quit, to collect EI (while also probably working under the table) and to free up their job for someone else who needs the qualifying weeks of work. As a result, Atlantic Canada suffers from a severe and

164

chronic shortage of skilled and semi-skilled workers willing to work year-round, even as unemployment rates are typically four to six points higher than the national average, leading to the travails that afflicted poor Mabel Gallant.[22] An insurance program that transfers money from workers in stable jobs to workers in seasonal employment, with the express intent of keeping them in their communities, is a social program, plain and simple.

And it is only one of many. The federal government accumulates more revenues from rich provinces with industries and affluent populations, and then distributes social spending on a per-capita basis, penalizing Alberta, Ontario, British Columbia, and Saskatchewan, and benefiting the rest. The equalization program, created to ensure that all parts of the country enjoy comparable levels of social services, encourages poorer provinces to provide health, education, and other services to communities that otherwise would not be able to sustain them, skewing the regional economy. Regional economic development agencies, such as the Atlantic Canada Opportunities Agency (there are others for other rural and impoverished parts of the country) have a lamentable track record in jump-starting sustainable economic development. They have a much better record of subsidizing marginal and declining industries, in order to keep workers from having to abandon small communities. In consequence, Ontario transfers twice as much wealth to other parts of the federation as do equivalent American states. The drain on Alberta is even worse.[23]

A necessary qualification: There is nothing inherently wrong with a resource-based industry. The Canadian fishery remains a $5-billion concern, and there is good money to be had from harvesting crab and shrimp.[24] Prince Edward Island potatoes remain a continental staple, and the demand for wood products from

Newfoundland to British Columbia, especially for the housing industry, is high. Finally, the stereotype of Canada outside the big cities, as dependent, resource-based, and chronically poor, while broadly accurate, misses some of the mark. Halifax's population has passed 350,000, and its unemployment rate in June 2005 sat at 6.3 per cent, below the national average. Saskatoon has Canada's only Synchrotron, used in applications from particle physics to structural biology. That province, thanks to diversification, but thanks even more to oil, entered the ranks of the "have" provinces in 2004.

But these facts remain: federal attempts to bolster the depressed regional economies, or at least to preserve the existing base, have not proven their worth. Federal investments in private-sector business have often failed to pay returns, while driving out the private-sector capital market. The transformation of EI into an income-subsidy plan for seasonal workers has kept those workers in a state of dependency and fostered a culture of benign, pseudo-legal fraud, while equalization payments have simply permitted provincial governments to fritter away tax dollars on propping up rural communities that are otherwise unviable. This is more than bad economic policy; this is bad social policy. And in any reweaving of the national social fabric, it must be taken into account.

There is another reason for limiting transfers of wealth from the richest parts of the country to the poorest. Everyone becomes poorer when the more productive regions have their wealth excessively taxed, with the tax dollars transferred to the less productive regions. This practice rewards failure and penalizes achievement.

It deters the successful from trying to become more successful, just as it deters the less successful from making hard choices about changing their circumstances. This same argument applies to individuals. Our progressive taxation system penalizes success by taxing the individual more heavily as he or she becomes more successful. Pushed too far, it reduces or even eliminates the incentive to work harder. Anyone who works in a job that pays overtime understands this principle. The more overtime you work, the less likely you are to ask for your reward in money, since the tax rate on overtime work is usually at the highest combined federal and provincial tax brackets, which generally equals about 50 per cent of the dollar earned. There is little to be gained by giving up evenings or weekends to make overtime, only to have half of what you make taxed away. You and your employer probably both agree that the overtime should be taken in time off. As soon as you make that agreement, you and your employer become less productive. Instead of working harder and making more money, you're working harder now so that you don't have to work at all later.

At this point, many conservative writers issue a clarion call for massive tax cuts. These writers need to get real. Thanks to provincial and federal restraint, personal and corporate tax levels in this country are roughly comparable to their American counterparts. And decades of experience suggest that Canadians are, on the whole, prepared to play slightly higher taxes than Americans, in exchange for health, education, and other publicly funded services that middle-class Americans pay out of their own pocket. Similarly, there is nothing to be gained by arguing for a flat income tax, in which all citizens pay the same rate of tax – say, 30 per cent of earnings – regardless of income. Canadians as a people accept the principle of wealth transfer, and however inefficient such transfers might appear to some bloodless econo-mist's calculations, the fact is that almost all of us would rather live under a social contract in which we agree that the better-off give a helping hand to the less-well-off, whether they want to or not. From 1993 to 2004, the Reform and Canadian Alliance parties, which preached lower and flatter taxes, never obtained more than a quarter of the popular vote. The Conservative Party of Canada, although it favours modest tax reductions, campaigned in 2004 and 2005 on a platform emphasizing continued support for social programs and equalization. Even so, Liberal warnings of a secret Tory "hidden agenda" kept many voters away.

So it is unreasonable to expect Canadians to swallow massive tax cuts and a total flattening of the income-tax system. But there is a compelling argument for *some* tax reductions and for *some* flattening. Just as too much wealth transferred from rich regions to poor harms the rich by robbing them of wealth and the poor by creating a debilitating dependency, so too an income-tax system that excessively punishes the productive and rewards the unproductive will in the long run harm both. In Canada, this dis-incentive is made manifest in a productivity gap between this country and the United States.

Productivity is a simple concept, the causes of which are devilishly hard to pin down. If you total the accumulated wealth that a country generates (its gross domestic product) and divide it by the number of people, you have measure of that country's productivity.[25] There is a pronounced productivity gap between Canada and the United States. Each American worker, on average, produces more each year than each Canadian worker. That makes Americans, on average, wealthier than Canadians, and explains why the best selling car in the United States is a Toyota Camry, while the best selling car in Canada is a Honda Civic.

Why are Americans more productive than Canadians? Here, everyone has an answer, and no one answer encompasses the whole situation. Partly it's luck: if your economy relies heavily on natural resources, as Canada's does, then your productivity will go up or down depending on the vagaries of natural-resource prices. No matter how state-of-the-art your smelting operation is, if mineral prices fall, the workers will appear to be less productive. However, the efficiency of that smelter is also a factor. Many analysts believe that, for a variety of reasons, Americans invest more in upgrading their industrial infrastructure than do Canadians, which makes American workers more productive than Canadians.

Again, however, Canadian governments have only a limited ability to correct the problem. Historically, many Canadian firms have been subsidiaries of American businesses, and Head Office naturally prefers to concentrate research and development on home soil. There is, as well, a seemingly intractable conservatism to the Canadian business class, which deters risky investments, even when threatened with loss of market share. There are many exceptions to these blanket generalizations, but common sense dictates that a conservative, subsidiary economy will be less productive than a dominant, entrepreneurial one.

What is to be done? Critics on the left argue that the federal and provincial governments lack an industrial strategy that would target incentives to advanced industries and away from low-tech natural resources and old-industry manufacturing. Right-wing critics warn that governments are notoriously incompetent at picking industrial winners and losers, and instead should focus on simplifying or reducing taxes. We'd be willing to work harder if we were able to keep more of our own money. Choosing which side to come down on doesn't need to depend on your ideology, however. In public policy, as in life, the maxim holds that the simplest solution is almost invariably the best. If your policy choice is between simplifying and lowering taxes, on the one hand, or creating an industrial strategy that will redirect the productive energies of the entire economy, on the other, go with the simple solution: cut taxes first, and see if that works.

And, in fact, we know it does. A groundbreaking 2005 Statistics Canada study discovered some intriguing reasons behind the Canadian/American productivity gap. The study found that, while Canadian productivity was only about 83 per cent of its American equivalent, about two-thirds of that gap could be accounted for by two factors: Canadians worked fewer hours than Americans, and Canadian unemployment was higher.[26] Does that mean Canadians are lazy and shiftless? Not at all. The study also showed that, between 1994 and 2002, the gap narrowed substantially. More Canadians had jobs and those with jobs worked longer hours. "Tell me something I don't know," the beleaguered Canadian worker moans, "I'm chained to this desk and I never see my kids." Indeed you are, but that's because there is work for you to do that you are willing to do. That was less likely to be true in the early 1990s, when unemployment was high, and so were interest rates, and so were taxes.

By the end of the decade, however, governments everywhere had cut spending and taxes while balancing their books. Interest rates came down, and unemployment rates as well. So if some is good, more should be better. If Canadians are to further close the diminishing productivity gap with the United States, we need to ease the penalties for working harder. The marginal tax rate[27] needs to be reduced, in order to remove the disincentive to work overtime or simply to work harder. Similarly, the jumps in tax rates between income levels need to be smoothed out. We all know what it is like to suddenly move into a new tax bracket, where it seems we were making lots more money in principle, but our take-home pay hardly changes at all. To the greatest extent politically possible, taxes should be shifted from income to consumption (the GST and provincial sales taxes). Before some left-winger out there gets all huffy, take a look at your beloved Sweden: that country places a much heavier emphasis on consumption taxes than Canada does, while its corporate income tax rates are among the lowest in the developed world.[28]

There emerges, from all this, the outline of a new social charter for Canada. The federal government would encourage provincial experimentation in health care, including more private delivery and perhaps even parallel private insurance and care, with any savings dedicated principally to post-secondary education, through the reform of the student-loan system, improved grants for low-income students, accompanied by increased diversification and competition among schools. Ottawa would, however, increasingly withdraw from post-secondary education, channelling funds to provincial governments, which could spend them in whatever way worked best for that jurisdiction. Similarly, the federal government would rethink its commitment to a national child-care program, transferring those funds as well to the provinces. In fact, a wholesale transfer of federal taxing power to provincial governments is probably in order, to redress the imbalance between resources and responsibilities. With it must come a reconsideration of the excessive and unproductive transfer of wealth from the prosperous regions of the country to shore up poorer regions, since these transfers are often ineffective as investments. Governments also need to acknowledge the improvement in overall wealth and productivity that balanced budgets, free trade, and lower taxes have generated over the past ten years, and look for ways to reinforce the prosperity and productivity that resulted. That said, the federal government must also recognize, as must conservative-minded Canadians, that principles of basic fairness dictate that some transfer of wealth, both vertically among the classes and horizontally among the regions is inevitable and desirable. And federalists of all kinds need to recognize that different provinces have different needs and capacities, which could lead to increasing autonomy for some provinces, and close federal-provincial co-operation for others.

Simple, really. The strange thing is that we seem to have so much trouble introducing, let alone carrying out, such straightforward, sensible reforms to the status quo.

CHAPTER FIVE

MAKING
CANADA
MATTER

I f the federal government were to pursue the path outlined in the previous chapter, some fear that there would be nothing left for Ottawa to do.

This is the sort of thinking that gave us executive federalism in the first place.[1] By this reasoning, the framers of the original Canadian Constitution made a big mistake by awarding the provincial governments all the powers that, in the nineteenth century, didn't seem so important but that, in the twentieth century, became the biggest game in town. Ottawa found itself in danger of being relegated to the sidelines as the great reforms in education, health, pensions, and welfare got underway. Fans of a strong, centralized federation feared that the national government might cease to mean anything in the eyes of its citizens.

To prevent that from happening, Ottawa used its spending power to intervene in spheres of provincial jurisdiction. We can now see that the federal intrusion did at least as much harm as good, by stifling provincial innovation, by creating an excessive transfer of wealth from successful jurisdictions to failing ones, and by creating fiscal crises at the provincial level whenever the federal power decided to reduce its financial commitment in an area of shared financing.

There are figures in the most senior ranks of the federal government who quietly agree that Ottawa has an ambivalent track record, at best, in the area of social policy; that the provinces are probably better able to manage social programs; and that the most efficient thing would be to give them the money, either through unconditional grants or through tax-point transfers, and let them get on with the job. Even so, apologists for the status quo continue to defend the federal role in this sphere as essential to national unity. Without a direct – or, at the very least, a strong indirect – say in social-policy development, the federal power would have nothing to do, it would mean nothing to the lives of Canadians, and the very notion of Canada itself would begin to dissolve.

This reasoning, though it permeates both the federal bureaucracy and the ranks of the Liberal and New Democratic parties, is flawed. First, it has been proven demonstrably untrue in Quebec, which has jealously protected its exclusive jurisdiction in the domestic sphere, and which remains part of Canada despite the separatist forces that seek a divorce. Second, federal interference in domestic policy creates more alienation than it assuages.

The warfare between the Ontario Conservative government of Mike Harris and the federal Liberal government of Jean Chrétien over health-care spending was often fiercer than that between Chrétien and Parti Québécois leader Lucien Bouchard. Federal policies from the Crow Rate to the National Energy Program to the Kyoto accord have angered and alienated Albertans, who, along with British Columbians, mostly want to be left alone.

At the root of this federalist fallacy lies a chronic lack of appreciation for the latent power of the national government. Even in domestic policy, Ottawa can play a complementary role that enhances, rather than competes with, provincial jurisdiction. (More on this will follow in the next chapter.) The greater tragedy is that its obsession with social programs has led Ottawa to waste years of effort and countless billions of dollars meddling in other governments' business, while ignoring its own, more important, responsibilities. The first duty of a national government, superseding all others, is to protect its people from external or internal threat. Its second duty is to represent its people to the world. Successive federal governments have wilfully neglected to carry out this fundamental task. In consequence, this nation's defence and foreign policies lie in a shambles, with Canada discredited in the eyes of its citizens and the world. Nothing that Ottawa has achieved or attempted in the realm of its internal relations can excuse the disrepair into which external relations have fallen. This is our national disgrace.

By the 1960s, it had become pretty clear that the Americans, with their military colossus, had assumed sole responsibility for the defence of the North American continent. That outcome had not been preordained. At the end of the Second World War, Canada was a major military power, with the world's third-largest navy and an army that had successfully taken one of the five beaches at Normandy on D-Day. Canada had played a significant role in helping to develop the technology that led to the creation of atomic weapons during the Second World War; this country could certainly have created its own nuclear deterrent, had it so chosen. Instead, Canada decided to concentrate on developing nuclear energy as a source of domestic power, a symbolically significant, as well as practical, decision. Similarly, Canada played an important role in the early days of the North Atlantic Treaty Organization, with major responsibilities in the North Atlantic, a fleet that boasted two aircraft carriers, and a permanent expeditionary force of ten thousand on the continent. The NATO alliance also led to a sharp increase in the export of Canadian military technology. The development of the AVRO Arrow proved, if nothing else, that Canadian engineers could compete with the best in the world. Finally, through NORAD (the North American Aerospace Defense Command), the United States and Canada assumed joint responsibility for patrolling North American skies, principally to deter Soviet attack.

All of this was frittered away in the 1960s and 70s, as the federal government turned its energies to domestic issues, halved its commitment to NATO, and ceded effective responsibility for continental air and coastal defence to the United States. The Americans believed that a modern industrial nation could develop a robust social safety net while simultaneously protecting allies and neutral powers from the ongoing threat of Communist expansion. Canada, especially once Pierre Trudeau became prime minister, believed the Soviet menace was exaggerated, and that the national government should focus on improving the lives of its citizens. Since the Americans would look after us anyway, there was no need for Canada to take any meaningful role in its own defence.

This rationale is, frankly, baffling, because it came – and still comes – from the very citizens who are most concerned with protecting Canadian culture and sovereignty. What is sovereignty, if not a state's ability to deter and repel foreign encroachments? Granted, Canada could never have resisted an American invasion, but such an invasion was inconceivable. Canada was, however, under threat from Soviet attack throughout the duration of that empire. Some of those missiles in Russian silos were pointed at Canadian cities and Canadian defence centres. By any reasonable definition of sovereignty, the Canadian government had an obligation to provide a robust defence of its coastline, to field a strong contingent on the European front line of the Cold War, and to assert Canadian control over and under the ice of the Far North. Instead, the very nationalists who were determined to resist foreign domination of the Canadian economy, and who trumpeted a distinct, if amorphous, Canadian identity, happily surrendered Canadian sovereignty over its airspace and coastlines to the United States, by eroding the Canadian military to the point of irrelevance.

The diversion of public resources from defence to social services accelerated when the cost of those services escalated and the tax base weakened during the 1970s and 80s. The deterioration accelerated even further in the 1990s, when all resources were diverted to eliminating the federal deficit. With the return of surpluses in 1997, the first priority was to restore funding to health care and to reduce taxes. The steady decline of the Canadian military became so serious that a Senate committee recommended in 2002 that Canada withdraw its forces from all overseas commitments, warning that our military had reached the point of effective collapse.[2]

There are tentative stirrings of renewal. The 2005 budget promised to increase defence spending from $13 billion to $20 billion over five years, with the money to be spent on increasing the size of the army by five thousand, and on upgrading the equipment on which they depend. This commitment largely rests on air, for most of the new money won't arrive until 2010, and it is an easy thing for a contemporary government to make a promise that a future government will be left to fulfill. Nonetheless, this commitment represented a long-overdue change of heart for the Liberals, and any Conservative government could be expected to honour the spending pledges, since Conservatives have long criticized the wind-down of Canada's military.

The generation-long degradation of Canada's defence capacity simply reflected national values: a casual disregard for something that other countries are obsessively concerned with – namely, the physical ability to protect the nation's borders from incursion; an acceptance that American continental security interests are identical with Canadian interests, accompanied by trust that the Americans will protect our interests along with their own, without abusing that trust; and most important, a strong emphasis on the necessity of protecting social programs at whatever cost, including the cost of national defence. There are few, if any, countries in the world where butter so thoroughly trumps guns.

But there are other Canadians values, values that are increasingly being compromised as a result of Canada's relentlessly deteriorating military. As citizens become aware of those compromises, we may expect to see increasing impatience with the current state of the nation's defences, and increasing pressure to accelerate improvements.

Simply put, Canadians care about what happens in the world. We always have; that is why it was important that the Canadian government independently sign the Treaty of Versailles; why Canada assumed responsibility for its own foreign police between the wars; why Canadian diplomats were heavily involved in designing the United Nations charter; why we were among the original participants in crafting NATO; why we have invested heavily in time and effort both within the Commonwealth and the Francophonie. Canadians are internationalists. Canadians are joiners.

In recent years, the nature of Canadian internationalism has evolved. When Canada was still ethnically a predominantly European country, our foreign policy centred on Europe: the defence of the mother countries, the protection of Western civilization and its democratic values against twentieth-century totalitarianism. But those threats have passed, and the Eurocentric nature of Canadian society has been eclipsed by the waves of immigrants from Asia and elsewhere. Canadian foreign policy in the Third World, and its accompanying foreign aid, has traditionally been based on a sense of *noblesse oblige* compassion. That, however, is dramatically changing. First of all, what is traditionally called the Third World is increasingly becoming integral to Canadian economic interests. China is now the second-largest market for Canadian exports. Chile, with which Canada signed a free-trade agreement in 1997, is a significant source of trade, currently just over $1 billion annually. The arrival of Mexico within the North American free-trade bloc in 1993 brought one of the world's largest and most important Third World states into close economic contact with this country. The federal Department of Foreign Affairs and International Trade has identified South Korea as an ideal candidate for a free-trade agreement. Most important of all, potentially, India is finally emerging from decades of stultifying protectionism: a new Asian tiger has awakened. International Trade Minister Jim Peterson led a delegation to the subcontinent in March 2005, hoping to capitalize on Canada's intimate links with a fellow Commonwealth member who exports tens of thousands of its citizens to Canada each year.

Immigration patterns are having a subtle but unmistakable influence on Canadian foreign-policy priorities. The efforts of Pakistan and India to defuse the tensions that could lead to a catastrophic exchange of nuclear weapons are of visceral importance to the 713,000 Canadians of Indian origin and 74,000 of Pakistani. There are 61,000 Sri Lankans in Canada, 40,000 of them of Tamil origin. The instability in that country has become a first-person concern for many Canadians, and for the Canadian government. Similarly, efforts of Latin American countries to stabilize their governments and grow their economies matter viscerally to the 244,000 Latino-Canadians. The Third World matters to Canadians because, demographically, Canada is becoming a Third World nation.[3]

For this reason, the Canadian response to the Asian tsunami that devastated the nations bordering the Indian Ocean in December 2004 will probably be seen as a watershed moment in Canadian foreign policy. Canadians had responded admirably to previous humanitarian crises, both natural and man-made. This country's extraordinary response to the Vietnamese refugees (the "boat people") who fled their repressive regime in the wake of the collapse of South Vietnam contributed to our being awarded the Nansen medal in 1986, the only time the United Nations High Commission for Refugees has bestowed that prestigious prize on an entire country. Canadians also opened this country's doors to immigrants and refugees from Somalia and Ethiopia, when war and famine rendered the Horn of Africa virtually uninhabitable.

The tsunami, however, was different. Not only was the scale of the calamity virtually unprecedented – in the end, the tidal waves cost more than 260,000 lives – but these were no longer foreigners caught in a vortex of poverty and natural disaster. These people were family – kith and kin to the Indians, Sri Lankans, Indonesians, and Thais living in this country. The immediacy that the crises represented for millions of Canadians – including the five members of Parliament of Indian descent who accompanied Paul Martin on his trip to the region – doubtless contributed to the exceptional outpouring of $200 million that Canadians donated to the relief effort, matched by the $425 million contributed by the Canadian government. And yet, despite this effort, we came up short.

The Canadian military had created an emergency response unit known as DART (Disaster Assistance Response Team), specifically created for such emergencies. DART comes equipped with a field hospital, desalination equipment, and trained personnel – exactly what the situation called for. That is why the Italian government deployed its version of DART immediately. Forty-eight hours after the waves struck, the Italians had a field hospital in place in Sri Lanka, and were sending Canadian-made water bombers to the region to deliver emergency supplies to cut-off areas.[4] But DART took two weeks to get to Sri Lanka. The military was not to blame; they had mobilized DART within hours of the first reports, and had even secured Russian-made transport airplanes to ferry the team to the disaster area. But senior figures in the Department of Foreign Affairs questioned the need to send DART. It would be expensive, went the argument, and no formal request had actually been received from any of the stricken nations. Better to start out by sending some field observers into the region to see where the need might be. This, at a time when it was clear to everyone everywhere that the fatalities numbered in the tens of thousands at the very least. When citizens and reporters began asking "Where is DART?" Defence Minister Bill Graham, who had actually favoured immediate deployment, was reduced to stuttering explanations that the cost of sending the unit was so high that the money could be better spent on immediate relief. In that case, came the question, what's the use of the thing in the first place? Caught off-guard, politicians scrambled to redress the mistake, but by now the Russian transport planes were no longer available. It took a week before the government was able to announce the deployment of the team, and another week before it landed in Sri Lanka. Once in place, the experienced troops and workers of DART did their typically fine job. But for many Canadians who had not paid much attention to the state of Canada's military in recent years, the DART incident was revelatory.

They didn't know that, despite federal surpluses that had averaged $11.5 billion over the previous five years, the Canadian military had become so rundown that huge gaps existed in its ability to carry out its assigned missions. Canada deployed five hundred troops to Haiti in 2004, as part of a multinational effort to bring stability to the Western hemisphere's most wretched country. A Defence Department report revealed that the troops lacked, and were forced to scrounge for, such basic equipment as flak jackets, proper boots, and latex gloves.[5] When Canadian soldiers arrived in 2003 to lead the multinational force bringing stability to post-Taliban Afghanistan, their poorly armoured Iltis jeeps were unable to protect troops from land mines, one of which killed two soldiers. The expeditionary force initially lacked a field hospital and other vital support services, which it had to scrounge from allies.[6] And in all of these so-called rapid foreign deployments, Canadian troops had to bum a lift, because this country lacks "heavy-lift capacity," the large airplanes needed to quickly transport troops and supplies to foreign destinations.

There are also notorious deficiencies at home. The Canadian Coast Guard lacks the equipment and mandate to intercept foreign vessels entering Canadian waters that are suspected of smuggling illegal goods or illegal immigrants. And yet the Canadian navy, with its three, three-decade-old destroyers (a fourth has been mothballed to provide parts for the others), twelve frigates, and the newly acquired second-hand British submarines – one of which, the HMCS *Chicoutimi*, caught fire in 2004, killing one seaman – is hardly up to the task either. The ancient Sea King helicopters, only now being replaced, are unfit for any military. (One airman told the author that friends of his spend their days working on a Sea King that sits in a hangar and is never expected to fly again.) And as Denmark contests Canadian sovereignty in the Far North,[7] and other nations contemplate the possibility of sending commercial traffic through the Northwest Passage whether Canada grants permission or not, it is abundantly clear that this country lacks the military capacity to protect national interests in the Arctic archipelago. It comes down to this: No matter what task the Canadian military might be assigned, it is not up to it.

The decline of the national defence capacity, which is only now being tentatively slowed, is bad enough on its own, but what the Afghan, Haitian, and Indian Ocean deployments reveal most clearly is that the deterioration of Canada's military has also led to the deterioration of this country's ability to project a coherent and respected foreign policy.

For a young nation, Canada has a distinguished record in foreign affairs. Apart from the examples cited above, the efforts of then foreign minister Lester Pearson in 1956 to defuse the Suez crisis by introducing peacekeeping troops won our future prime minister the Nobel Prize. More recently, Canada led the fight among the developed nations within the British Commonwealth to impose sanctions that helped end apartheid in South Africa. We spearheaded the campaign to develop a treaty banning the use of land mines, and we were an important supporter of the new International Criminal Court. Our ratification of the Kyoto Protocol on global warming was central to its final passage, while Paul Martin helped fashion the G20 meeting of finance ministers from developed and developing nations. (Mr. Martin has also floated the idea of inaugurating a G20 of heads of government, but with less success. It seems everyone is just too busy to meet one more time each year.) These foreign initiatives are part of what has been dubbed "soft power." According to the theory, Canada influences the world, not by virtue of its military prowess or economic clout, but by promoting Canadian values of diversity, tolerance, and human rights in international forums.

Perhaps the most important manifestation of Canadian soft power was "Responsibility to Protect," a United Nations report sponsored by the Canadian government and submitted to the world's governments in 2001. The document sets out a framework through which the UN and its member states could intervene in countries where governments were unable or unwilling to protect their own people from natural calamity or internal violence.

Response to "R2P" has been wary from many Third World countries, who suspect it may be used to legitimize neo-colonial interventions. Nonetheless, the philosophy behind the Canadian initiative will become increasingly dominant in the coming decades. In the twentieth century, nations emerging from colonial pasts jealously guarded the prerogatives of sovereign states, including rigid non-interference in internal affairs. The United Nations, whose General Assembly is dominated by these governments, has traditionally respected this principle, even when it has led to mass slaughter in Rwanda, or the more petty persecutions that African governments so often enjoy visiting on their own citizens. As more countries enter the privileged club of functioning liberal democracies, the atrocities committed by the holdouts against their own people will become less and less tolerable in the eyes of the international community. After all, if we could safely liberate the people of North Korea from that murderous dictatorship, which literally starves its own population while it develops nuclear weapons, wouldn't that be a blessing? Don't the people of Myanmar and Zimbabwe deserve every bit as much as you or I to live in free societies governed by the rule of law? God willing, the day will come in this century when citizens of all nations feel a responsibility to protect the most persecuted on the planet.

That day might come sooner rather than later, if Canada is able to persuade the General Assembly and Security Council to accept, at least in principle, the precepts of R2P. Unfortunately, this country is ill-positioned to press the case, for when it comes to contemporary foreign policy, Canada is something of a failed state of its own. Canadian foreign policy today is marked by so much contradiction and hypocrisy that it's hard to take anything that Ottawa says to the rest of the world seriously, which is why no one does.

First and foremost, Canadians have only belatedly begun to realize that a country's foreign policy is primarily its defence policy. Unless a nation is able to protect itself and to project force abroad, it will not be listened to, which is why Canada is not listened to. The reader might well ask: how can this be? Surely a nation is not respected or ignored based on its ability to wage war. Surely Canada won't be given a more respectful hearing if it demonstrates its capacity to invade Norway. Of course not. But projecting force in the twenty-first century is an evolving concept, one with which Canada is failing to keep pace.

Canadian officials point to the atrocities being committed against the people in the Darfur region of Sudan as a textbook case of how the R2P doctrine can be applied. The rape and murder of innocents by government-backed militias in 2004 appeared to be careening toward genocide, and continues to be – or at least should be – one of the more important areas of international concern. The global community has supported troop interventions by the African Union to protect the citizens of Darfur, and an international peacekeeping force is to be deployed to monitor a peace settlement between the Sudanese government and southern rebels. If that peace holds, it could also lead to a reduction in violence in Darfur.

But although Paul Martin personally visited Sudan in 2004, and although Canada has pushed hard for international action on Darfur, Canada's own contribution, in terms of financial support and of peacekeepers, has been largely symbolic: A token force of one hundred troops to assist the African Union in training and logistics, and $170 million in aid over two years. (And even this commitment, made in the midst of the spring 2005 political crisis, was as much a futile effort to retain the support of former Liberal MP David Kilgour as it was an act of considered altruism.) Most Canadians may not be fully aware that Canada, the country that invented peacekeeping, is no longer a significant contributor to peacekeeping activities around the globe. Canada ranks thirty-fifth among nations contributing peacekeeping forces, behind Nepal and Bangladesh. In fairness, the statistic is questionable, since it doesn't include Canadian forces stationed in the former Yugoslavia, who are there under the auspices of NATO. Nonetheless, the fact remains that Canada, which once committed peacekeeping forces whenever asked, from Cyprus to Cambodia, is often no longer able to respond to UN requests – or, more accurately, has to ask the UN not to ask us – simply because our military has deteriorated to the point where we have neither the troops nor equipment. Former journalist Andrew Cohen observed in *While Canada Slept* that "while Canada once supplied 10 per cent of the world's peacekeepers, it now contributes less than 1 per cent."[8]

The truth is that soft power only works when it is backed by hard power. The people of Darfur can be protected from the janjaweed militia only if the African Union is willing and able to carry out its mission to protect them. In this or other conflicts, First World military intervention may be needed to protect civilian populations, as happened in Haiti in 2004 and East Timor in 1999, or to provide financial or material support for regional coalition forces, as in Sudan. Anti-neo-colonialists may decry what they see as naked imperialism disguised in humanitarian robes, but these imperialists may often be the only ones able to prevent mass starvation or slaughter. Responsibility to Protect means protecting with a strong arm.

In fact, although many critics would deny it, a principle similar to that enshrined in Responsibility to Protect has already emerged over the past fifteen years. It has done so tentatively, inconsistently, and highly imperfectly. It has often originated in American determination to protect its own interests. But it has emerged nonetheless.

Kuwait. Somalia. Bosnia. Kosovo. Afghanistan. Haiti. Iraq. In all of these conflicts, an American-led international force – sometimes with United Nations approval, sometimes without – has intervened to deter aggressions by rogue governments, or to protect civilian populations from their own government. The interventions have sometimes failed. They have sometimes been prompted more by American perceived self-interest than collective altruism. They have always been attended by complications and unforeseen setbacks. Yet the principle is slowly emerging: coalitions of willing states, in the presence of an international emergency, have intervened to correct situations deemed intolerable. With the exception of the invasion of Iraq, Canada has participated in all of these coalitions. But that participation has probably done little to burnish Canada's image abroad. In every instance, our contribution was limited, not by our commitment to the cause, but by the forces we were able to contribute. Too often, the paucity of our resources rendered that contribution negligible.

If Canada truly does believe in a Responsibility to Protect, then it must develop the *capacity* to protect. At a minimum, this country must develop the ability to dispatch at least one brigade of troops, fully equipped for action in hostile territory, and able to deploy at very short notice without having to bum a lift or beg for supplies from allied forces. It is well understood that this brigade would never be deployed in a unilateral action, and would be trained and equipped to act in concert with, and in support of, larger allied militaries. Nonetheless, the Department of National Defence must have the resources, including naval and air units, sufficient to support that brigade and to contribute to the defence and supply of international peacemaking forces, without compromising the nation's capacity to defend itself, and without beggaring other peacekeeping operations overseas. Even this would be a small fraction of what the British and Australian defence establishments – to name two of our English allies – are capable, but it would be a start.

It's about more than military might, though, or the lack of it. Canada's global profile in recent years has diminished in any number of ways, through our own inconstant and ill-chosen actions. Consider foreign aid. The developed nations committed, back in the 1960s, to devoting 0.7 per cent of their gross domestic product to foreign assistance. What most Canadians probably don't know is that Lester Pearson headed the commission that came up with the figure, and all prime ministers since Pearson have committed to meeting that target. In 2002, the world's richest countries renewed their pledge, promising to greatly reduce global poverty and its side effects by 2015. Canada was one of the nations that ratified this pledge. How dare we? This country has never come even remotely close to meeting the original target set by Pearson forty years ago. Instead, foreign aid has been steadily cut – Jean Chrétien's government slashed it by half from the level it was at during Brian Mulroney's tenure – until today it sits at around .28 per cent of GDP. Other nations have met the Canadian standard, including Norway, Sweden, Denmark, the Netherlands, and Luxembourg. Still others, including Britain, France, Spain, Finland, Ireland, and Belgium, have set firm targets and are on their way to reaching the goal. But although the Martin government has finally reversed the lamentable decline in foreign giving, Canada has no concrete, achievable plan for reaching the benchmark that this nation set for the rest of the world, and that Europe, at least, is largely on the way to meeting. Even as he affirmed Canada's determination to focus and reinforce foreign aid, in the spring of 2005, Martin admitted that the 0.7 target was simply unrealizable. Neither the blandishments of rock stars, the urging of editorialists, nor the gentle encouragement of other heads of government could get him to change his mind.

Critics of Canada's foreign-aid policy also rightly bemoan its lack of coherence or focus. As Andrew Cohen observes, our paltry contribution to overseas development should be concentrated on a few key countries where Canadian dollars could substantively help. But just as Canada can't resist joining every international forum that will have us, so too we can't resist being part of every relief effort, no matter how small our contribution might be. The Canadian International Development Agency delivers aid to more than one hundred countries, including China, which at last look was hardly a struggling, backward state. Canadian foreign aid must not only be increased, but it must be targeted to reach those countries where help is most needed and can do the most good. For example, Canada can be proud of the passionate advocacy of Stephen Lewis in bringing home to the developed world the magnitude of the HIV/AIDS holocaust in Africa. Jean Chrétien's far-sighted plan to deliver anti-retroviral drugs to the region at low cost will be remembered as one of his most positive legacies. Canada might well conclude that combating HIV/AIDS in Africa is its principal goal in foreign aid. If so, then other programs, such as those in Latin America and Southeast Asia, might have to be wound down, so that all available resources can be focused on this particular fight. Encouragingly, the foreign-policy review released in spring 2005, after much delay, promised to increase foreign-aid funding (though not to the 0.7 per cent level) and to focus efforts largely on the poorest states. However, as with all the other noble principles espoused in this foreign policy and defence review – including the promise to increase the size of the military by five thousand regular troops – the promises are far distant and dependent on the will of future governments. Intentions, at least, are finally headed in the right directions. But when it comes to Canada's posture before the world, the only thing missing, usually, is meaningful action.

To its credit, the federal government has finally moved to exploit one special area of potential that will involve little cost and could make a significant contribution. In Ukraine, in 2004, an exasperated population rose up against rigged elections, demanding a free and fair vote, open and democratic government, and closer ties to the democracies of Europe. That Orange Revolution overshadowed equally promising elections in Romania, leaving Belarus the last totalitarian holdout in Eastern Europe (Russia partially excepted). It is not being naive to predict that, with each passing year, more and more countries will progress steadily closer to democracy and the rule of law. In fact, this is the trendline.

Canada has an important and unique role to play in encouraging the spread of democracy around the globe. This country has considerable experience in election monitoring – our observers were at elections both in Ukraine in December 2004 and Iraq in January 2005 – and a solid record in training police forces and judges in emerging democracies. More important still, our Constitution, with all its faults, has proven well adapted to managing the needs of a bilingual and multi-ethnic nation. We have lessons to teach and help to give in the development and coordination of local, regional, and national governance. This is why many voices, from universities and non-governmental organizations to journalists (in particular, the *Globe*'s Jeffrey Simpson) and the Aga Khan, have promoted the idea of centralizing Canadian expertise and initiatives in an independent organization devoted to exporting what Canada has learned about governance to nations around the globe. Different voices offer different conceptions, but, in general, all agree that such a centre would draw on the experience of national and provincial elections commissions, police forces, academics, public servants, and politicians, to coordinate and promote good governance in nations seeking help in developing it. A few American-based institutions (the National Democratic Institute, for example) offer similar services. But Canada can go into places where Americans – or even the British, French, or Russians – are not always welcome. A Canadian Institute for Democracy could help monitor elections, train judges, advise constitutional assemblies, devise education programs, and provide advice for all who asked for it on Canadian federalism as a vehicle for incorporating diverse populations within a single state. Such an institute would have many supporters, both inside and outside government. The Martin government took a significant first step in April 2005, partnering with the Aga Khan Development Network to establish a Global Centre for Pluralism, based in Ottawa, aimed at exporting Canadian experience in accommodating minority populations to Third World countries struggling with ethnic tensions. The Centre's mandate is too narrowly focused, and the federal contribution of $30 million insufficient for a meaningful, long-term contribution to democracy-building, but a start is a start. The onus will be on future governments to sustain and expand this initiative.

Foreign policy is also an instrument of economic development. Between 1993, the year NAFTA was signed, and 2004, Canada signed three free-trade agreements: with Chile, Costa Rica, and Israel. The United States, on the other hand, despite George W. Bush's reputation for unilateralism and protectionism, signed twelve, and was hard at work on ten more. China is the new international buzzword; its seemingly exponential economic growth has made it the world's second largest exporting nation. And yet despite considerable advantages (including early Canadian recognition of the Chinese Communist government, which preceded American recognition), the Canadian market share of Chinese trade has diminished, from 1.25 per cent to 0.82 per cent. Expanding trade links with China should be a top international-trade priority. Equal attention needs to be paid to India, which has a robust (if flawed) democratic tradition and intimate links to Canada through the Commonwealth and immigration from the subcontinent to this country. Following on, Canada should be able to negotiate free-trade agreements with anyone and everyone who is interested, from Australia to Brazil. But the Department of Foreign Affairs and International Trade has been repeatedly hampered by internal disputes, insufficient funding, a confused mandate, and domestic pressures. Efforts to ink a free-trade deal with South Korea, for example, are being hampered by fears that Canadian shipbuilding jobs (which are themselves heavily subsidized) could be lost. Few nations are more dependent on trade than Canada, with more than 70 per cent of its GDP based on exports or imports. To fail to pursue trade opportunities with important potential markets is to risk economic suicide.

Strangely, those who oppose the expansion of global free trade are almost invariably the same people who oppose closer ties between Canada and the United States. What these anti-American, anti-globalist critics would have us do – cease to trade entirely? learn to live off the land? – remains a mystery. Fortunately, supporting an expansion of Canadian trade in other markets need not and should not entail reducing Canadian political, cultural, and economic relations with the United States. Instead, the time has come to strengthen and deepen those ties.

There is a dark side to the celebration of Canada's growing ethnic diversity and cultural tolerance. Some observers, not content to celebrate this country's strengths, feel compelled to contrast the ongoing evolution of Canadian society with its American counterpart. They use it to rebut conventional wisdom that Canadians are, in most respects, pretty much like Americans. Canadians and Americans are *not* alike, these critics maintain. In fact, the two peoples are quite different in fundamental respects, and are growing further apart with every passing year, polarizing into opposing and incompatible camps. Implicit in this argument is the assumption that Canadians are not just different from Americans, but Canadians are *superior* to Americans, that American culture and society have embarked on a downward spiral even as Canada ascends toward Utopia.

This is mostly a new take on an ancient, tired argument. There is a saying that Americans know who they are, while Canadians know who they are not – they are not Americans. There is nothing to be gained by rehashing the brand of Canadian nationalism that manifests itself in self-conscious anti-Americanism. We know it's a regrettable part of the fabric of Canadian culture: it influences the editorial and programming decisions of the *Toronto Star* (and sometimes, sadly, the *Globe and Mail*) and the Canadian Broadcasting Corporation; it is rife in some of the better drawing rooms of Toronto; a strain of it runs through both the federal Liberal Party and the federal public service. Its most ardent advocates are, fortunately, in a small minority, and it has not prevented Canada and the United States from developing the closest relationship between any two countries in the world. But it exists, and will always exist, and lately has been on a bit of an upswing that we can only hope is temporary.

The reason for that upswing is, as usual, the presence of a Republican president in the White House and a Liberal prime minister at 24 Sussex Dr. Just as Canadians in general seem most comfortable with Liberal prime ministers, so too Canadians in general are uncomfortable with Republican presidents, who personify the most conservative aspects of American culture, throwing the differences between the two countries into relief. Canadians in general were discomfited by the re-election of

George W. Bush, who seemed a bit of a non-entity when he defeated Democratic challenger Al Gore in 2000 (Raymond Chrétien, then Canadian ambassador to the United States and the nephew of the prime minister, simply reflected Canadian attitudes when he appeared to endorse Gore during the election campaign), but who was transformed into an aggressive and activist president in the wake of the attacks of September 11. Bush had Canadian support when he overthrew the Taliban government in Afghanistan; Canadian special forces took part in the hunt for Osama bin Laden and other al-Qaeda leaders, and Canadian troops were prominent in the international effort to stabilize and rebuild the country. But there was less support for the American government's decision to remove Saddam Hussein from power in Iraq. Chrétien refused to endorse the invasion unless the United Nations did likewise; when it did not, Canada stood aside, a move that was widely popular in this country. There appeared to be a collective sigh of disappointment when Bush defeated John Kerry in the 2004 presidential election, and that election only intensified the chorus of voices in Canada, and in the United States as well, who proclaimed that America was devolving into a militant, conservative, theocratic rogue empire, and that now, more than ever, Canada should keep its distance.

The personification of this line of reasoning can be found in the writing of Michael Adams, president of the polling firm Environics, and the author of several books on Canadian social values. His 2003 bestseller, *Fire and Ice: The United States, Canada and the Myth of Converging Values*, used polling data to assert that American society and culture are steadily deteriorating, while Canada (along with Europe) is steadily progressing toward a more socially just and enlightened society. The 144 pages of *Fire and*

Ice, though based on carefully accumulated polling data, are rife with a knee-jerk fear and loathing of all things American. "Canada strives to be an upstanding citizen in the world while the United States has, under George W. Bush, reaffirmed its commitment to brash unilateralism;" "although Americans may make a more impressive living, Canadians have better gotten the hang of how to live." American lives "appear (from above) relentlessly competitive, perilously chaotic, perennially unfulfilling," while we Canadians "cherish our separateness – our unassuming civility, our gift for irony and understatement in a world of exaggerated claims and excess."[9] And that's just the Introduction.

These and similar claims are echoed in analyses as diverse as Jennifer Welsh's *At Home in the World: Canada's Global Vision for the 21st Century*, an otherwise-incisive analysis of Canadian foreign policy marred by its portrayal of Canada acting in concert with other nations to limit some of the excesses of American protectionism and unilateralism; in the political critiques of authors such as Margaret Atwood; and in various newspaper columns. Fortunately, all of this incestuous chatter is ignored by most Canadians, who wisely skip the page and get on with their lives. But over time, unless counterbalanced, it can have a corrosive effect on Canada–U.S. relations. Already, the wildly popular Fox cable-news network has made Canada-bashing an occasional sport, although even the most self-righteous among us had to smile at Pat Buchanan's description of this country as Soviet Canuckistan.

Of course there are cultural differences between Canada and the United States. How could there not be? Our nation has not been scarred by the curse of slavery and the entrenched racial tensions it engendered. Nor can Canadians fully comprehend the mindset of a people who collectively preside over the most powerful and wealthy nation in all of human history. (And how differently would we manage things if *we* had such power?) Americans place a greater emphasis on individual liberty than Canadians, who are more attracted to the collective security of government intervention and communal rights. Although the American political system in theory separates church more emphatically from state than does ours, the political influence of evangelical Christianity has always been strong in that society and appears to be growing, leading to a more socially conservative country, while Canada is steadily dismantling the former institutional ties between church and state, especially in Quebec, and there is no evidence, as yet, that religious fundamentalism is on the rise, at least as a political manifestation. (The fruitless efforts of the religious right to galvanize the Opposition to federal same-sex marriage legislation in 2005 only served to reveal the weakness of the movement.) It is perfectly true that even Canadian conservatives would mostly vote Democrat in the United States. It also doesn't mean a thing.

For the truth is, Americans and Canadians are so inextricably intertwined as to be inseparable. Now this has to be parsed, for there are several Americas, just as there are several Canadas. Atlantic Canadians share strong cultural and historical links with New Englanders. Quebeckers historically moved back and forth between the home province and Maine, New Hampshire, and Vermont. Ontario has been described by the political economist Thomas Courchene as an integral part of a de facto Great Lakes region-state, with closer economic ties to Michigan, New York, and Pennsylvania than to Quebec or Manitoba. Winnipeggers travel to St. Paul–Minneapolis for big-city shopping, while Prairie farmers know their compatriots south of the border understand better than anyone the challenges of farming in the North American Midwest. Alberta is closer than any other part of Canada to emulating the social conservatism, raw entrepreneurship, and petro-wealth of Texas, while Vancouver and Seattle are so closely intertwined that the local PBS station has hosted fundraisers in Canada. Canadian political elites like to point out that the dominant Canadian political ethos is most closely mirrored in the Democratic states of the Northeast, the Great Lakes, and the Pacific Coast, but that doesn't exactly hold, for there is equal resonance between Alberta, plus parts of Saskatchewan and Manitoba (all hotbeds of the original Reform movement), and the Red Republican states of the South and the Midwest. It would be more accurate to say that Canadians resemble, politically and culturally, the Americans they live closest to. And remember, just about everyone lives close to the Americans. Eighty per cent of the Canadian population lives within two hundred kilometres of the American border.

The similarities are based on more than geography. Snobbish Canadians may sniff at American excesses, but no other culture anywhere in the world more clearly mirrors its American mentor. Canadian actors integrate seamlessly in Hollywood, just as American filmmakers happily take advantage of a low dollar and government tax credits to shoot their movies in Canadian cities. (Try to think of another country in the world where you could film a TV series without giving away the fact that the city streets are not American. Australia, perhaps, but where would you find extras with matching accents?) Many Canadians probably aren't aware that the hilarious satire *Trailer Park Boys* depicts the lives of trailer trash in Nova Scotia, not Kansas. The North American music industry is more integrated now than the cattle industry, while poorer countries often purchase Canadian television programming, because it looks just like its American counterpart, but is cheaper.

As for economic linkages, they are so intimate as to hardly require repeating. Forty per cent of Canadian GDP is tied to trade with the United States, which accounts for 85 per cent of Canadian exports. Since the signing of the 1988 Free Trade Agreement, Canadian exports to the United States have grown from $99 billion to $279 billion in value (counted in 2005 U.S. dollars). Trade between Ontario and Michigan alone surpasses $1 billion a day, with the Ambassador Bridge between Windsor and Detroit the world's busiest border crossing. Canada is the United States' biggest supplier of imported energy. Our automotive industries are fully integrated. The Americans have $239 billion of capital invested in Canada, while Canadian investments in the United States total $191 billion. Canadians and Americans are business partners, friends, and family, all rolled into one.

This inescapable fact undermines the core argument made by those who favour keeping a healthy distance in American and Canadian relations. That argument is predicated on the assumption of different and diverging social values, displeasure with American foreign policy, and fear that Canada will lose its sovereignty – cultural, economic, and ultimately political – and its soul if it draws any closer to the American behemoth. The danger, however, is not that Canada will grow too close to the United States, but that we are growing too far apart. Trade irritants such as those that have emerged over softwood lumber, wheat, and the aftermath of the BSE cattle crisis threaten to rile the mostly calm waters of Canada–U.S. trade. More important, both Mexico and China could surpass Canada as America's largest trading partner in coming decades, diminishing Canadian influence in Washington. And as America signs more and more trade agreements with other countries, Canada becomes simply one of a number of states with most-favoured trading status. We recede, rather than progress, in America's consciousness. One way to compensate, as mentioned above, is for Canada to seek trade agreements with other countries, and this is a policy worth pursuing aggressively. But it would be naive to imagine that Canadian trade will ever shift substantively from its American focus. Trade between Canada and the European Union, for example, is already mostly tariff-free. Yet trade with the EU represents no more than 1.8 per cent of Canadian GDP. The truth is, there isn't a lot that we have to sell them that they want to buy. They're just not into Ontario wines.

Beyond the economic, there is the moral. That word will raise eyebrows among foreign-policy aficionados. Nations, we all know, do not have friends, only interests. To the extent that it is in America's interest to treat with Canada, or in ours to treat with them, they and we will. But to negotiate from an assumption of shared values, obligations, duty, and trust is dangerous in the extreme. Just ask anyone who helped negotiate the Free Trade Agreement.

Yet to argue that Canada should approach its relations with the United States in the strictly bloodless context of national self-interest is itself dangerously naive. Academics in think-tanks, and even deep thinkers in Foreign Affairs, might like to cast the Canada–U.S. relationship in the amoral light of state interests, but any mature discussion of the subject must take into account our shared values, the simple yet profound fact of mutual identification, admiration, friendship. Yes, these are empty words when mouthed by politicians at public ceremonies, but they are also deeply complex truths that inform the way Canadians and Americans feel about each other. If Americans lose their temper at Canadian standoffishness, if Canadians lament that Americans don't pay us enough attention or treat us with enough respect, these complaints simply speak to the profound depth of attachment between two peoples enmeshed in an intense, complex, and permanent relationship.

Here's another way to put it: It is dangerous and impossible to contemplate the Canadian and American relationship in terms of national self-interest rather than shared values because interests *are* values. It is not only in both countries' self-interest to co-operate in securing the North American perimeter against terrorist incursion; it is morally necessary for the two nations to co-operate. The Canadian government has an obligation to protect its own citizens *and* to protect American citizens as well from terrorist attack, and is obligated, therefore, to spend whatever it costs to bolster border security. Anyone who argues that the imperatives of sovereignty limit the extent to which Canada should divert scarce resources to perimeter defence, or the extent to which the two countries should share information and coordinate policies, is putting forward a values-based argument: the value of sovereignty, whatever that might be, versus the value of protecting ourselves and our friends from attack. And Canadians would make short work of any governing party that put such an argument forward, not only because our citizens want to be protected from terrorist attack themselves, but because they would be horrified if Canadian negligence led to a terrorist attack on the United States. That is why both countries have, in fact, worked closely and successfully since the attacks on New York and Washington to keep the wrong people and the wrong objects out. Better yet, that co-operation has actually improved the flow of trade across the Canada–U.S. border, through programs that pre-clear low-risk goods and people, and by instituting policies that limit the right of refugee claimants to use one country as the launching pad for a bid for asylum in the other country. Needs are identified, both sides work on joint solutions, values and interests intermesh.

In that context, what specifically are the next steps that Canada and the United States could take to improve trade and security? On the trade side, three issues dominate: dispute resolution, regulatory harmonization, and labour mobility. On the first, there is little to be done. Canada has continually pushed for a swift, fair, and binding dispute resolution mechanism that would resolve issues such as the softwood lumber dispute[10] quickly and simply. It won't happen. The American Congress, whose members are beholden to many powerful interests, would never cede the power to impose tariffs or other penalties to an arbitrary body. Besides, these disputes are often about science as well as trade. The question of when, or if, the American market could be fully re-opened to Canadian beef after cases of BSE were discovered in three Canadian cows depended as much on when the American Department of Agriculture decided that there was no scientific basis for concern, as it did on efforts by elements in the American beef industry to keep the market closed to Canadian competition. And even then, a capricious judge in Montana temporarily closed the border back up again, demonstrating the capacity of caprice to frustrate even the best bilateral intentions. Finally, a no-appeals panel could work against Canada's interest in future disputes. Our hands are not always clean, when it comes to accusations of government subsidies. A better approach is to incrementally build up a body of evidence and precedence through appeals against American punitive tariffs through both NAFTA and the World Trade Organization. Any attempts at more emphatic reform would probably meet with failure, at least in the near future.

Both the American and Canadian governments are interested, however, in breaking down regulatory barriers that hamper the free flow of goods across the border. President Bush's NAFTA-plus agenda, as it is called, is an important priority in his second term, and Paul Martin appears willing to push the file, as he should. Bush, Martin, and Mexican president Vicente Fox mutually agree that incremental progress is more realistic than big-bang agreements, which is why, at a March 2005 summit in Waco, Texas, they established joint ministerial task forces that could identify and propose solutions for specific irritants – a more pragmatic, if less exciting, agenda than rewriting NAFTA entirely. This incremental approach should bring progress on such important, if mundane-sounding, issues as coordinating regulations, so that their red tape is the same red tape as our red tape. And there is room to go further, in particular through joint regulatory approval processes, in which common continental agencies could study and approve new hybrid cereals, for example, or propose new drugs to combat depression, or any other patent or regulatory application. Once approved, that approval would automatically extend to both Canada and the United States (and Mexico). Regulatory harmonization makes eminent sense: both countries have confidence in the competence and integrity of the other's inspections and approvals processes. Mexico would no doubt also be able to contribute finances and expertise to support any NAFTA-based approvals process, while that country would benefit from the quality of inspections and the stringent approval standards employed by both Canada and the United States. A continental inspection and approvals system would save time and money and speed the delivery of important new products that would improve the quality of life in all three societies.

Labour mobility is an issue whose time has not yet come, but that could soon change. To discuss this issue honestly, we have to be blunt. One impediment to eliminating restrictions on the free flow of labour between Canada and the United States has been an unspoken but widespread fear among some Canadians that an open border would lead to a mass exodus of African-Americans into Canada. For much of the twentieth century, Canadians watched with a mixture of horror and self-satisfaction as a massive black exodus from the Jim Crow south to the industrial north produced racially defined, crime-ridden, and explosively violent ghettoes, whose residents periodically rioted, often destroying entire sections of their respective cities' downtowns. This country had no similar racially defined underclass, and no desire to import one. While some Canadians were frustrated with the difficulty of acquiring the treasured American green card, or work permit, few were willing to take the risks of opening the Canada–U.S. border to the free flow of workers.

Much has changed. Canadians have seen their own cities become home to a broad range of ethnicities, who often choose to live in their own communities (at least in the case of new arrivals; their children tend to move away), without any serious descent into ghettoization or violence. In the meantime, a black American middle class has emerged; although there is still a serious problem of racially defined poverty in urban America, both blacks and Hispanics are making significant progress. There are no longer any reasonable fears (if those fears were ever reasonable in the first place) that opening the border to unfettered labour mobility would lead to any mass exodus of either African or Hispanic Americans into Canadian cities. After all, unemployment levels are lower in the United States than in Canada. And the weather could always be counted on as a deterrent.

A NAFTA-based labour mobility agreement would ensure that professional and skilled workers could move freely between Canada and the United States, as market conditions warranted, which would improve productivity and living standards in both countries. In many ways, it would be a return to the border that existed before the First World War, when farmers and factory workers traversed between the two countries without giving it much of a thought, and families migrated back and forth between family landholdings in provinces and states. Although rules would need to be in place to ensure that Americans, in particular, didn't move here under false pretenses simply to access public health care, for all intents and purposes, the Canada–U.S. border should be as invisible as possible.

However, the more invisible the border gets, the more secure it must get also. As mentioned, the Canadian and American governments have already taken steps to protect both countries from people and weapons who could do us harm. But security cooperation is about more than anti-terrorism measures. It extends into the areas of defence and even foreign policy as well. For many Canadians, proudly at odds with the rambunctious actions of the Bush administration, the more distance Canada can put between us and the United States, the better. This attitude is both wrong and dangerous.

First, it ignores linkages. Among other attendant ills, Canada's decision to permit its military to deteriorate to the point it could no longer protect itself or contribute its fair share to collective defence impaired bilateral relations with the United States. It made us an unreliable partner, an object of derision in the Defence Department and White House, and a less reliable and consequential ally, to the point where Australia now ranks higher in the counsels of American foreign and defence policy. That country not only supported the United States in its invasion of Iraq, it backed up that support with troops, while investing heavily in upgrading its military. Not only was Australia rewarded with a free-trade agreement with the United States, in May 2005 the U.S. Congress approved 10,500 special visas for Australians workers and their spouses. The United States typically only issues 65,000 such work visas each year for all countries. No other country in the world – certainly not Canada – could expect such privileged treatment, which will increase the number of Australians working in the United States tenfold.[11]

Contrast that with the U.S. State Department proposal in April 2005 to require Canadians to carry passports when entering the United States. The move threatens to significantly impair cross-border traffic because, if implemented, Americans visiting Canada will also require passports (otherwise, they won't be able to get back home), and a far smaller percentage of Americans than Canadians hold passports. The tourism industry, alone, could suffer a major hit. Fortunately, because of the impact it would have on American travellers, the proposal is unlikely to be adopted, but that it was even raised is a warning signal.

It may be mere coincidence that the American move came just weeks after Canada announced it would not participate in the U.S. missile defence program. More likely, the move resulted from a lack of any real concern over the impact it might have on the border, or on bilateral relations. But those who believe that Iraq, missile defence, and passports are completely unrelated are deluding themselves, or trying to delude us.

Paul Martin's decision not to bring Canada into the American Ballistic Missile Defense (BMD) program in some ways was more egregious than Jean Chrétien's decision not to join the American coalition in Iraq. At least in the former case Canada had been warning well in advance that, without Security Council approval, Canada might not be able to participate. But Martin had repeatedly signalled his desire and intention to sign on to BMD, which proposes to establish a ring of radar and missile installations that could intercept and destroy a small number of ballistic missiles fired at the United States, most likely from a rogue state such as North Korea. Because of Canadian reservations about the program, which critics warned could lead to a new arms race, the Americans did not propose to install radar or interceptor facilities on Canadian soil.

Despite the warnings of Canadian critics, who maintained BMD was an expensive folly that wouldn't work and would destabilize the balance of power, Martin supported the idea of joining the BMD command structure, arguing that any attempt to shoot down an incoming missile would probably happen over Canadian soil, and it was in the interest of Canadian sovereignty to be a part of the decision-making process.

But so strong is the strain of anti-Americanism within the Liberal caucus and parts of the Canadian public that Prime Minister Paul Martin became paralyzed with indecision, delaying a debate on the matter in the House until internal dissent within his own party forced him in February 2005 to tell the Americans that Canada would not be signing on.

Some Canadians took enormous satisfaction in this country's decision not to support American actions in Iraq or on missile defence. The rest of us should ponder the costs of these triumphs in lost goodwill from the one country in the world that no one should want to be on the bad side of.

Despite tensions, disappointment, and mere fitful progress, Canadian and American co-operation in one sphere could eclipse all others. In essence, a made-in-Canada environmental policy makes no sense. Nowhere is this more apparent than in this country's approach to the Kyoto accord on global warming. Let us assume that carbon-dioxide emissions are warming the global atmosphere, with potentially ruinous consequences. (Some scientists doubt the claim, but when it comes to a potential apocalypse, better safe than sorry.) Canada, in concert with other developed nations, has agreed to reduce greenhouse-gas emissions to 1990 levels by 2012. The Kyoto Protocol was always flawed, however, because such major emitters as China and India and Brazil never signed on, and it became even more problematic when the United States and Australia withdrew. It is also now abundantly clear that, despite the vague promises contained in the 2005 Liberal budget and subsequent documents, this country has no plan in place to meet its Kyoto targets, simply because such a plan would have ruinous consequences for the Alberta energy industry and the Ontario manufacturing industry. Canada will not live up to its Kyoto obligations. The only consolation, if that is the right word, is that the Europeans and Japanese will do no better.

Nonetheless, carbon-dioxide emissions must be curtailed. And the Americans, although they have not signed on to Kyoto, are moving on their own to reverse the trend of global warming. The big problem of Kyoto, however, is that it fails to address what is, for many, an even greater threat: the worsening quality of urban air, thanks to smog. Smog shares a common origin with CO_2 – coal-fired power plants, industrial emissions, and auto exhausts – but its core components are nitrogen oxide and sulphur dioxide, or NOX and SOX.

Canada and the United States have already demonstrated their powerful joint capacity to improve the environment. Both countries took major steps in the last decades of the twentieth century to clean up their lakes and rivers, while working together to reverse the deterioration of the Great Lakes. (Remember when Lake Erie was declared dead? Today, it boasts the largest freshwater commercial fishery in the world.) As it was with water, so it could be with air. Sooner or later, the federal government is going to have to accept that its commitment on Kyoto exceeded its fiscal capacity. Apart from being the right thing to do, it would also be politically savvy for Ottawa to deflect attention from that unpleasant truth by entering into treaty negotiations with the Americans on an improved Air Quality Agreement, which would require either that coal-fired generating stations be closed or that new technologies be installed that drastically reduce harmful emissions; and that vehicle emissions be steadily reduced (with tax incentives for alternative technologies), with an overall goal of slowing the rise in, and then reversing, the levels of both CO_2 and NOX and SOX in the atmosphere. The treaty would need to include an enforcement mechanism that imposed strict financial penalties on either government, if it failed to meet the treaty's emission targets. Such an agenda might well appeal to a president looking for an environmental legacy. At the least, Canada could make it clear that any progress in increasing energy exports via new pipelines, or of Canadian acquiescence in petroleum extraction on environmentally sensitive lands in Alaska[12] is contingent on progress toward a comprehensive clean-air treaty. The Canadian government could also lobby state governments – especially California, which leads the continent in emissions standards, and the New England states, who must breathe in both Ohio Valley and central Canadian emissions – to support Ottawa in pressuring the administration and Congress to negotiate a clean-air pact. Smog is a worsening health problem that is also lowering the quality of life for millions of Canadians and Americans. A strong and consistent Canadian initiative to eliminate the scourge will resonate with urban dwellers on both sides of the border. Progress will initially be slow; there might be little sign of momentum before the end of the decade. But if Canada must admit in 2012 that it failed miserably to meet its Kyoto obligations, then ratification of a North American Clean Air Treaty would be more than adequate compensation.

A revived, consistent, and dynamic reshaping of Canada's role in the world would be reflected in a substantial upgrading of the Canadian military; an expanded and refocused program in foreign aid; improved efforts to export the Canadian experience in democratic governance; new trade agreements with other countries;

and broader and deeper economic, security, and environmental co-operation with our friend – yes, our *friend* – and ally, the United States.

Such an aggressive expansion of Canada's role in the world would not come without a price. Federal subsidies in the domestic sphere would certainly diminish as a result of increased expenditures in defence and foreign aid. Any broad expansion of federally directed national social policy would have to be curtailed.

But fears that the federal government's importance in the lives of its citizens would diminish are misplaced. Canada is an outward-looking nation; its heritage as a settler country has made it so. As Canada bolsters and amplifies its role in the family of nation states, as its foreign policy, foreign-aid programs, and foreign presence becomes more credible, as its role matures within the United Nations, NATO, NORAD, the Commonwealth, the Francophonie, the G8, and new international forums yet to emerge, Canadians will look to Ottawa with pride and confidence, as the voice of Canada in the world, in a century when Canada can and should mean more to the world. This country has a unique role to play as liaison: a first-world, European culture increasingly dominated by polyglot races from around the globe; a bridge between English and French, European and Asian, American and everyone else. Canada, as the country that embodies the world, is the country that can make the world finally understand itself. And in that mission, the very thing that so many fear is being lost – the national identity, the national soul – will finally have been found.

CHAPTER SIX

THE

DEMOCRATIC

PARADOX

I n the 2004 U.S. presidential election, voters in thirty-four states considered 162 referendum questions. The citizens of Alabama rejected a referendum to cleanse their constitution of language requiring racially segregated schools.[1] Voters in eleven states passed resolutions banning the legalization of gay marriage. Californian voters approved $3 billion over ten years for stem-cell research, along with proposals to limit the awards for damages in certain kinds of lawsuits; Colorado voters rejected this proposal but approved a referendum to expand public transit. Arizona voters adopted a motion cracking down on welfare benefits for illegal immigrants. Voters in Florida, Nevada, Oregon, and Wyoming passed measures that made it easier to sue for medical malpractice, and measures that made it harder. Sometimes, voters in the same state passed both kinds of measures. There were votes to increase the minimum wage that passed, but votes to increase funding for education that failed.

Are Canadians any less flighty, when it comes to referendums? In 1980, the Quebec government presented the people of that province with a referendum proposing sovereignty, accompanied by an ongoing association with Canada. Voters defeated it. In 1992, they voted down a federal referendum that would lead to greater autonomy for Quebec within Confederation. In 1995, they rejected a second referendum on sovereignty-association.

The wisdom of electors, as expressed through direct democracy, is inscrutable. American voters seem to want increased funding for education, public transit, medical research, law-enforcement, and infrastructure, along with lower taxes and balanced budgets. Quebec voters have twice rejected sovereignty for their province, but also rejected the Charlottetown Accord, which would have protected the distinct status of Quebec within Confederation. When the people speak, the result can be cacophony.

All the more reason, perhaps, to embrace the representative democracy bequeathed us by the Mother of Parliaments in Westminster. But consider this: since the end of the First World War, Canada has had fifteen majority governments at the federal level. But in only four instances did the governing party actually receive 50 per cent of the vote. Three times in the 1990s, parties that came second in the popular vote actually formed majority provincial governments. In the 2000 federal election, it took on average 30,000 votes for the Liberals to win a seat, but 130,000 votes for the Progressive Conservatives to win one. More people voted for the Canadian Alliance in Quebec than in Saskatchewan, yet Saskatchewan voters elected ten Alliance MPs, and Quebec voters not one.[2] In the 2001 provincial election in British Columbia, the NDP received 21.6 per cent of the popular vote, but won only two of seventy-nine seats in the B.C. legislature. And everyone remembers that in 2000, George Bush lost the popular vote in his battle with Al Gore, yet became President of the United States.

And in case you retort that, whatever the apparent distortions, voters support the electoral outcomes they provide, then please account for the fact that in the 1960s, voter turnout at Canadian federal elections averaged 77 per cent; in the 1970s it fell to 74 per cent; then to 73 per cent in the 1980s, after which it plummeted to 66 per cent in the 1990s.[3] In the 2004 federal election, one of the most hotly contested in recent memory, with a reunited Conservative Party posing a credible alternative to the governing Liberals, the turnout was 62 per cent, the lowest ever. Given that not all potential voters were registered, less than half the eligible voters might have cast a ballot.

This is the democratic paradox of the twenty-first century. Centuries-old institutions fail to reflect the reality of voter intentions at elections. And yet experiments in direct democracy have led to inconsistent and sometimes plainly wrong-headed results, suggesting that voters cast their ballots without taking the time to become properly informed on the issues at hand. Sometimes, the People just aren't very bright. Meanwhile, the general population – especially those under thirty-five – is steadily disengaging from the political process, raising questions of whether modern liberal democracy is democratic at all.

There are no simple explanations for the decline in voter turnout, but the root of it, sadly, appears to be the result of what could be called the decline of citizenship. When Statistics Canada compared the percentage of citizens who volunteered for community service in 2000 with a similar study from 1987, it found a sharp decline among people under forty-five who gave of their time to help their community. Similarly, church (and mosque and temple and synagogue) attendance had declined (from 41 per cent among all age groups to 34 per cent) between 1988 and 1998. In 1980 37 per cent of Canadians identified themselves as having a strong affiliation with a political party; by 2000 that number was down to 18 per cent. The authors of one Elections Canada study concluded: "To the extent people are declining the opportunities to vote in Canada, they are also illustrating a lowered commitment to the Canadian community."[4] Add an ongoing decline in trust in the political process – be it for political parties, leaders, or government in general – especially among the young, and you get a glimpse of what ails us. One consequence of the breakdown of ethnic homogeneity, of the migration from smaller communities to large, impersonal cities, of the decline in deference toward political elites (not to mention religious leaders, educators, and other traditional community leaders) has been an erosion of the legitimacy of our political institutions in the eyes of the population, leading to apathetic or even hostile voters – or, to be more accurate, non-voters.

We also know that voter turnout is lower, and is falling more quickly, in Westminster-style democracies, where candidates are elected using the first-past-the-post method, as opposed to countries that elect their legislatures through some form of proportional representation. In the three most recent elections prior to 2004, voter turnout in the United States hovered around 50 per cent (55 per cent in 1992; 47 per cent in 1996 and 49 per cent in

2000. In the 2004 election, however, the turnout was just under 60 per cent). In the United Kingdom, the popular vote has plummeted in the past four elections from 78 per cent of the electorate in 1992 to 61.5 per cent, in the May 2005 vote. In Germany, however, which employs a form of proportional representation to elect the Reichstag, it has remained steady at about 80 per cent, while in Sweden, which also uses PR, it has dropped from 88 per cent to 80 per cent. Only in Australia does virtually everyone vote, but that is because they are required to by law, with sharp penalties for shirkers.

Canadians would probably resist a law compelling them to cast a ballot in municipal, provincial, and federal elections. And such a law might prove counterproductive. The best way to measure whether reforms in governance increase citizen engagement is by watching the turnout. When and if it starts to go back up, without the citizenry being coerced, we'll know we're on the right track.

So what is the right track? As a start, Canada needs to experiment with switching its voting system to some form of proportional representation.

After all, the existing first-past-the-post method of electing parliamentarians (in any given constituency, the candidate who wins the plurality of votes wins the seat) is becoming an anachronism. Only Great Britain, Canada, the United States, and India employ it. And yes, they're worried about the decline in voter turnout in India, too. The problem with FPTP, simply, is that the majority of the votes cast are wasted, since in many ridings, an MP can win the riding with 40 per cent of the vote or less. The legislature in no sense reflects the proportion of votes cast for each political party, leaving voters disenchanted with, and detached

from, the electoral process. Although there are several forms of
PR, all of them result in a legislature that more or less corresponds
with voter intentions. If Party A received 15 per cent of the vote,
it has roughly 15 per cent of the seats in the legislature.

There are two principle criticisms of PR, both of them cogent.
The first is that governments are less accountable for their actions.
A governing party may campaign on a given platform, but then
largely fail to implement it, claiming it had no choice, since in
order to form a government that commanded a majority of seats
in the legislature it was forced to form a coalition with a smaller
party that opposed aspects of the larger party's platform. Similarly,
legislatures can dissolve as a result of non-confidence votes,
budgets can run red with deficits, important but unpopular
reforms can be stymied, with each party blaming others in the
House. (Although the American Congressional system, in which
Congress and the executive are separate, sometimes combines the
unrepresentativeness of FPTP with the paralysis of PR.) And it has
to be said that many European governments appear to have
difficulty implementing contentious legislation, such as pension
reform or cutbacks to unproductive subsidies, in part because
governing parties know that such measures, and the government
itself, would never survive a vote in the legislature.

A second, related criticism is that legislatures elected through
proportional representation are inherently unstable – the Italian
Disease, some call it. Coalitions can consist of several parties with
differing agendas, making it difficult to establish a credible legislative program, as mentioned above, and leading to repeated defeats
of shifting coalitions of government, accompanied by frequent
elections that fail to resolve impasses, and general chaos. Defenders
of the status quo argue that only FPTP leads to majority – or at least

stable minority – governments that have the will and legislative capacity to make tough decisions. Without Westminster, would the federal government have been able to eliminate the deficit in the 1990s, or impose the Goods and Services Tax (a necessary precursor to balanced budgets) in the 1980s?

These are compelling arguments, and the responses to them are only partly satisfactory. On the question of holding parties to account, voters clearly do not feel under the existing system that political parties can be trusted, or that those that break their word are properly disciplined. The Liberal hegemony that has dominated Canadian politics for most of the past century has made it possible for prime ministers to repeatedly reverse their stance, without being punished for their actions in the next election. On the other hand, the Liberal government elected in 2004, while allowing the party to pursue an election agenda that principally involved giving money to everyone, was racked by political instability, almost collapsing after the Throne Speech in October 2004, and again during the budget debate in May 2005. But then legislative stability appears to be more the product of the culture than of the political system. Italy and Israel have often suffered from volatile legislatures and unstable governments, not so much because they use PR, but because PR reflects the divisions and polarizations within these two societies. Germany and Japan, on the other hand, manage their PR-based systems with little disruption. (Indeed, some would argue a little more disruption would be healthy in both countries.) In the end, PR-based legislatures simply reflect the divisions within society itself. And its compromises are reflective of the necessary compromises within society. Sometimes tough choices have to be delayed until a necessary consensus emerges as to how they should be tackled. The inability to pursue strong measures without popular support may be the greatest immediate strength of FPTP; it might also in the long haul be its greatest weakness.

There is, in addition, an argument in favour of moving to proportional representation that is unique to Canada's situation. This country may have already arrived at a state of permanent instability at the federal level, making it virtually impossible for any political party to form a majority government, except under exceptional circumstances. For reasons already explained, both the Liberal and Conservative parties are currently incapable of forming a broad enough coalition to earn either party substantial support across the country. The Liberals have alienated soft nationalist support in Quebec that the Conservatives no longer seem able or willing to exploit. The Liberals dominate in urban Ontario, but the Conservatives have regained control of the more rural parts of the province, while continuing to dominate in the West. The Bloc has its bastion in Quebec, while the NDP picks up a seat here, a seat there, across the country, reflecting the marginal fate that awaits a party unable to attract more than one voter in five, and that's on a good day. All three federalist parties grab their share of votes in Atlantic Canada. Unless and until one political party can establish a strong presence in Quebec, while holding a majority of seats in Ontario and make a respectable showing in the West and Atlantic Canada, majority governments could be a rarity in Ottawa for several elections to come.

The Liberal Party remains the best equipped to once again cobble together such a coalition, but that in itself is a compelling argument for moving to PR. The twenty-first century simply can't be a repeat of the twentieth, with Liberals in power federally a large majority of the time, while the Conservatives fracture and coalesce, waiting for a perfect storm of opportunity that could see them actually win power, at least until the coalition dissolves in acrimony once again. Proportional representation, at the least, would ensure that Liberal majority government was a rarity. It might also lead to the rise of smaller parties that, for better or worse, accurately represent the contending interests within Confederation. Under PR, there would almost certainly always be a party representing the interests of sovereigntists in Quebec. The Conservative Party might permanently fracture into its natural components: an economically libertarian and socially conservative party that defends Western interests, and a fiscally conservative but socially liberal party whose base of support was in Ontario, with additional support coming from Atlantic Canada. Such a conservative coalition might more easily form a government in tandem with Quebec sovereigntists – or even with Quebec federalists – than any of the existing, non-Liberal combinations.[5]

The news would not be necessarily rosy for conservatives, however, for the legislature as a whole might tilt to the Left. The New Democrats, representing the interests of silk-stockinged socialists and some elements of blue-collar and pink-collar labour, could easily command between 45 and 60 seats in the legislature (the current House of Commons contains 308 seats), if it does not lose support to a surging Green Party, which might offer a more appealing choice to voters who want government to emphasize environmental stewardship as well as economic redistribution. The Liberals, governing in coalition with parties of the Left, could be pushed permanently to the Left, with fell consequences for the recent fiscal probity that has made Canada the envy of the world.

But then, the Liberal Party itself might not survive a move to proportional representation. Internal party divisions have been sapping Liberal strength for a generation now; with the Martin wing (fiscally conservative and somewhat decentralist) and the Chrétien wing (socially liberal and centralist) pitted in acrimony so intense that it even infected the deliberations of the Gomery inquiry. (The Chrétien wing viewed the exercise as a blatant attempt by the Martin wing to discredit and destroy the former's influence.) Without the discipline of the prospect of power, the party itself could dissolve into factions, which could emerge as separate parties in the House of Commons.[6]

Some would regard a Parliament consisting of half a dozen parties or more, representing a mosaic of regional and class interests, with horror. Others would say that such a mosaic accurately reflects the nation itself, and whatever compromises were needed to achieve political stability and a legislative agenda would reflect the national will in a nation built on compromise. Already, no fewer than five provinces, representing two-thirds of the Canadian population, are at various stages of considering proportional representation in their own jurisdictions. The first test came in May 2005, when 57 per cent of voters in British Columbia supported a move to a form of proportional representation. The vote was not sufficient to force the change, since Premier Gordon Campbell decreed that 60-per-cent support was required.[7] But, as Mr. Campbell acknowledged, the solid majority support had to be taken seriously, and some form of electoral reform remains a strong possibility. Meanwhile, Quebec is considering moving to its own form of PR-based elections, as is Prince Edward Island. Ontario and New Brunswick are also making rapid strides toward transforming their electoral systems.

There are both similarities and differences in the provincial approaches. The various electoral commissions in all five provinces favoured a form of what is called mixed-member PR. Ridings are retained, although there are fewer of them, and several members may be elected to each riding. The British Columbia variation was known as the Single Transferable Vote, with ridings containing multiple members who are chosen based on a complex redistribution of ranked ballots, while in other jurisdictions only one member would represent each riding, with other members elected directly to the legislature, based on overall party percentage of the vote.

There are strengths and weaknesses to each of the variations. The extreme complexity of the British Columbia system – more people understand the theory of relativity than grasp the complexities of the Single Transferable Vote[8] – probably account for its failure to reach 60 per cent support. And of course, some will argue that all are inferior to the status quo. Fortunately, Canadian federalism offers splendid opportunities for experimentation and comparison. The best course might be for each province to adopt the system that seems right for its circumstances, and then to watch a few elections and judge the efficacy of the results. The federal government could then strike its own electoral commission to assess what reforms, if any, would be best for the federal government itself. Ideally, the federal government would not move on reform until assessing the success of the provincial experiments. However, one or two more elections that result in unstable minority Parliaments and recurrent political crises could accelerate this timetable. The preferred option should, of course, be subject to a referendum. If the referendums on sovereignty and the Charlottetown Accord achieved nothing else, they at least

established the welcome precedent that, in matters of fundamental reforms to government, the people should be directly
consulted.

Transforming the electoral system to one based on proportional
representation might help to retard or even arrest the decline of
civic participation in the political process, but no one single
measure will restore public interest in, and faith in, the system.
Fareed Zakaria, the editor of *Newsweek International*, argues in *The
Future of Freedom: Illiberal Democracy at Home and Abroad* that liberal
democracy in both the developed and developing world is placing
too great an emphasis on democracy and not enough on the institutions that keep democracy liberal – that is, constrained by law
and custom. Political parties, he argues, have lost their mediating
function, traditional elites have surrendered their influence (or
had it stripped from them), and government is becoming captive
to capricious – and sometimes dangerous – majoritarian whims.
One solution he puts forward is to remove some of the more vital
but politically troublesome elements of decision-making from
elected legislatures and hand them over to impartial, non-elected
bodies. This may sound authoritarian and elitist, but all democracies already employ the practice – at the very least by remov-
ing the judiciary from the direct influence of the legislature. As
well, most advanced democracies, including Canada, have discovered the wisdom of transferring monetary policy to a central
bank independent of legislative influence. That single act appears
to have permanently defeated inflation, and may have succeeded
in smoothing the peaks and valleys of the economic cycle, preventing major recessions.

Although Canadians are, as a whole, far less deferential than they were in previous generations, when the Masseys ruled on behalf of the masses,[9] the people of this country still demonstrate, far more than their American counterpart, a respect for impartial third-party adjudication. The Auditor General and provincial auditors have become critical components of Canadian politics, keeping a watchful eye on government waste and abuse. Independent ethics, information, and privacy commissioners monitor and judge the actions of elected politicians and bureaucrats, and protect citizens from unwarranted intrusion by the state; so important is their impartiality that when Jean Chrétien created an ethics watchdog who answered only to him, the poor fellow was ridiculed by the Opposition and rebuffed by the public, until new legislation created an ethics commissioner who answered directly to Parliament. The independent inquiry, especially, has become such an integral part of the political process that it almost constitutes a fourth branch of government. At any given time, half a dozen federal and provincial inquiries can be underway across the land, convened by governments (often reluctantly, as a result of pressure from opposition parties and the public), and presided over, in most cases, by sitting or retired judges, who investigate the causes of and assign responsibility for alleged mistakes or misdeeds by politicians, bureaucracies, businesses, police, or even the courts themselves. Coupled with professional disciplinary bodies and Royal Commissions that investigate broad subjects of national importance, they constitute a parallel system of governance; without them, there would be little legitimacy left to the political process at all.

And yet, like all good things, watchdogs and inquiries can be abused. Ultimately, stripping our elected bodies of authority and politicians of their responsibility, while vesting their powers in impartial tribunals, weakens the already frayed bonds between the elected official and the voter, distancing the citizen even further from his government. Beyond that, public inquiries, and even the Auditor General, are starting to lose their lustre, with inquiry commissioners accused of bias and auditors questioned on their overheated use of language.[10]

We need a way to bind the body politic more intimately to its government, while avoiding the abuses of direct democracy, limiting reliance on unelected tribunals, and promoting sound decision-making. British Columbia might have come up with the very thing.

Liberal premier Gordon Campbell arrived as premier of British Columbia in 2001 determined to prevent the recurrence of a previous outcome in which his party had won the popular vote but, thanks to vote splits, lost the election to the NDP. He handed the job of coming up with a method for investigating electoral reform to Gordon Gibson, a former leader of the party, and fellow at the conservative Fraser Institute. Gibson recommended the creation of a citizens assembly – in essence, a large jury of randomly selected citizens who would study the electoral system and recommend what, if any, reforms were needed, with those recommendations submitted to the public for ratification through a referendum. The selection process was slightly manipulated to ensure that one man and one woman would be chosen from each riding in the province, and two places were reserved for aboriginal representatives among the 160 citizens who ultimately agreed to join the assembly. For a year, while keeping their regular jobs and family responsibilities, members of the assembly pored over academic studies, listened to experts, and met regularly to discuss the strengths and weaknesses of both the existing FPTP system, and possible alternatives. It was they who, in November 2004, recommended that the province adopt the form of proportional representation known as Single Transferable Vote. STV turned out to be a hard sell in British Columbia, thanks to its mind-boggling complexity. The assembly members, it seems, became such experts on the subject of voting systems that they ended up choosing a form of proportional representation that only purists could admire. (More prosaically, members of the assembly explained that STV tended to weaken the power of party elites, which they considered desirable.) Nonetheless, the 57-per-cent support that their proposal received clearly showed that British Columbians were ready for a change.

Despite the ambiguous result in the referendum, citizens assemblies hold enormous potential to become an important new tool for solving some of the more intractable problems of Canadian democracy. For example, Gibson has argued that a national citizens assembly should be convened to investigate the question of Senate reform.

Even the Fathers of Confederation knew they'd botched the job when they designed the Senate. It was "just the worst body that could be contrived – ridiculously the worst," one contemporary parliamentarian commented.[11] The Upper House was intended to represent regional interests within the federal government. But liberal reformers, objecting to its geographic rather than popular composition, pushed through a proposal to have senators appointed for life by the federal government. This, they knew, would discredit the body entirely, ensuring that the House of Commons reigned supreme. And they were right. Close observers of Parliament know that many senators are thoughtful, relatively non-partisan, and reasonably hard-working. Their committee reports are generally better researched, more objective, and more insightful than those that come from the House. And the Senate has occasionally stayed the hand of the House, rejecting legislation that it believes has been too hastily drafted or poorly thought-through, and occasionally (as during the 1988 Free Trade debate) vetoing legislation that it believes lies outside a government's existing mandate. However, whatever its tangible accomplishments, the Senate has an entrenched reputation as a political Valhalla for (almost invariably Liberal) party bagmen, defeated candidates, and friends of the prime minister. It is the most discredited component of the Canadian political system. And since it is incapable of effectively representing the regional interests of the nation, the provincial premiers have taken their place, often becoming – even more than other political parties – the de facto opposition to the federal government of the day.

Some reformers would simply like to see senators elected; others want more radical reform, such as the Triple-E proposal (elected, equal, and effective), which would lead to a wholesale reconstruction of the Senate, with the West receiving a portion of Senate seats equal to its population. (It is currently underrepresented and Atlantic Canada overrepresented, simply because representatives of the latter were at the table when the thing was crafted.) But that would require a constitutional amendment, and Quebec, in particular, would balk at any constitutional changes that weakened its strength in the Upper House.

One solution put forward by Gibson and others would apply the citizens-assembly precedent set in British Columbia to the question of Senate reform. An assembly of, say, three hundred citizens from across Canada, weighted to ensure gender and age

balance and aboriginal participation, would spend the year exam-
ining proposed reforms: studying reports, hearing from experts
and advocates, and periodically meeting (by teleconference as well
as in person) to discuss options. If a consensus emerged, that
proposition could be put to the electors, with the first ministers
committed to reforming the Constitution if the solution received
majority support in all five regions (Atlantic Canada, Quebec,
Ontario, the Prairie provinces, and British Columbia). If the
assembly could not reach a consensus, or if their proposal was
vetoed in one or more region, then at least we'd know that Senate
reform truly was a hopeless proposition.

Citizens assemblies could become a valuable, even integral,
tool in reforming democratic institutions or solving intractable
disputes. They combine the populist element of citizen participation and ratification, with the impartiality of the unelected
tribunal. Just like a courtroom jury, a body of our peers would
deliberate on our behalf and render a verdict – or, in this case, a
recommendation. And they could help to convince Canadians
everywhere that the people, not the politicians or the bureaucrats,
were in charge of reshaping our institutions of governance.

A citizens assembly on Senate reform would have even more
authority if it received its mandate from the Council of the Federation. A new entity, the council has confounded skeptics, rapidly
emerging as a formidable, if sometimes flawed, counterbalance to
the centralizing and intrusive tendencies of the federal power.

Nothing delights an Ottawa-based columnist more than a
meeting of premiers. All of the tools of condescension, sarcasm,
and supposedly superior insight that are the pundit's stock-in-
trade can be brought into play. Premiers are provincial politicians
in every sense of the word, in the eyes of these jaded journalists;

their bureaucrats rank amateurs in the field of statecraft (or so the federal bureaucrats confide, in whispered tones); their incessant demands for more power, more cash, and less accountability self-evident proof that the Imperial Centre must protect is powers and prerogatives, lest these local buffoons be allowed to run away with the country. It's all rubbish, but it is very comforting.

In fact, for as long as this country has existed, premiers have successfully confronted and constrained Ottawa, defending their rights as sovereign governments in the spheres of their jurisdiction, and seeking to wrench back from that Imperial Centre the taxing authority taken from them during and after the Second World War, and never given back. Since the nineteenth century, premiers have met at regular intervals in search of a common front with which to confront the federal power. Because Jean Chrétien, especially, disliked convening first-ministers meetings, premiers conferences became an entrenched annual event, as the provincial first ministers drew on each other for moral and political support in their dealings with Ottawa. In July 2003, Jean Charest, the newly elected Liberal premier of Quebec, proposed creating a Council of the Federation – in essence, a permanent secretariat to help provincial premiers coordinate relations with Ottawa. The Council effectively kept the premiers united during the arduous negotiations leading up to the health-funding agreement with Paul Martin in September 2004. Centralizing federalists, and their apologists in the press, have gone from dismissing the Council with contempt to viewing it with alarm. Provincialists have found the whole thing deeply satisfying.

The Council can't always be effective, since some provinces want things that others don't. And Paul Martin discovered an antidote to provincial power, by inking individual deals with provinces that took asymmetrical federalism past the bounds of reason and into a nightmarish world of chaos driven by his own political needs. But there is a way to make sense of all this.

First, the Council should renew an early, tentative offer to invite the federal government to sit at its table, at least as an observer. This would represent an important, if subtle, evolution in federal–provincial relations. Rather than summoning the premiers to Ottawa whenever there was something the prime minister of the day wished to discuss – as though the federal first minister were some Bourbon king assembling the Estates General for a tax levy – the federal government would instead become part of the ongoing provincial dialogue. That dialogue, ideally, would promote economic co-operation among the provinces and the expansion of national standards in the field of social policy.

Second, the federal government and the Council could work together to replace the patchwork quilt of one-off agreements, special deals, and temporary transfers into a coherent and permanent devolution of the federal spending power to the provincial governments. The deal could provide individual components for individual provinces – New Brunswick, for example, might wish to let Ottawa retain some tax points (as the policy wonks call them) in exchange for predictable transfers, while Alberta might prefer to take back its tax room, and be left alone. This proposal will horrify centralists, because Ottawa's role in domestic policy would diminish. Worse, a portion of the federal bureaucracy might be transferred to provincial governments along with the tax room. People might have to move from Ottawa to Regina, an idea that for the federal mandarinate simply does not bear contemplation.

To scare us out of agreeing to such a devolution, the centralists argue that transferring tax points will lead to the end of national standards in social programs. This is bosh to start with, since each province interprets the Canada Health Act, for example, its own way: Quebec is festooned with private MRI clinics, which are banned in Ontario. But if national standards are such a Holy Grail, then the best way to preserve them is through the Council of the Federation, where provincial governments could meet, with Ottawa in attendance but not in charge, to decide among themselves what appropriate national standards they wish to share. National standards, after all, need not be federal standards.

Ottawa can still have a role. It can act as a liaison, bringing different sides together and leading the discussion. It can offer its expertise in areas where provinces struggle to grasp complex problems; it can promote best-practices, so that all jurisdictions can benefit from one jurisdiction's success; and it can serve as a neutral referee, in areas of interprovincial dispute. The trick is for Ottawa to work with the provinces, through the Council, rather than to dictate to them, through a first-ministers' meeting.

Already, the provinces are learning to co-operate in a limited fashion. Because Western provinces banded together to develop a common curriculum in education (mostly to save money on textbooks) in the early 1990s, and because the Atlantic Canadian provinces did the same, and because the two groups consulted each other and shared ideas, and because Ontario drew from both their examples when it revised its curriculum, there is now in English Canada at least the potential for developing a common national curriculum. Not only would such a curriculum promote shared perceptions, it would make it easier for children to pick up their studies where they left off when a family moved from Saskatoon to Bathurst. Were the federal government to attempt to impose a national curriculum on the provinces, there would be riots in the legislatures. But the provinces could succeed where Ottawa would surely fail.

The Council is also at work on one of those perennial bug-bears of federalism: free trade among provinces. Many provincial governments put up so many barriers against workers and busi-nesses from other provinces entering their domain that it is sometimes easier for a province to trade with the United States than with another province. People who think the Americans are nefarious in their efforts to impose tariffs on softwood lumber should examine the obscene lengths the Quebec government has been willing to go to to keep out Ontario construction workers.

Critics sneer at provincial efforts to break through inter-provincial trade barriers (as though Ottawa has had any more success). But the Council of the Federation is like a precocious infant, weak and dependent at present, but with enormous poten-tial. Developed wisely, it could become a vital forum for advanc-ing the cause of binding the country together voluntarily rather than with federally imposed chains.

Another way to expand citizen participation in the political process is to lower the voting age.

Sometimes an idea can languish on the margins of debate for decades, until suddenly someone shines a light on it and it becomes sexy. Lowering the voting age is just such an idea. Its attractiveness is rooted both in history and in contemporary concerns. The history of English democracy is the history of an expanding franchise. Prior to the nineteenth century, anyone could cast a ballot, as long as they owned property, which only a better sort of people possessed. The American franchise was, in theory, broader, but there was the small problem that blacks not only did not own property, in the South they were considered property. Canada had property restrictions of its own: in 1867 only 11 per cent of the citizenry was eligible to vote. Not until 1874 was the secret ballot introduced, which was a major inconvenience to party strongmen wishing to bribe or intimidate voters. The property qualification was abolished in 1876, but, although Manitoba expanded the franchise to women in 1916, Quebec didn't see the light until 1940. South Asian, Chinese, and Japanese citizens were prohibited from voting until 1948. The Inuit received the right to vote in 1950, Indians on reservations were added in 1960, although, again, Quebec didn't extend the right to native women until 1968. Courts have intervened to extend voting rights to inmates and to the mentally disabled, and in 1970 the federal voting age was lowered to eighteen. There is, in other words, an entrenched momentum toward expanding the franchise to the widest reasonable limit. The question, then, is what's so special about eighteen.

After all, the age of sexual consent is fourteen. Political parties typically permit party members fourteen or older to cast a ballot in leadership contests. Sixteen-year-olds are entitled, with restrictions, to drive a car. They can also join the army. Why should someone who can drive a car, choose a prime minister, fight for their country, or pick a lover not be able to vote? Lowering the voting age will increase voter participation, by getting young people into the habit of voting early and often – municipally, provincially, and federally, that is.

On the other hand, the age group that votes the least currently is the eighteen to twenty-five cohort. Expanding the pool to include sixteen- and seventeen-year-olds might actually drive the participation rate down: why would these teenagers be any less apathetic than their older brothers and sisters?

They might be less apathetic if the school curriculum placed a greater emphasis on teaching them civics and Canadian history. Now this suggestion is itself fraught with danger. First, everyone with a cause wants to get their hands on the education system. Music is vital to developing teamwork (band practice) and an aesthetic sense; without more math and science we won't be able to compete; physical education must be re-emphasized to fight juvenile obesity; without heritage courses immigrant Canadians will lose their connection to their place of origin. With all these pressures, no wonder history is now relegated, typically, to a single mandatory course in high school, with civics occupying a half-course, if that.

In some ways, this is not so bad a thing, since history as taught in schools is mostly pure propaganda. History courses are how adults instill approved prejudices in the young. The very oldest among us will remember when history courses taught students of the glories of our British heritage (and warned us against fraternizing too closely with the lawless rebels to the south). In more modern times, history courses have been used to instill Marxist theory, feminism, victimization, and assorted other mechanisms of class consciousness and guilt in students. Media courses are captive to Chomsky conspiracy theorists, while civics courses provide lessons on the evils of polling, political advertising, and lobbyists. No one can accuse the typical provincial history or civics curriculum of Pollyannaish naïveté.

Nonetheless, unless we consider Canadian democracy expendable, an increased emphasis on civics, especially, must be part of our package of democratic reforms. This is particularly true given the present high rate of Chinese immigration. It is well known within political circles that immigrants from the Indian sub-continent are politically active, while immigrants from China are less so. That isn't surprising, given India's lively democratic tradition, and the lack of it in China. Voter apathy from immigrants whose mother country has little or no experience with democracy could be contributing to the decline in voter turnout; if so, it could have dangerous long-term consequences for the health of Canada's political institutions. The solution is to entrench civics lessons in the curriculum early and reinforce it often. Lowering the voting age to sixteen will only help reverse the decline in turnout if students thoroughly understand why their vote is important and how the system they are supporting with that vote works. Although this book has defended a certain measure of ahistoricism as the necessary price of preserving a multicultural Canada, new Canadians and young Canadians do need to know that the tolerant and diverse society that we enjoy today came at a price and as a result of deliberate choices made at pivotal moments in this country's history. They need to know this in order to appreciate the importance of their democratic and multicultural inheritance, and the responsibility that will reside with them to preserve it.

Whether it is the chicken or the egg, Canada is also witnessing, along with other democracies, a steady decline in the power of political parties. There is irony in this, for the erosion of the party system is itself the result of improved governance. Political parties traditionally expanded their base and their coffers by rewarding their supporters on assuming office. The joke in Prince Edward

Island has long been that with every change of government, all the snowplow operators are fired and new ones hired. Up until the 1980s, it was well nigh to impossible to get a coveted job at a government liquor store in Ontario unless you had connections to the Progressive Conservative Party. And it sure didn't hurt to be a good Liberal if you wanted to make your way up the ladder at the Post Office.

But with each succeeding scandal, the power of government to employ the tools of patronage has been circumscribed. The public service has been steadily professionalized; Crown corporations are less likely to do political favours for their political masters (and the abuses revealed by the Auditor General and investigated by the Gomery inquiry will ensure that arm's-length means an even-longer arm); the symbiotic relationship between political parties and big business has been constrained by campaign finance reform. Although you would never know it from reading the rants of pundits in the newspapers, government has been getting steadily cleaner for decades. The scandals of the quiet present would make a nineteenth-century party boss laugh with scorn.

At their traditional best, political parties helped cement the nation. The local MP or party boss knew the concerns of his riding's constituents, and communicated those concerns to the national caucus or party leadership. Political parties helped broker regional compacts, while articulating a common national purpose. But this conception of the party has been in decline for decades. Broadcasting technology has made it both easier and more important for the party to sell its leader directly to citizens. Polling has replaced the front porch for gathering information on the mood of the electorate. And as each patronage tap has been closed, the tangible benefits of party membership have diminished. No wonder even the Liberal Party is having trouble keeping its members loyal, its debt manageable, and its troops united.

Still, there's nothing for it. The days of brokerage politics by party elites are fading away, to be replaced with mechanisms exquisitely tuned to voter preferences, even if the voters themselves don't know exactly what it is they prefer. In some ways, the real problem is that the mechanics of democracy haven't kept pace: institutions, habits, and values created in the nineteenth century must adapt to a twenty-first-century world in which ideas are communicated instantaneously. Why on earth must we still trudge to high-school gyms, community centres, and church basements on election day to vote, when we can do our banking on the Internet?

A healthy democracy will not be afraid to exploit new mechanisms better suited to the age. So let the experiments begin. Bring on the citizens assemblies; let the voting age be lowered; introduce proportional representation; try out alternative methods of voting. And if all else fails, then we may have to adopt the Australian expedient of requiring people to vote by law. Democracy is too precious, and too fragile, to let it be compromised by neglect. Besides, the Australians hardly have a reputation for being a nation of sheep.

LET'S GO FURTHER

At the bottom of each article written by a staff columnist, the *Globe and Mail* publishes the e-mail address of the writer. I typically receive from twenty to forty responses from readers each day (although that number can skyrocket if the subject is abortion, gay marriage, Jewish or Muslim Canadians, Western alienation, French-language rights, or Atlantic Canadian dependence).[1] Many of the letters are thoughtful rebuttals, but some are simply snarls – from Alberta separatists, aggrieved Newfoundlanders, infuriated Anglo-Saxons, insulted immigrants, zealots from a variety of religions, insufferable gay-rights activists, insufferable homophobes, or people who don't seem to realize that their real problem is they lead unhappy lives.

In febrile moments, I imagine an immigration policy that would truly transform Canada. Each time a new arrival gratefully set foot on our soil, one of the complainers would be deported. We'd make sure they weren't sent to a country that practises torture (although sitting beside one of these malcontents at a dinner party is a form of torture all its own), but we'd also ensure that their new hosts did not speak their language, so that no one would have to listen to them.

Of course, we'd have to give the countries we sent these people to a lot of money, but it would be a sound investment to diminish the incessant, nasal whines of those who seek to tear Canada down rather than build it up. And such a law would certainly withstand a Charter challenge, for what could be more reasonable and justified in this free and democratic society than to banish these sour souls?

Unavoidably, this book has spent some time diagnosing the ills that beset the Canadian polity. It has recommended solutions to many of those problems. But let's go further. Let's imagine the Canada that could be, and the things we could do to make that Canada a reality. Some of the suggestions that follow are essential if this country is to transcend its current limitations; others are, well, out there. But all are aimed at pointing us toward the Canada that we can become. Take a deep breath, and let's get started.

This book has argued for increasing the emphasis on immigration, as a solution to economic and demographic challenges, and as the foundation of Canada's amazing experiment in diversity. Yes, there are problems: the refugee determination system is open to abuse; failed claimants too often use legal loopholes to delay their departure for years, or disappear entirely. Political opportunism — yes, that's you, Liberals — leads to too great an emphasis on reuniting families, resulting in elderly arrivals who speak neither official language, have few job prospects, and who add to the strain on health care and other social services. Meanwhile, economic migrants risk descending into poverty, in part due to delays in recognizing foreign credentials. These chronic obstacles to progress need to be fixed, and it is a testament to the sclerosis of the federal government that Immigration Canada is unable to fix them.

But let's not obsess about the negatives. Immigration remains Canada's biggest success story. Let's build on that success. Let's commit right here and now to increasing the intake of immigrants in Canada by 10 per cent a year, until we reach a level equal to 1 per cent of the population. That would entail an increase of about 100,000 people a year over the current level of approximately 225,000, and would entrench Canada's enviable reputation as the world's most immigrant-friendly country.

And then, let's go further.

Atlantic Canada's economic decline will not be reversed until it starts to bring in its fair share of immigrants. Let's commit to ensuring that 10 per cent of Canada's immigrants, or about thirty-two thousand people, settle in Atlantic Canada each year. Imagine: In five years, that would represent an influx greater than the current population of Prince Edward Island. In less than twenty years, the intake would equal that of Newfoundland's population. In a single generation, Atlantic Canada would be transformed.

It would not be to every Atlantic Canadian's liking. Too many of the citizens of the region continue to cling to their Celtic past. They celebrate their proud heritage oblivious to the impact it is having on present prospects. Asian immigrants don't care about the Auld Alliance; they aren't interested in seeing tax dollars wasted on propping up rural communities whose *raison d'être* vanished years ago. They're all for keeping the pretty buildings, but not for retaining the mindset that accompanies them. They want to live in a place that looks forward with confidence, not backward with resentment.

It was probably a mistake for the federal government to cede to Quebec control over the selection of its economic-class immigrants. But the precedent has been set, and what was done for reasons of expediency in Quebec's case could be exploited for purposes of renewal in the Maritimes and Newfoundland. Atlantic Canadian provinces, acting as a region, should negotiate a new immigration arrangement with the federal government, aimed at reaching and sustaining the 10-per-cent target. The points system used to rate potential immigrants could be modified, even lowered, to make it easier for applicants to qualify for entry to Canada, provided they are willing to settle in one of the four Atlantic provinces and provided they agree to live there for a period of at least five years.

Inevitably, such an arrangement would be challenged in court, as a violation of the Charter guarantee of freedom of mobility. If the challenge succeeded, then federal and provincial governments should invoke the Charter's notwithstanding clause. Some purists object to any application of that constitutional hammer, citing Quebec's decision to apply it to protect legislation limiting English-language rights. But the truth is that the clause has also been invoked by the Yukon, Saskatchewan, and Alberta, for such prosaic and uncontroversial purposes as permitting women to collect pensions earlier than men, and enforcing back-to-work legislation. Protecting legislation that encourages immigration to Atlantic Canada would be exactly the sort of pragmatic purpose the clause was intended for in the first place.

This is the sort of aggressive immigration policy that Atlantic Canada needs, to invigorate its stagnant culture and revive its moribund economy. Such change can't be forced on Atlantic Canadians: they must embrace it themselves. But immigration is the necessary and almost-sufficient condition for Atlantic renewal. Yes, historical memories will be lost. But history is mostly misery; it is the story of your tribe against all the other tribes. Toronto has paid the price of ahistoricism, in pursuit of a genuinely multi-cultural society. And Toronto has proved it's worth the price.

Like people everywhere, Canadians sometimes hobble their freedom of action with sterile arguments about the past. This is especially true of the challenge facing us in improving the quality of life for native peoples. Both sides are to blame. First Nations leaders cultivate exquisite grudges about past injustices, and dream of recovering lost sovereignty, as if either could guarantee health, happiness, and prosperity to a native child born today. White Canadians, guilty over past sins, resentful over aboriginals' special status, and in despair over prospects for improvement, try to pretend the problems of poverty and discrimination don't exist, or assume that nothing can be done. New Canadians simply don't understand the predicament.

Many observers argue that the Department of Indian and Northern Affairs should be dismantled. But the leaders of

Canada's Indian, Métis, and Inuit peoples are equally intractable. That said, the Paul Martin government is the first in a generation to attempt real reform. And in its proposals lie the seeds of renewal, including meaningful investments in education, health care, and housing.

But let's go further. Let's give every aboriginal child the very best education this society has to offer. Let's get the federal and provincial governments to sign an education charter, in which both sides promise that on-reserve schools will meet or exceed provincial standards. Let's give on-reserve parents educational vouchers, so that if the reserve school cannot meet their children's needs, they can send their children to the school of their choice.

Some reserves are in locations too remote for families to access an off-reserve alternative. Let's shut them down. Not only are these communities unable to provide a decent education and a decent living for their people, they are too often riven with alcohol, drug, physical, and sexual abuse. If it is illogical for provincial governments to prop up communities that make no economic sense, it is sheer insanity to subsidize remote reservations that offer their young nothing but dependence, addiction, and suicide. Stubbornly clinging to mythical pasts while refusing to face the tumultuous present is a trap of false expectations into which too many indigenous Canadians fall. Reserves that are economically viable – and there are many of them – should sell off their lands to their residents. The best way to improve the housing stock on reserves is for Natives to own their houses. Indigenous communism in land ownership is as inappropriate to this country as indigenous defence of racial purity. Let's settle the land claims. Let's encourage self-government. Let's introduce private property on reserves.

Let's insist on the very best in aboriginal education and economic development. And where that isn't possible, let's move on.

As mentioned earlier, half of Canada's aboriginal population now lives off-reserve, part of the ongoing emptying out of the spaces between Canada's large cities. It is a military axiom not to reinforce failure, yet a disproportionate amount of Canada's wealth is diverted to rural and remote areas, while its cities struggle to accommodate the influx of internal and foreign migrants. In part, this is due to well-intentioned attempts to renew the decaying and declining parts of the country; but in large measure it also results from the influence of rural politicians on federal and provincial legislatures. There are economic and immigration policies, and revisions to the federal power balance, which could mitigate this distortion. But let's go further. Let's enlarge the House of Commons by one hundred members, with Elections Canada directed to ensure that the new electoral boundaries equalize existing disparities in riding size. Prince Edward Island would retain the four seats it has been guaranteed, but its effect would be diluted. We might have to get rid of the desks in the House of Commons, of course, but they're hardly needed, since most of the honourable members devote all their time to playing with their BlackBerrys.

More substantially, the federal government should fold all regional assistance into a simplified equalization program that will limit, by statute, the extent to which taxpayer dollars from contributing provinces can be transferred to receiving provinces. The Employment Insurance system should be returned to its original purpose of ensuring against temporary job loss, rather than propping up economies based on seasonal employment. The ethos of the federal government must change from maximizing to minimizing transfers of wealth from one part of the country to the other. Rural communities must either become self-sustaining, or extinct. Prediction: Although there will be temporary dislocations, the freeing up of resources will benefit, not only the already-rich parts of the country, but the poorer ones, as well. Halifax, Moncton, and St. John's are all, in different ways, burgeoning cities that are being kept from reaching their full potential by wasteful transfers of wealth to their own hinterlands. Minimizing horizontal transfers will change this six-city country into a ten-city country. And a generation from now, people will wonder why the politicians wasted so much time and money trying to prop up outports and family farms.

Just as much of the Canadian Constitution is unwritten – being derived, instead, from British precedents – so too Canada embraces an unwritten social charter based on principles of universal access to health care and education, combined with an accepted right to some form of accommodation and income for those who cannot provide for themselves. This Charter is national. The question is: Must it also be federal?

In the depths of the Depression, with the provincial government bankrupt, Mackenzie King reluctantly agreed that the federal government should assume responsibility for unemployment insurance. With each succeeding decade, and with ever-greater enthusiasm, Ottawa gathered to itself responsibility for crafting the elements of the Canadian social charter: old-age pensions; universal public health care; access to post-secondary education; welfare and social housing; and now daycare. The whole thing is a mistake.

Albertans, who are wealthy and independent, want to run their health-care system as they see fit. So do Quebeckers, who are poorer but even more independent. New Brunswickers, however, are poor and dependent, which is why they defend the principle of national standards. What they're really defending is the right of New Brunswickers to a health-care system as good as Alberta's, even though they can't afford it, which is why the money inevitably comes from Alberta (and Ontario, and sometimes Saskatchewan and British Columbia), via Ottawa. The same is true, though to a lesser extent (because Ottawa interferes to a lesser extent) in post-secondary education, social assistance, subsidized housing, and child care. National standards are invariably federal standards, set by Ottawa, and financed through transfers from richer to poorer. Is it fair? That depends on your perspective. But the system has been conclusively proven to be inefficient, draining money from productive to unproductive parts of the country, with no demonstrable improvements to show for it.

The solution, argues the Conservative Party, is for Ottawa to stop interfering in areas of provincial jurisdiction. But this is a half-hearted solution, and half-hearted solutions are the worst solutions of all. Let's go further. Let's pursue a realignment of federal and provincial powers that will ensure each is doing what it does best. Let's reshape the federation.

It would begin with a comprehensive downloading of federal tax points to the provinces. Ottawa, in effect, would be giving back to the provincial governments the tax room it gobbled up more than half a century ago, during and after the Second World War.

As well as righting this fiscal imbalance, Ottawa would abandon its claims to set and maintain national standards in health care and child care; it would relinquish its role in funding post-secondary education; it would get out of the subsidized housing game; it would make welfare an exclusively provincial jurisdiction. It would maintain the constitutionally protected equalization programs, but it would eliminate seasonal Employment Insurance, regional development agencies, and all other forms of targeted funding. It would, however, continue to deliver funds to provinces that, for lack of a tax base, are unable to provide the social services that have devolved to them. So while Alberta, Ontario, B.C., Saskatchewan, and Quebec assumed exclusive control over social policy, Manitoba, Atlantic Canada, and the territories would probably continue to receive limited federal assistance. Ottawa would still monitor social programs and encourage shared goals and standards, in co-operation with the Council of the Federation. But these standards would be voluntary, achieved by consensus rather than financial coercion. As a test of how the new system might function, the federal government could work with the provinces on a voluntary and co-operative basis to expand the national curriculum, ensuring that students in all parts of Canada learned roughly the same thing at roughly the same time.

This federal download of funding and responsibilities must not, however, be one-sided. There are areas of shared federal–provincial jurisdiction that Ottawa is ultimately more competent to handle. In exchange for ceding tax room to the provinces, the federal government would assume greater responsibility over environmental regulation. After all, not only do fish swim, but water flows and air circulates. Ottawa already has considerable powers in this area, but all provincial governments should explicitly acknowledge, as part of an environmental accord, the primary responsibility of the federal government to legislate and regulate to protect land, air, and water. The federal government should also be given greater responsibility for inspection and regulation, whether of food or drugs or consumer products or businesses. There should be only one, national securities regulator, and the provinces should finally and explicitly agree to drop all non-tariff barriers between themselves, ceding to Ottawa the power to penalize or disallow any actions that hamper the free flow of goods, services, and people across provincial borders. Ottawa should continue to regulate communications and transportation. It should have exclusive direction over preventing and responding to pandemics and other invasive health threats. It should continue to fund scientific research, inside and outside the university (though such grants should avoid becoming regional development programs in disguise). It should assume exclusive authority for regulating the professions: a lawyer who passes the bar in Newfoundland should be able to practise law anywhere in Canada outside Quebec (whose legal framework is based on the Napoleonic code rather than English common law). It should assume exclusive responsibility for the justice system, eliminating provincial crimes, provincial courts, and provincial jails. And the provinces should abandon their encroachments on the federal power to manage foreign relations. Shut down the overseas trade missions. Stop demanding seats at La Francophonie. Abandon all claims of veto over international agreements affecting areas of provincial jurisdiction.

Can't you just hear the premiers howling? They want Ottawa simply to "right the fiscal imbalance" by ceding tax points and letting them get on with their respective jobs. In principle, they have a case: Ottawa is implicitly violating the Constitution by using its spending power to interfere in areas of their jurisdiction. But politics is about horse-trading. If the provinces want Ottawa out of social policy, then they are going to have to surrender some powers that they currently share with Ottawa. The result would be a less ambiguous federation, with each level of government responsible for what it's responsible for. What reason is there for not doing it, other than that nobody has yet tried?

A cleaner, clearer division of powers would allow Ottawa greater freedom to focus on the things that should matter to it most. And nothing should matter more than the environment. Canada has done everything with the Kyoto Protocol on global warming except meet its commitments. Only half of the estimated $10 billion required to reduce greenhouse-gas emissions to 1990 levels has actually been set aside; nor is there any realistic hope that even the full $10 billion would do the job. Carbon-dioxide emissions in Canada have steadily increased every year since the protocol was signed, and yet by 2012 we must somehow have magically reversed this process. The time has come for the federal government to admit the truth. Canada will not meet its Kyoto targets.

Nonetheless, Canadians have both a moral and personal responsibility to identify, target, and improve the most serious threats to our environment, those that threaten both our planet and our quality of life. Today, the single most pressing environmental issue affecting the Canadian population is smog.

The Canadian and American governments must assign, as their highest bilateral priority, reversing the buildup of smog.

Already, they have taken steps to limit sulphur-dioxide emissions, and the Ontario government has committed to closing its coal-fired generating plants by 2007. Let's go further. Let's reopen the 1991 Canada–U.S. Air Quality Agreement, imposing rigorous new standards on nitrogen-oxide emissions (and we should get tough with mercury emissions, while we're at it). Let's improve bilateral monitoring and impose tough new penalties for industries that fail to meet standards. Let's work in lockstep to impose major improvements in vehicle emissions (goodbye, Hummers and SUVs), while the federal government, with or without provincial consent, expands its regulatory control over air quality. Not only will these steps reduce smog, they will reduce carbon-dioxide emissions as well. Who knows? One day we might even meet our Kyoto targets.

A comprehensive bilateral air-quality agreement might help to reverse the recent deterioration of trust and collaboration between the Western Hemisphere's two developed nations. Trade disputes and botched diplomacy over Iraq and ballistic missile defence have left relations between Canada and the United States no better than frostily correct. Paul Martin's pragmatic approach has been to work with presidents George W. Bush and Vicente Fox in tri-lateral negotiations that target specific irritants and search for means to ease them. But we must go much, much further. North America's future hinges on a dynamic, elastic, and Teflon-smooth trading relationship between the two countries. The federal government should approach Washington with comprehensive and far-reaching proposals: to integrate our regulatory regimes; to craft a continental labour-mobility agreement, permitting

Canadians and Americans to move freely between the two countries; to harmonize professional standards and accreditation.

One key element of restoring an attitude of mutual trust between the two governments is for Canada to reverse a generation of decline in the quality of its military. The Paul Martin government has already taken significant steps, but there is, as has already been mentioned, much further to go. If Canada is not prepared to make its contribution to continental security by participating in the missile defence system, there are other steps it can take. We need to consistently increase defence spending by at least 10 per cent a year each year for a decade. With that money, we need to fashion a well-trained and well-equipped rapid-response force of at least battalion strength, complete with heavy-lift capability, bolstered by naval support and supply, able to immediately deploy overseas for extended periods, in co-operation with allied forces, be they part of a United Nations, NATO, or an ad hoc coalition.

The ability to project military force, even at this modest level, will give teeth to Canada's commitment to its own doctrine, the Responsibility to Protect, of intercession by concerned governments in failed states whose leaders are unable or unwilling to protect their own people from violence and danger. We can go further. The federal government has already committed to participating in Aga Khan's Global Centre for Pluralism. We can expand and complement this notion, by fostering a Canadian Institute for Democratic Development. It could involve private as well as public financing and participation; could be headed by an eminent Canadian (rather than a bureaucrat); could draw on the resources of Foreign Affairs, the Canadian International Development Agency (CIDA), the military and police; as well as universities and non-governmental organizations to centralize and focus Canadian efforts to foster democracy around the world. Such an institute could help monitor elections, train police forces and judiciaries, offer advice on building legal and governmental systems that protect the rights of minorities in multi-ethnic communities. Democracy is on the march around the globe, from Ukraine to Brazil. Canada should be second to no nation in nurturing fledgling democracies, until they mature into stable liberal-democratic societies.

This country is finally, tentatively, reversing the steady decline of its foreign profile and its foreign aid. We have not gone nearly far enough. The federal government must produce a clear plan to bring foreign-aid spending up to 0.7 per cent of Gross Domestic Product, a commitment we first proposed and that other nations, but not Canada, have committed to meeting. Direct foreign aid should target the region of greatest need: sub-Saharan Africa, where the scourge of HIV/AIDS and poverty walk hand in deadly hand. The greatest emphasis should be placed on educating women and helping to protect them from abusive partners. Education and lower birth rates are the ultimate solution to African poverty and disease. Canada should have no greater foreign-policy priority.

Foreign and defence policy matter as much at home as abroad. We must increase our efforts to protect our continent, by sharing intelligence and coordinating continental security policies with the Americans and Mexicans. But we must go past that. The Canadian government should enlarge the capacity and mandate of the Canadian Coast Guard beyond search-and-rescue to include patrol and deterrence – of poaching, drug smuggling, or trafficking in illegal immigrants. We must pay special attention as well to our northern perimeter, improving the capability of the Canadian Forces to defend our Arctic territories, in the air, on land, and under the sea.

Foreign policy, defence policy, and environmental policy all intersect in one crucial spot: those portions of the Grand Banks that currently lie outside Canada's coastal jurisdiction. Over-fishing by foreign vessels in these waters continues to deplete fish stocks, threatening to turn what was once the richest ocean resource in the world into a desert. Repeated efforts to obtain stricter control over fishing off the so-called nose and tail of the Grand Banks, and of the Flemish Cap, have been rewarded only with promises in principle and obstruction in practice. It's time to go further. After giving fair warning, Canada should extend its jurisdiction over fish stocks to include the nose, tail, and Cap. Fishing is to be strictly controlled, with Canada doing the con-trolling. No nation is to be discriminated against and none, including Canada, favoured. But our impartial yet firm steward-ship is the only hope for preventing one of the principal sources of our food supply from exhaustion. At first, the rest of the world will excoriate us. In time, they'll thank us.

Once we have sorted out the jurisdictional conflicts at home, and defined a more confident and assertive voice in the world, the final major task is to reform our democratic institutions and processes. Civic engagement is nowhere on the decline more than among the young, on whom the future of democracy rests. The federal government must encourage provincial governments to include both civics and Canadian history as core components of their curriculum – not, however, through tied grants. (We're putting a stop to all that, remember?) Let's take it another step. Let's provide funding that ensures every Canadian student, regardless of where he or she might live, is able to visit the national capital at least once as part of a school trip. Let's reduce the voting age to sixteen, expand programs that encourage students to work in other parts of the country, and make it possible to vote on the Internet. Let's experiment with new electoral systems based on proportional representation at the provincial level, convene a citizens assembly on Senate reform – with their recommendations to be put to a vote that will require majority support in all five regions before it can be passed. And let's go further than anyone has yet been prepared to go: let us introduce legislation at the federal level that sets a ten-year window for restoring turnout at federal elections to a minimum of 70 per cent. If that target isn't met by the assigned deadline, voting at the next and all subsequent federal elections will become compulsory.

In May 2005, the *New York Times'* Canadian correspondent, Clifford Krauss, dared speak the unspeakable. Canadians, he suggested, were hypocrites. "No other country puts such a high premium on its own virtue as does Canada," he wrote. And yet, as he observed, the seamy revelations of the sponsorship scandal had Canadians themselves wondering whether they are any different, or any better, than anyone else.

But there is more to it than political scandal, Krauss went on. Canadians celebrated the environment while shipping toxic asbestos to Europe. (Who knew?) We celebrate free trade and criticize agriculture subsidies, while propping up agricultural marketing boards. And while Canada celebrates its multicultural diversity, "corporate boards and senior political bodies on the federal and provincial levels remain overwhelmingly dominated by people of European stock."[2]

A timely reminder. Canada's self-image is often as divorced from reality as that of any other nation, be it stoic Britain, cultured France, or freedom-loving U.S.A. Nonetheless, nations need these self-embracing myths, which are true to the extent that their citizens believe them to be true and act as though they are true, thus translating the myth into daily experience. What matters about the Canadian mythical self-image is that we finally have one: that after years of muddle and confusion, as we let go of one empire, and tried not to be swallowed by its successor, a picture of Canada emerged in the minds of Canadians, a picture of tolerance and diversity and creativity and good humour – all wrapped up, of course, in an exquisitely cultivated sense of insecurity – that makes Canadians feel, on most days, good about themselves. This is something that, until recently, we lacked. In some countries, it's called patriotism. It feels good.

Perhaps, objectively, Canada is not the world's most successful country. Perhaps it's Finland, or Slovenia. Maybe the United States is right in believing it is the world's *only* true success story. But Canada, for the first time in its history, can at least stake its own claim with a straight face. We can stack our economic performance, our artistic accomplishments, our political stability, against the best of them. And in our invitation to people from all parts of the world to come join us, in our cosmopolitan, outward-looking, boisterous, splitting-at-the-seams cities, in our confidence that there is nothing ahead but future, no one can touch us.

Because the future is Canada.

N O T E S

INTRODUCTION: And Here We Are

1. Tom Barrett, "Portrait of an immigrant-driven, urban nation: New Canadians lead way in growth, census shows," *Vancouver Sun*, 13 March 2002, p. A1.

2. Elizabeth Thompson, "Canada's population is more people diverse than it's ever been: stats," Montreal *Gazette*, 22 January 2003, p. A2.

3. A. Bélanger and É. Caron Malenfant, *Population Projections of Visible Minority Groups, Canada, Provinces and Regions*, Statistics Canada, March 2005, p. iii.

4. In more recent years, Canada has ranked as low as eighth and as high as fourth. But the statistics for measurement are sufficiently crude – life expectancy, literacy, school enrolments, and standard of living, as measured as gross domestic product per person – that the top-ranked countries are always within statistically insignificant fractions of each other. More important, perhaps, Canada always leads all other G8 nations in the rankings.

5. Though in the city's best dives, indie music lovers mourned the overexposure.

6. Actually, he is usually misquoted. The exact words were: "Canada has been modest in its history, although its history is heroic in many ways. But its history, in my estimation, is only commencing. It is commencing in this century. The 19th century will prove to be the century of the United States. I think we can claim that it is Canada that shall fill the 20th century."

7. Jennifer Hyndman, "Immigrants are not a problem," *Globe and Mail*, 4 July 2003, p. A15.

8. Its Germanic roots were transformed by the invasion of the Norman French, who injected Latin and Greek as well, while Imperial English (blessed by a simple grammar devoid of gender or complex conjugations) has imported words from Australia (*boomerang*) to the Arctic Circle (*kayak*), giving English vastly more words in its vocabulary than that of any other tongue. See Melvyn Bragg, *The Adventure of English: The Biography of a Language*. London: Hodder & Stoughton, 2003.

9. Hamida Ghafour, "For Dutch Muslims, there's a chill in the air," *Globe and Mail*, 19 March 2005, p. F3.

10. The two former colonies that have reached Western levels of economic development, but are not composed primarily of British settlers, are Singapore and Hong Kong, which had been dependencies of Great Britain.

11. The guilt and confusion that accompanied the expulsion of French Acadians from New Brunswick in the 1750s might also have been a factor. Besides, deporting a few thousand Acadians was one thing; trying to depopulate what is now Quebec was obviously impossible.

12. Jack Jedwab, *Migrating North and South: The Impact and Nature of Population Exchanges Between Canada and the U.S.*, Association of Canadian Studies, March 2002, p. 2.

13. There are approximately 415,000 people of Italian origin in the Toronto area, according to Statistics Canada, whereas the population of Bologna, Italy's seventh-largest city, is about 385,000.

14. "Overtaxed and underfunded," *Canada and the World Backgrounder*, 1 May 2004.

15. That country has been able to retain the birth rate of 2.1 children per woman needed to maintain its current population thanks to high birth rates among Hispanic immigrants.

16. Ben Wattenberg, *Fewer: How the New Demography of Depopulation Will Shape Our Future*. Chicago: Ivan R. Dee, 2004.

17. Magomed Omerof, "Depopulation," *WPS Russian Media Monitoring Agency*, 29 November 2004.

18. With Israel, Chile, and Costa Rica.

19. The others are Australia, Ireland, and New Zealand – another British legacy, perhaps? See Niall Ferguson, *Collossus*. New York: Penguin, 2004, p. 337, note 36.

20. Sangeetha Ramaswamy, "Canada dodged recession through trade: Goldman Sachs report," *Bloomberg News*, 31 August 2004.

21. *Nafta Works*, International Trade Canada, 29 December 2003.

CHAPTER ONE: The Politics of Dysfunction

1. That said, the margins of society receive little if any representation in the political process. The very poor, the mentally disabled, the incarcerated are neither courted by nor attracted to any political party, and often feel no attachment to the political process whatsoever. However, many others who choose not to vote – sadly, about half of all electors – nonetheless find their interests represented by one political party or another.

2. The Social Democratic Party (Sweden) and the Liberal Democratic Party (Japan) have dominated the political life of these two countries since the Second World War.

3. The aberrations of Arthur Meighen, Joe Clark, and Kim Campbell are ignored for the purposes of this argument, as they have been by history.

4. Joe Paraskevas, "Stay away from seat projections, pollsters told: Last-minute shift in opinion blamed for botched vote call," *Ottawa Citizen*, 15 September 2004, p. A10.

5. Bill Clinton, *My Life*. New York: Knopf, 2004, p. 144.

6. The speech was reprinted in the June 2003 issue of the now-defunct *Report Magazine*. The Liberal Party gleefully makes it available, at www.liberal.ca/pdf/shse.pdf.

7. In 2004, the high-profile activist MP confessed to, and was convicted of, pocketing a ring from an auction house.

8. James Cowan, "Ethnic voters foil Tories' 905 hopes: Follow tradi-tional voting patterns," *National Post*, 30 June 2004, p. A8.

9. However noble its intention – the program was launched in the wake of the horrific murder of fourteen women at the École Polytechnique at the University of Montreal in 1989 – the plan to register all long guns in Canada was naively conceived and incom-petently executed. Worse, when the Liberal administration realized that costs were escalating beyond all reason, it actively conspired to hide those costs by burying the program's expenses in special esti-mates. Not until a report by the auditor general in 2002 detailed the extent of the debacle – a program that was supposed to pay for itself with fees had already eaten up $1 billion, and was costing more than $100 million a year – were efforts made to bring the program under control.

10. Elizabeth Thompson, "Tories dream big in Quebec," Montreal *Gazette*, 27 November 2004, p. A15.

11. Harper promised to introduce legislation that would permit civil unions for homosexuals, while reserving marriage for opposite-sex couples. Such a law would almost certainly run afoul of the Supreme Court, which would back the provincial appellate courts in declaring the distinction a Charter violation, leaving a Conser-vative government with no choice but to invoke the Constitution's notwithstanding clause. Harper refuses to say whether he would do so.

CHAPTER TWO: Four Solitudes

1. Gerald Hallowell, ed., *The Oxford Companion to Canadian History*. Toronto: Oxford University Press, 2004, p. 625.

2. A. Margaret Evans, *Sir Oliver Mowat*. Toronto: University of Toronto Press, 1992, p. 173.

3. Ingrid Phaneuf, "Public meetings on Windsor start next week," *eSource Canada Business News Network*, 21 March 2005.

4. John Ibbitson, "Fiddling on the Island: Free Mabel Gallant," *Globe and Mail*, 16 December 2002, p. A17.
5. The oil refinery opened in 1974, with considerable federal assistance, employing upwards of five hundred people. But it was poorly designed and badly run, and shut down after only a couple of years of operation. After being handed over to a private consortium in 1987, the factory reopened and employment is back to previous levels, although future prospects are uncertain.

    In the early 1990s, Premier Brian Peckford's lavish ($18-million) public investment in a scheme to grow cucumbers hydroponically not only turned out to be economically unsound, but turned the province into a laughingstock.
6. *Canada's Ethnocultural Portrait: The Changing Mosaic*, Statistics Canada, January 21, 2005.
7. Nutriscience studies how elements in plant life can be used for medical or commercial purposes.
8. Maria Barrados, *The Senior Civil Service System in Canada*. Presentation given at the Conference on Senior Civil Service Systems, Seoul, Korea, 9 December 2004.
9. For example, in April 2003, when the Americans were headed for a quick and easy military victory, and the insurgency had not yet taken root, an Ipsos Reid poll found that only 29 per cent of Quebeckers supported the war, whereas 54 per cent of Canadians outside Quebec supported it. Fifty-four per cent of Ontarians supported the war, and 68 per cent of Albertans. Kim Lunman, "Canadians split on war, poll finds," *Globe and Mail*, 7 April 2003, p. A7.
10. Konrad Yakabuski, "Population key to province's health," *Globe and Mail*, 9 January 2004, p. B2.
11. Close political associates of the French president have been accused of illegally profiting from the oil-for-food program, in which billions of dollars intended in humanitarian aid were siphoned off through corruption and kickbacks.

CHAPTER THREE: Migrations

1. It is the first sentence to his *Mémoires de guerre*.
2. Actually, it was Gen. Sir Edward Spears, Churchill's liaison officer with de Gaulle, who made the remark.
3. The data is taken from *World Population Prospects: The 2002 Revision*, United Nations Population Division, 2003; and from *State of World Population 2004*, United Nations Population Fund, 2004.
4. Michael Meyer, "Birth dearth," *Newsweek International*, 27 September 2004.
5. Immigration and skills data taken from Statistics Canada, as compiled in *Immigration and Skills Shortages*, Canadian Labour and Business Centre, 2003.
6. "Large-scale retirements to help Quebec trim government – Premier," *Dow Jones International News*, 2 October 2003.
7. Andrew Duffy, "Fears of an underclass," *Toronto Star*, 28 September 2004, p. A6.
8. Christopher Worswick, "Immigrants' Declining Earnings: Reasons and Remedies," *Backgrounder*, C.D. Howe Institute, 2004, p. 3.
9. Martin Collacott, "Canada's Immigration Policy: the Need for Major Reform," *Public Policy Sources*. Fraser Institute, 2003, p. 42.
10. Eric Beauchesne, "'Employment barriers' could cost Canada skilled immigrants," *National Post*, 15 September 2004, p. A6.
11. Marina Jimenez, "A star immigrant gives up on Canada," *Globe and Mail*, 19 April 2005, p. A1.
12. Tom Kent, a former Liberal policy adviser, expands on these thoughts in his paper, "'In the National Interest': A Social Policy Agenda for a New Century," *Policy Options*, August 2004, p. 28.
13. "Study: Demographic Trends in Canada's Communities, 1981 to 2001," *The Daily*, Statistics Canada, 31 May 2005.
14. Figures obtained from the Canadian Real Estate Association.
15. Data obtained from Robert Schwandl, "Fifty years of Toronto subway," *UrbanRail.net*, 2004; Steve Munro, "Transit's lost decade:

How paying more for less is killing public transit," *RocketRiders*, 23 April 2002; and the Toronto Transit Commission.

16. Robert Harris, "Bridges of Greater Vancouver," *Discover Vancouver*, 2004.

17. Patti Edgar, "City of disrepair," *Winnipeg Free Press*, 4 April 2004, p. B1.

18. Taylor Lambert, "Calgary needs to grow up, not out," *Calgary Herald*, 27 March 2005, p. A12.

19. A word, here, on nomenclature. Canada's 760,000 Status Indians are officially recognized as Indians as defined by the Indian Act. They are also called, by choice, First Nations. Non-status Indians have lost Indian status, due to marriage, but are still considered part of Canada's aboriginal community. There are also 26,000 Inuit (according to Statistics Canada) living in Canada's North and at least 350,000 Metis (according to the Metis National Council) who are the descendants of the original co-mingling between Indians and the first French explorers, traders, and settlers.

20. *Basic Departmental Data 2000*, Indian and Northern Affairs Canada, 2001.

21. John Ibbitson, "Canada's vanishing people," *Globe and Mail*, 21 September 2004, p. A4. Data obtained from Manitoba, Saskatchewan, Alberta, and federal databases. Researchers wishing to pursue the subject are advised to consult the Indian or aboriginal affairs websites of the relevant jurisdictions.

22. Peter Frayne, *1981 and 2001 Census Tabulations – Aboriginal Lawyers/ Doctors*, Statistics Canada.

23. Data provided by Tyendinaga Band Office and County of Hastings.

24. Lisa Schlein, "Grim picture painted of native health in Canada," *Toronto Star*, 27 November 1999, p. A1.

25. Jon Bricker, "Off-reserve natives in poor health: Study," *National Post*, 28 August 2002, p. A5.

26. Rod Mickleburgh, "Mortality rates among natives under 65 higher than those for other Canadians," *Globe and Mail*, 30 December 1992, p. A5.

27. Data provided by Department of Indian Affairs and Northern Development.

28. Bill Curry, "Minister turns his attention to contentious issue of Indian status," *National Post*, 3 January 2005, p. A7.

CHAPTER FOUR: A New Social Charter

1. Tom Olsen, "Klein sets agenda," *Calgary Herald*, 30 July 2004, p. A3.

2. Liberal democracies are ones in which governments are elected by the broad citizenry (hence the noun) but constrained by laws and institutions such as constitutions and courts that protect the rights of minorities and individuals from possible majoritarian tyranny (hence the adjective).

3. For example, see Joseph Bream, "52% back private care: Quebec, B.C., Prairies favour a user-pay alternative: poll," *National Post*, 26 April 2005, p. A1.

4. Tim Naumetz, "CBC audience less than 6% despite nearly $10 billion in subsidies," *National Post*, 2 April 2004, p. A5.

5. In fact, a broad range of medical services, from dentistry to prescription drugs, lie wholly or partially outside medicare. The more precise definition of socialized medicine is one that, in the delivery of doctor and hospital services, limits the application of private insurance to supplement the publicly-insured system.

6. In 2002, health care consumed the equivalent of 9.6 per cent of the Canadian GDP, as opposed to 14.6 per cent in the United States. However, Canadian health spending equals or exceeds that of many European countries, which often provide superior (and privately supplemented) service.

7. This 1983 legislation, passed by Parliament in the wake of rising concerns over doctors who were charging extra for services, permits the federal government to cut funding to any province deemed to

be violating the act's requirements that health care be government-administered, comprehensive, universal, portable, and accessible.

8. The University of Phoenix has established campuses in British Columbia, and is expanding into Ontario and Alberta, offering degrees principally in business.

9. Ontario Ministry of Education.

10. Data obtained from the Association of Universities and Colleges of Canada, based on data from Statistics Canada and the National Center for Education Statistics in the U.S.

11. Data obtained from the Institute of Higher Education, Shanghai Jiao Tong University.

12. Heather Sokoloff, "Elementary students' test scores improving," *National Post*, 11 November 2004, p. A5.

13. *Measuring Up: Canadian Results of the OECD PISA Study*, Human Resources and Skills Development Canada, Statistics Canada, and the Council of Ministers of Education, December 2004.

14. In post-secondary education, the federal government funds the Canada Student Loans Program for students in financial need, runs the Canada Millennium Scholarship Foundation for superior students in financial need, funds the Registered Education Savings Plan, which helps parents save for their children's education, and supports research projects and programs.

15. Bob Rae, *Ontario: A Leader in Learning*, Government of Ontario, February 2005.

16. Some readers might question the lack of a more direct comparison between Canadian and American educational systems. As in health care, however, the differences between the two systems are so radical as to limit the fruitfulness of such discussion. Racial divisions, class tensions, and middle-class migrations have left the American public education system in a shambles, while the greater reliance on private universities at the post-secondary level also inhibits apples-and-apples discussion. As in most fields of social policy, a more valid comparison can be made with other OECD

nations, whose mix of public and private social services more closely approximates Canada's.

17. Peter Shawn Taylor, "The next Medicare?" *National Post*, 7 December 2004, p. A1.

18. Alberta premier Ralph Klein and Newfoundland and Labrador premier Danny Williams both walked out of the conference, complaining that the federal government wasn't listening to their respective demands, but that's another story. And both provinces signed on to the agreement.

19. Duplicitous in that federal finance ministers Paul Martin, John Manley, and Ralph Goodale fell into a consistent pattern of grossly underestimating the annual federal surplus. The windfall that resulted when the books were finally balanced had to be applied, by law, to the debt – an efficient, if mendacious, approach to deficit reduction.

20. Although the raft of spending announcements contained in the February 2005 budget, coupled with the Liberals' Faustian bargain with the NDP in April 2005 in their efforts to avoid being defeated in the House, threatened to undermine the federal government's fiscal foundations.

21. *The Economist*, 25 September 2003.

22. For more, see Brian Lee Crawley, "Employment insurance causes unemployment," *Halifax Chronicle*, 10 September 2003. Also available at the website of the Atlantic Institute of Market Studies (www.aims.ca).

23. David Naylor and Roger Martin, "A better way to share," *Globe and Mail*, 10 February 2005, p. A25.

24. Jacqueline Thorpe, "It's back to the drawing board," *National Post*, 28 August 2004, p. FP5.

25. A variation is to divide GDP by total number of hours worked by all workers, which is known as labour productivity.

26. J. Baldwin and J.-P. Maynard, "The Output Gap Between Canada

and the U.S.: The Role of Productivity, 1994–2002," *Canadian Economic Observer*, Statistics Canada, January 2005.

27. What is the marginal tax rate? Let's say you make $75,000 a year. Let's say you don't pay any federal or provincial tax at all on the first $15,000 of earnings. From $15,000 to $35,000 your tax rate is 20 per cent. Let's say that from $35,000 to $70,000 the tax rate is 35 per cent, and after $70,000, you are taxed at 50 per cent. Your marginal tax rate is 50 per cent, because every additional dollar you earn will be taxed at that maximum rate, even though your overall income tax rate will be lower, because not all of your income is taxed at that rate, and some of it isn't even taxed at all.

28. Roger Martin, *Taxing Smarter for Prosperity*, Institute for Competitiveness and Prosperity, March 2005.

CHAPTER FIVE: Making Canada Matter

1. Executive federalism is the kind that takes place when the federal and provincial first ministers or their representatives, meeting in private, hammer out policy in areas of joint concern. It's how most of the big decisions get made, these days.

2. Daniel Leblanc, "Keep troops at home, senators say," *Globe and Mail*, 13 November 2002, p. A4.

3. Data obtained from Statistics Canada, which adds the caveat that ethnic origin "refers to the ethnic or cultural group(s) to which the respondent's ancestors belong. An ancestor is someone from whom a person is descended, and is usually more distant than a grandparent. Ethnic origin pertains to the ancestral 'roots' or background of the population, and should not be confused with citizenship or nationality." There are 963,190 people who reported South Asian ethnic origins either alone or in combination with other origins in 2001.

4. Hugh Winsor, "'Can do' general right choice for forces," *Globe and Mail*, 17 January 2005, p. A7.

5. Kevin Bissett, "Canadian troops left to beg for basic equipment," Canadian Press, 17 October 2004.

6. Stephen Thorne, "Canada seeks NATO help to run Kabul peace-keeping operation," Canadian Press, 21 February 2003.

7. Hans Island, a barren bit of rock between Ellesmere Island and Greenland, is claimed by both Denmark and Canada. War is unlikely, but both countries consider the island important. Ownership could affect control over future shipping routes, especially in the event of global warming, and there is always the possibility that oil or gas lies offshore.

8. Andrew Cohen, *While Canada Slept: How We Lost Our Place in the World*. Toronto: McClelland & Stewart, 2003, p. 29.

9. Michael Adams, *Fire and Ice: The United States, Canada and the Myth of Converging Values*, Toronto: Penguin Canada, 2004, pp. 1-2.

10. This chronic irritant stems from differing patterns of land ownership in the two countries. Most of Canada's forests are Crown land, while most American forests are privately owned. Canadian governments charge lumber companies licences, or "stumpage fees," to harvest lumber from Crown lands. The Americans complain that the fees are too low, and constitute a subsidy, and so impose tariffs on the import of Canadian softwood lumber. This hurts the Americans as much as the Canadians, since the tariffs increase the price of housing construction, but the American forest industry is a powerful force in Washington.

11. Michael Gawenda and Tim Colebatch, "U.S. creates special Australian work visas," *The Age*, 12 May 2005.

12. The Bush administration is determined to drill for oil in the Arctic National Wilderness Refuge (ANWR), despite opposition within the United States and protests from Canada, which is concerned about the potential effect on the Porcupine caribou herb, which migrates between the two countries.

CHAPTER SIX: The Democratic Paradox

1. Ellen Goodman, "A patchwork quilt of civil rights," *Washington Post*, 19 December 2004, p. G5.
2. The above data obtained from Fair Vote Canada. (www.fairvote canada.org).
3. *Citizen Participation and Canadian Democracy: An Overview*, Centre for Research and Information on Canada, August 2003.
4. Ibid.
5. Some worry that several regionally based parties in the House would only lead to the further devolution of federal power to the provinces as the necessary price for brokering region-based political coalitions. But then, such a devolution in the field of domestic policy is one of the key recommendations of this book.
6. The need to reduce the prospect of unending Liberal majority governments is the reason for rejecting a third system of electing representatives, known as alternative voting. In this system, used to elect the House of Representatives in Australia, voters rank their candidates in order of priority. If, after the first round of counting, no candidate has secured 50 per cent of the vote, the candidate with the fewest votes is dropped from the ballot, with voters' second choices redistributed among the remaining candidates until one candidate has the support of a majority of electors, and wins the seat. Alternative voting combines the principle of fairness embodied in PR with the principle of strong government promoted by FPTP. The problem for such a system in Canada is that, federally, the Liberal Party is the second choice of the overwhelming majority of voters who vote for other parties, which means that under an alternative-voting system the Liberals would be even more entrenched in power than they are already.
7. As well, the rules required that a majority of voters in 60 per cent of ridings endorse electoral reform. In fact, seventy-seven out of seventy-nine ridings voted Yes.

8. Which may be why only Ireland, Malta, and some Australian elections employ stv.

9. A phrase coined in the nineteenth century by an anonymous writer.

10. Auditor general Sheila Fraser, for example, was criticized for the extreme language used in comments to the media when her reports on the sponsorship program were first released. Critics warned that her remarks appeared to put the entire public service into disrepute, which is one reason her subsequent reports and comments were more temperate in tone. More famously, former prime minister Jean Chrétien brought an unsuccessful legal challenge against Mr. Justice John Gomery, claiming that his comments to the media and in the inquiry displayed bias against Mr. Chrétien and others implicated in the sponsorship scandal.

11. Christopher Moore, *1867: How the Fathers Made a Deal*. Toronto: McClelland & Stewart, 1997, p. 107.

CONCLUSION: Let's Go Further

1. This gives me, finally, an opportunity to apologize to those assiduous souls (perhaps ten a year) who send letters through the mail. I cannot reply. My penmanship is execrable, and while our bureau has a manual typewriter, it doesn't work very well, I have largely forgotten how to hit the keys, and we lack stamps.

2. Clifford Krauss, "Was Canada just too good to be true?" *New York Times*, 25 May 2005, p. A4.